Entertaining MOMMY?

A Child's Abusive Memories Revealed

Gemma

Copyright © 2023 Gemma
All rights reserved
First Edition

Fulton Books
Meadville, PA

Published by Fulton Books 2023

ISBN 979-8-88505-843-8 (paperback)
ISBN 979-8-88505-844-5 (digital)

Printed in the United States of America

For my sisters who have helped with the memories I have lost, the childhood we lived through, and to have struggled with me throughout our pain and ordeals, thank you from the bottom of my heart.

To my husband who held my hand through all of my pain, thank you for all the support. I love you.

Thanks to my children for all the support you gave; the respect this part of my life needed but mostly for the love you have shown me. I love you dearly.

To my dad who we lost the year I started to write this, you will be forever missed.

Last but not least, my therapist, for all the support I needed to get started and get through this painful time, thank you all.

Contents

Acknowledgments vii
Author's Special Notes ix
Memories 1
    Chapter 1: Awakened from My Hellish Nightmares 3
    Chapter 2: The Hurting Never Stops,
                     The Healing Now Begins 9
    Chapter 3: Starting Out 18
A Mom Should Be… 29
    Chapter 4: Being Selfish 31
    Chapter 5: More Ways to Hurt Me 36
Retrieving a Memory 46
    Chapter 6: Remembering Three 47
    Chapter 7: What Really Happened? 54
A Note to My Mother 58
    Chapter 8: The Moving Memories 59
    Chapter 9: A Scary Place 65
    Chapter 10: Finding the Right Place 69
    Chapter 11: I Was Seven 75
    Chapter 12: The Gravel Pit 81
    Chapter 13: Jealous of Her Daughters? 85
    Chapter 14: Only Part of My Feelings 91
    Chapter 15: The Good One 95
    Chapter 16: Always the Cynic 99
    Chapter 17: Feeling Someone's Pain 105
I Am Done 110
    Chapter 18: Feeling Uncomfortable 111
    Chapter 19: Being Bribed 116
    Chapter 20: Getting Even 123

- Chapter 21: The Nightmares Start 129
- Chapter 22: I Had My Chance 135
- Chapter 23: Wanting to Be Alone 140
- Chapter 24: What Can I Do? 145
- Chapter 25: This Would Get Me in Trouble? 153
- Chapter 26: He Hurts Me 160
- Chapter 27: A New Game 165
- Chapter 28: The Circle Fights 171
- Chapter 29: A Mother's Compassion 177

My Mom's Compassion 181
- Chapter 30: My Mother's Nightmare 182
- Chapter 31: It Gets Even Worse 186
- Chapter 32: How Could She? 193
- Chapter 33: Getting Out with Regret 197
- Chapter 34: Not Going So Well 204
- Chapter 35: Starting All Over 211
- Chapter 36: It's My Fault? 222
- Chapter 37: My Rage 229

Controlling My Rage 234
- Chapter 38: The Voice Inside Me 235

To Have a Wish 239
- Chapter 39: Mom's Rage 240
- Chapter 40: The Hits Keep Coming 251
- Chapter 41: Having Enough 258
- Chapter 42: My Last Assault 270
- Chapter 43: Accountability 281

I Did It 289
- Chapter 44: I Did Not Understand 290
- Chapter 45: Mom's Way 296
- Chapter 46: Getting Me Through 302
- Chapter 47: Understanding the Hat 311
- Chapter 48: Control 316
- Chapter 49: I Found My Voice, the Coward Lives No More 327

Find Your Voice 335
Nationwide Hotlines for Abuse 337

Acknowledgments

I appreciate the courtesy, love, and support from my family and friends through my journey while remembering. No one could have gotten me through this like all those whom I have talked to about my puzzling, complex journey. Thank you all for the deep conversations, the chilling reminders, and the unfortunate episodes you may have witnessed through your eyes. I deeply appreciate your kindness and decency. Thank you to all who inspired me for all of your support, love, and advice. Some of my family still live in that old house we grew up in. Now that I know and remember… I never want to go back!

    A very special thanks to my sister, who spent the most time with me on this. For all your feedback, special stories, times, and places. All the time you took to help me through this, just as you did while growing up, being my bodyguard, my hero, my friend. I could not have done it without you, then or now. I love you always.

Author's Special Notes

My privacy is very important to me, as well as the privacy of my family and friends. I used no names or locations to help protect all who have been involved. I only wanted to tell my story without shame or ridicule of anyone who may have been tangled up in my complicated life, to protect the very few innocents.

Just possibly it may help a parent or teacher become more aware of the signs to look for, especially when it comes to child abuse, physical abuse, or bullying. Please be observant! Watch for signs! Unfortunately, it is still going on in our world today. Look for a child's pain. A child might be crying for your help right now. Please open your eyes.

Look for signs of distress, fear, pain, tears. Listen! There are always signs that a person may not be able to hear or see if you don't know what to look for or to listen to. Help someone if you can, always. You could save an adult or a child from any kind of abuse, maybe even save a life. I am only asking that you be observant. So many years had passed for me when no one heard my cries. Could I still get help? Did I even want to? I was too afraid of what that coward would say to me, what horror I would have to handle next. To tell my story as I tried to remember would be so painful for me, too frightening, too raw. Remembering it for the first time felt like I was reliving it all over.

I guess the only thing that held me back was fear, trying to destroy all that I have worked so hard for in my life, all I had happily forgotten. Only I found out I am stronger and more powerful than any voices or monsters that I thought held me captive for so long. I have set myself free of all I have felt chained to! My voice is the only

Gemma

voice I listen to now. No one else is allowed into my thoughts, especially that controlling coward… Gone forever is that part of my life.

I hope you all enjoy my very first book.

Memories

When you are a child,
you should have memories
that leave you with a smile
once remembered.

Hopefully, they make you happy
when you think about them.
They'll reflect back in your mind
like a picture.

They should mirror back to you
as something beautiful.
I had very few of these.
Without some help,

I would never have
retrieved any
of the ones
I had left behind.

I assumed, our moving memories
were pleasant.
A few bumps in the road
that call to mind.

Others, I have lost forever.
I think we all may have
some of those.
A couple I wished
remained hidden.
But…
Here we go.

Chapter 1

Awakened from My Hellish Nightmares

"What kind of person am I?" I mumbled as my body began its first series of trembles.

All of a sudden, I felt panic, anxiety, even fear rushing through me like a tornado. My heart was beating out of control as my ears began drumming to the beat of the same rhythm. I could not stand the pressure I was feeling right now. Even though I have had this same reaction, the same dread in the past, this felt like it was gripping my heart like a vice, reveling in knowing I was about to explode from the pain I was reacting to. I thought I knew what was happening to me this time as well. I was just not as sure now. Was I just beginning a full-blown panic attack again? Was that all this could be too? I have had hundreds of these before.

Never knowing how to begin to stop them or what the hell ever caused them to start with in the first place. What was so different about this one? Why did this seem to scare me so much more? No, something did not feel right this time, but what else could it be? I just couldn't seem to put my finger on it. My head was beginning to pound again. Great, another migraine, just what I also needed today! I only knew I'd never felt anything like this before. Whatever I was sensing right now was something I just could not explain, even if I wanted to. It's so damn frustrating. I could barely hear the words "calm down" as she spoke them. But I certainly felt the vomit now making its way up.

I somehow kept it down as I have done so many times in the past when I have felt attacked in this way. I cannot begin to explain what this was doing to me right now, and how the hell do I know it is different? When I just do! I don't understand, damn it!

"This can't be true," I suddenly screamed at her, jumping her and shocking myself that it came from my mouth as if this was her fault. "You're lying," I whimpered as the tears began to flow, my breath catching, *certain* I was taking my last, all the while my hand grabbing my throat, clutching it, feeling like it was going to close up any minute. I could not stand the force of it all. She opened her mouth to say something as I focused my watery eyes on her.

"No! Stop talking!" I screamed at her again. "I have to think," I said as my mind began to crawl out of what felt like an underground murky hole.

I began to feel it, what she was trying to tell me. How? Why? That was the scariest factor of this whole "experiment," she called it, something she had been trying to get me to do now for years. This was only one of the reasons I resisted for so long. I knew it was nothing I wanted to know. Certainly, knowing not one good thing could come from finding out the existence of what I thought I feared. Why did I say yes this time? The dreams, fear, the nightmares? Because of just not knowing? Why did I do this, damnit! Then again, I was curious as to what the hell it was she could be talking about! Like what coward? What neglect? What abuse are you discussing right now?

She was making it sound like I had to have been in a comatose state while I was young. I had blacked out or not even been there for what I thought was my own childhood

"How could this have possibly happened? You're saying I just shut this all out? You're actually telling me that this all happened to me, and I do not remember any of it? What did you call it? No, never mind. It will just confuse me more! I already feel like I'm trying to claw my way out of some desolate, forbidden place. I can't take any more at the moment."

"I do not think there is any other possible explanation," she gently tried to explain as she spoke quietly.

"I believe it was such a tragic childhood that you must have had, that you wanted to just forget it ever happened. Considering it does seem you have blocked it all out the way I think you have," she whispered. "No one would ever blame you."

"No, there definitely is something wrong with me," I whispered back.

"No, no," my therapist said in her most comforting soft voice.

"Why! How could this have been happening to me without me knowing anything about it?" I hollered at her. "What could be wrong with me that I could have forgotten something so life-changing?"

I began to cry harder before she could answer. I started feeling so terrified. It just couldn't be true as I interrupted her answer I didn't want to hear.

"I just don't understand what it is you're telling me that I may have told you just now. It just can't be true!" I screamed at her. "That can't be me. What did you do to me? Damn it, I told you I did not want this! I'm sorry," I suddenly said through my sobs. "I know none of this is your fault. Please, if you ever wanted me to understand, if you ever wanted to help me, help me now. I'm begging you! Explain this to me if you can. You're the expert here," I said in such a desperate voice it didn't even sound like my own.

I knew she must have seen it on my face—the panic, the anxiety rising in my voice again. I could tell by the worried look she had on her face and the breaking up of her voice as she spoke.

I had to ask, "Did you record this from beginning to end? Capture every panicked word, every painful dream, my memories I remembered?" I asked her, talking through my sobs, as if she could understand me right now, already knowing the answer before she spoke.

"Yes," she explained with a concerned look on her face. "You remember, we agreed we would record everything. It was our deal when we started. You never wanted to hear them until now."

"Well, I'm sorry I did! There must be some mistake," I told her as I raised my voice louder and felt nothing but fear while still sobbing like a child. "How could I have told you any of this? There is no way this is how my life could have started out. I do not care what age I was. That I could possibly have grown up with any of this *horror* and somehow forgotten it all. There is just no chance that was me," I explained to my therapist, looking her straight in the eyes.

I was now trying to find a clue, a hint of her ready to burst out laughing, telling me it was all a joke, that she was pulling a prank. After all, it felt like we were almost friends. To me it did anyway. Couldn't she just be joking? I would have forgiven her for it. Feeling so happy that I was really not crazy to have truly forgotten my whole childhood; that I would not have been mad at her at all if she had been joking.

"Please let this not be true," I said to her, terrified. Even though cruel, yes, but it would have been a better alternative than what she was trying to make me believe. "I really did tell you all of this? That I should just accept what you have told me as truth?" I said as I somehow began to believe it myself.

The more I thought about it, the more I saw visions, flashes of…

"What was that? Did you see that?" I said in a panic.

"No, but it's probably just flashes of your nightmare. You just awakened in your subconscious."

Great, I thought, *something else for me to be afraid of.* I understand she started to say, interrupting my thoughts.

"You can't begin to understand!" I instantly screamed at her. I had two older siblings. They had to know something about this terror of a childhood before I did. They would have said something to me about this. As adults, even as children, we would have talked about something so serious. How could I not remember? What kind of person could I be to have forgotten something so tragic?

"No! I don't believe that's what I told you! It is someone else I heard talking just then and what you said I told you could not be true. It just couldn't have happened like this. I don't remember anything like that in my younger years. They're such painful memories. You're lying," I screamed at her again. "You did something to me, or the recording." I began to cry uncontrollably once more, not able to stop my tears or my thoughts.

But even as I was going through the motions, saying the words, feeling the pain, I could not stop the tears when I could almost feel the pain and agony of raw wounds opening after I saw flashes.

Visions of a small, blond little girl, huddled in a corner, crying, "Please stop! I'm sorry." She was yelling as loud as her small voice could muster while holding her arms over her head and face to protect herself from the blows she could almost feel again, not yet knowing who it was that was hurting her. I couldn't see a face right now. Who was this mean person? What have I done? I now began to realize that this nice, truthful woman sitting across from me was repeating back to me something she had heard coming from my own lips. She would not have made it up. I trusted her more than anyone in the world right now.

How could I not? What would she gain by lying? Why purposely hurt me? Throughout my adult life, I knew I could not have had the best childhood with seven kids, then an extra one later in life. But this?

"You're saying I could have blocked all of it out? People really do that?"

I never imagined that could be true. This is so absurd! I went on to have my own children. They had what I thought as fairly normal, decent lives. I began to think about how I raised them. All that could have gone wrong, or maybe it did and I just didn't remember! I couldn't remember anything cruel I had done, could I? Maybe I was a horrible mother too! Oh no, maybe I blocked out what I thought my good parenting skills were also. What if I'd done that to them?

Should I even have become a parent after now finding out the way I was raised and not remembering anything about it? I began to realize what I had just witnessed in my dreams, my nightmares while I was asleep, or under as they call it. This could have turned out to be a disaster waiting to happen. What the hell have I done! My childhood, my children, my god! Even though my upbringing was not my fault, I know that in my heart, it's just something I would not have been able to live with had I hurt or harmed my own children in any way. I will have to talk to them. I know there have been a lot of family members on their father's side that never would have tolerated any kinds of marks on my sons or letting me get away with it.

I could swear I have heard them tell I was a decent enough mother. What about when my sons were really young? Too young to know what kind of mother I really was? I shook it off, literally. No, my sons have told me in the past I have been a good mother to them. They wouldn't lie about that! I must have been a decent enough one; my boys treat me with respect and love. I began to forget about any bad thoughts. I just now felt something good that was very unexpected. I felt great about myself for the first time in a very longtime. All of a sudden, I felt something happening to myself. Things were not so cloudy now. What was this strange thing happening to me? I was not so frightened! It was only making me smile.

Something or someone was trying to tell me something exceptional, some kind of extraordinary fascination of appeal washing my body and mind clearer. I felt the pulling of a stronger power all of a sudden, an allure of calming. Something wonderful just came over me. I literally felt it! I only felt like smiling because of it. I would have happiness in my life now. How strange. I didn't know what this was, but I liked it; it felt so serene. I couldn't explain what was happening, but I knew a great significance was going to happen for me. I sensed new life, new beginnings for me. I just woke from the most terrible, hellish nightmares, still trying to poke out through my thoughts and call to me. Looking up at my therapist at that moment, at that very second without any kind of fear, I suddenly felt a lull come over me, a sort of peace I had never felt before.

She smiled without either of us saying a word or her waiting for me to explain. Finally, she broke the calming silence filling the room.

"Do you think you are ready to finally do this now?" she asked with such joy on her face for the breakthrough she'd known I just had. I feel ecstatic.

Everything was very clear, and I was wide awake for the very first time—a feeling I didn't think I had quite felt before. Almost feeling too happy, knowing the dread of responding to what I now knew would be following, even so, I said "Yes," as I still smiled. "I think I am…"

Chapter 2

The Hurting Never Stops, The Healing Now Begins

My story did not start with just myself as being the only abused child. Of that I was certain. But then again, was I really? I had to think long and hard about this, it still being so cloudy in my mind. I began thinking about my siblings. Why did we not talk before now about any of this? Or did I just not remember talking to them about it? It seems I have forgotten everything since I was a child. I just know my older sister would have told anyone any kind of abuse she may have received throughout her childhood without anyone's help or coaxing, as well as any she might have witnessed or could hear going on behind closed doors. She was bold and sassy, that one!

    She wouldn't have let anything happen to herself without making a big thing of it. So I do not understand why no one knew. She was also the kind of child who would see an opportunity and take it. She would have told if this were true. Of that, I am sure! While I would still remain silent without any kind of guidance, I am certain. Staying afraid, the way mother liked me best. The oldest sibling? He is a much different story. He would protect our abuser no matter what the cost. For he did and has most of his life. It didn't matter what he saw, heard, or even if he was the one being abused, which didn't happen often but did go on. My other siblings could also tell you a thing or two about what it was like to be abused.

    Growing up with a monster like we lived with, my thoughts bring me back to times when I didn't know who it was in front of me because it certainly changed daily. We never knew who it was going to be facing us from one day to the next. Sadly, what we called the monster, you probably knew best as mom. I sure wished now I had used my voice to try and stop the hurting she was causing and allowing, as I now remember her being the monster in most of my dreams, the flashes of terror, and the visions. She sure knew how to frighten me, always having more than one face to share with all of us as I now remember, all of them scaring me, especially her smile, that fake smile she always used.

She did have so many distinct faces I would not dare try to count them all, the ones I do remember, like the one she wore when important people were around, people she wanted to impress—yes, she used that one a lot to let them see what a great mother and wife she wanted them to believe she was. What a joke that one turned out to be! Then there was the one she wore when she wanted something. Mom truly could put on the charm whenever she was determined to get something from someone. Oh, I remember how nice she could be when she needed something from just about anyone. Usually, it would be our dad she fooled all those times for so many years, getting her way a lot of the time.

Although she sure laid it on thick with others too. She knew exactly how to manipulate people. Then there was the one the children saw the most, the mean, evil, and seemingly very unhappy one. It appeared sad at times as I look back on it now. I can't image we ever saw a true, happy smile. At least I didn't think I had ever seen a real one looking back at me, only seeing those cold black eyes, she had when she looked at me. Although it was my mother's mouth I disliked the most. It always looked so angry.

Those straight, puckered-up, tight lips letting me know just how enraged she was in the moment, I would watch that mouth of hers; that vicious mouth full of what felt like hurt, hostility, and resentment; that mouth that spurted out swear words at us with such hateful, mean names, hurting me as she wanted, like I am sure it did my siblings also. It's a wonder we remembered what our real names truly were. The terrible screaming that came from that mouth of hers, past her lips, it sometimes seemed as bad as the beatings to me. Well, for me, it did anyway. As for myself? I was hurt mostly by the look of hate when she would look right at me, or was it right through me? Yes, I remember that look all too well. Oh, don't get me wrong, the beatings and punishments were horrifying and painful.

I've often wondered if I just got used to them after time and only cried when she looked at me in that way. That is what I told myself whenever I allowed myself to look at her face, that is. It would seem she only looked at me like that—I always thought so anyway—like I was nobody, someone she did not know, she did not love, a child she could possibly hate? It is truly what I felt and believed. I knew we were all such similar children. How was it that I was that much different, I wondered? I just didn't know why or how I could be estranged from them in any way or how her daughters could be so different from her sons as far as children go? Like for instance, another of her children, her youngest child, another boy, the baby of the family, the one she probably treated so much better than the rest of us.

He, too, has protected our mother no matter what she has done, even now as an adult, to this day, sometimes making me sick to my stomach because of it, especially with him knowing she was not a perfect mother to him either. Her own son, her baby—she also mistreated and abused him, just not as much or as often but it did happen. Unless it served her to be nice to the boys, she liked to use them to her advantage, we figured out, sometimes paying them! She knew exactly how to get them to tattle on all the girls or anything else she wanted them to do for her. It is the very same way today. She is still being evil and hurtful, telling things about each one of her children to the other, gossiping, untrue slander, always stirring the pot, especially with telling the boys, as if still having them under her spell almost. I do get why those two stuck together right to this day, why they may have even formed a pact. They knew they were truly opposite of us. Mom had us all sensing it from day one. She let them know it, feel it, see it. Yes, we all believed it from the beginning. Mom treated them so much better, and she let them and us know not just why but how she could do it day in and day out! She told us daily she would raise ten boys to one girl any day. It hurt us back then, not so much now, even though she's still saying it to this day! I am so sick of hearing that statement, and she knows it used to hurt to the core.

She liked that a lot too, knowing it hurt. We know you loved them more, Mom! You showed it enough, always trying to hurt us time and again. That, for some reason, always made me especially feel dirty. No matter what I did. I could feel her eyes on me. I did not dare to look up at times, fearing yet another nightmare to wake up from, crying, screaming, or both, or the pounding inside of my body as I woke, making me sweat and sick to my stomach If I did not look into her eyes, I know that horrifying laugh was always meant for me, stinging my heart with pain, knowing she would have enjoyed that, had she only known! What do I know? Maybe she did. These were the kinds of days that made me think Mom hated me most. That somehow she knew exactly what she was doing to me, even as a young child. I felt it in my heart, as I now think back on my memories that keep surfacing, just another way to torture me. We also knew anything the girls did would never be right or good enough. No matter if she told us to or we did something special for her, I don't think the words "thank you" ever escaped her lips when it came to her daughters. We did all she asked of us and more. Damn right, it hurt! To her, we were her servants, like we owed it to her for being our mother. She sure made us feel that way treating us in that manner. No matter what, we girls were never going to please her, no matter how hard we worked or tried.

Nothing was going to make her happy when it came to the girls! What kind of mother would do all she has done, all she has said, and how the hell did she live with herself? I still wonder how she could change so quickly when it came to the boys. The smiles, the hugs, the affection—fake or real, why would her boys say anything bad about her even now? They did not live with the same kind of mother that we did! That is exactly how she wanted it—her boys treated well with a mother she thought they deserved. My guess is, the girls supposedly did not! We were not allowed to forget it for one minute either.

The foster child she eventually took in, also a boy. I believe he, too, was treated better, as did my sisters. Even some adults felt this way. Everyone could see it. You didn't have to be a genius. "Anything with a penis is" what the five of us girls finally thought, and would say only when we were older and only to each other. Strange, though, we thought Mom appeared to hate our dad. We knew he was a boy. Mom screamed at him almost as much as she did her daughters, not understanding why. She called our dad such horrible things, swearing at him, sometimes I think more than she did the girls. We were aware he must have been the same as our brothers, not like her girls. We were just kids. Still, we felt something was wrong between the kids and adults.

With no understanding of any issues they may have had with us, we only knew something was not right with our family. The true love and affection she was able to show the boys was not something we would understand or receive, then or now. This is how we felt. We still do to this day. Nothing has seemed to change for any of us as of today. Now that I am an adult, with knowing my childhood as I do, it still hurts some. I am very thankful my brothers did not feel the same kind of abuse we received, as none of us deserved it, or that they did not witness her anger and hate that we could see and feel coming from her eyes, voice, her mouth. Her actions were certainly worse whenever she was around the girls, especially me for reasons we had not figured out. Not only was it painful and torturous at times, it made all of us feel less than human throughout our young, innocent lives.

I remember as memories become clearer, as if it were yesterday. So I thought of a plan, sadly. As a young child, I thought about ending my life more than once so my mother could not hurt me anymore or be so angry at me all the time. I saw it on TV a few times. I heard about how people take their own lives and wondered if that could help my family. What would be the best way to do it? She would never be able to hurt me again. How damaging and sad for a child so young to imagine something like that for themselves; to be made to feel so negative in such a way they would even think about taking their own life. I thought maybe that could put her in a better mood for her loved ones, be happier, maybe more caring to everyone, be able to show more love toward her family. Maybe she would possibly want to be with all of them after the bad seed was gone, that she might be happier and not be so threatening or mean toward my sisters and hopefully anyone in my family if she did not have me to look at or be mad with all the time—they might have a better life—that I could sacrifice myself for them in a way. It did appear to us all that Mom had it out for me for unknown reasons no one has yet to figure out.

So I thought I was the one that put her in this bad mood she was in all the time. I just couldn't figure out why or how I was doing it. I did think of running away a lot. Then in the back of my mind, I knew, as evil as she seemed, she would track me down and be even angrier when she got ahold of me. The only other way was if I was gone for good. That was when I began to think, *If I were just not here anymore, gone somehow. If only I could be out of this family forever. Mom might be happier and not be so uncivilized with others around her. Yes, that would solve the problem.* My young mind told my heart. I felt it was the right thing to do. I just had to find a way to make it happen. I would just have to think about this and how to do it without causing myself a lot of pain. I never told anyone about my thoughts. I kept it all inside, like all my lonely secrets.

My younger sister must have had this feeling because once I decided I would get rid of myself, she began to cling to me like lint on a sweater. I couldn't believe this. She seemed to always be watching me, like she didn't want anything else bad happening to me, acting as if she could hear my thoughts. Though she was always the kindest to me and always stuck up for me. Not that my other siblings did not if they saw someone mistreating me besides my mother. No, this sister was closer to my age, only ten months apart. We did just about everything together. We were even in the same grade together for one year. We became even closer during that year. I do remember kindergarten as one of my favorite grades in school. At least the year we were together. One reason was, sis did not tolerate anyone even looking at me the wrong way. Knowing how shy and timid I had become, scared of my own shadow, as they say, she tried so hard to make a fighter out of me to at least stick up for myself. I was just too afraid; I couldn't do it! So she became my sort of bodyguard. I did not like fighting. I did not want to see it, feel it, or hear it. I have had enough of it in my life already, even at the age of six. The pain, the brutalization of it all—it made me feel so weak, so scared, so terrified.

Thinking the way I did, I thought all the kids could somehow see all the things that were done to me through all the stages of my life, that they somehow knew and were laughing at me because of it. How cruel I thought they were. So I became somewhat of a loner; a chicken was what they would call me most. Then I decided to put the idea of killing myself away for a while. I felt like a coward, too afraid to even think about it sooner! My only friends for some time became my siblings. I felt safe with them when we were out of our house, outside playing, feeling free.

I knew Mom could not touch me then. She could probably holler our names, then I would panic and freeze, but we hid from her as much as we dared to. I would not have hidden by myself. My siblings encouraged me, promising I would be safe with them; and they were right, I always was. When we were home and younger, there was not a lot anyone could do to save one another from her savage mouth, her brutal hands, the weapons she began to use. If we did not scream or cry exactly how she wanted us to, we would get it until we did. It seemed to never stop! It was so confusing; we never knew what she wanted us to do at that moment. So we always had to wait to see what to do.

I did not know back then that all mothers were not the same, that all children were not treated this way. I did not know that children did not have nightmares of their mothers chasing them, children running for their lives while moms screamed your name, telling how you would be dead if she ever caught you; that you just run for your life while you slept, feeling like you never slept at all, making dark circles forever under their children's eyes. Why did I not know? Why did I not share this with someone when she frightened me so? My sister who was always there for me, I trusted her with my life. I should have told her, my older sister who I could talk to about anything.

I know now she would have helped me in some way. As children, we do not think like that. Who could have known had we stuck together had I told, it might have been different for all of us?

I remained silent, like the coward I thought I might have become. I never shared anything while I was terrified or suffering. We just do not go against our parents! We are made to believe we should trust that they know what is best. We do not ask, tell, or even dare speak bad about them. Besides, who could I tell that did not already know? At that age, everyone who was supposed to love me already knew, and they were not going to help me, or they would have by now.

After all, I thought my life meant nothing in my own eyes. Why would it mean anything to any of them? If not for my siblings, I know I probably would have attempted to end my life right at that young age. Many times, in many ways, I would have thought of some type of plan. I knew I was a coward and taking the easy way out, as I had also heard on television. My oldest sister helped me through many rough times. I am so thankful to her. But I give the most gratitude to the sister who was closest to me in age. I believe she saved me not only from not wanting to be there anymore but from many beatings that I believed should have been mine. The beatings would start out to be for me, but whenever my sister was around or knew what was going to happen, she stepped in and took the beatings for me. Also sad but true. She was such a courageous young child.

My sister was so brave, standing up to that woman while she was on one of her tirades. I could not even imagine all the good my sister would do for me as we grew up. All those sacrifices and pain she took for me. She did become my hero. This was just the beginning of all the joys and heartbreaks of my sister who saved me. She would go on to sacrifice herself many times to save me from pain, in more ways than one.

As we grew older, I would see more of her kindness and strength just to help me. At the time, I did not think I was worth all that saving, or the pain that I know it caused her to do so. I still thought I had done something truly bad or evil to make our mother feel the way she did about me and that my sister was wasting her time, offering herself to save me. There was a reason my mother looked at me that way. I had no idea why. I did not know yet that she enjoyed this torture she made me feel. Was I that different from my siblings? What did I do or say that could have upset her almost every day?

Even though she was my mother also, I did not know back then that she did not have the right to do all she had done to us. Especially to me! I will never know why she singled me out the most. The lighter hair? The blue eyes? Then again, that could not have been the reason because as we got older, the sister who was ten months younger than me had begun to be beaten as much as I was, maybe more. She had dark hair and brown eyes. My other sisters were abused as well, but I think because the two of us who were so close in age, who played together the most, caught together the most, she who stuck up for me, got it more often. This is how this part of the story goes…

Sis just could not stand to see anyone pick on me, even our own mother. It had begun with how she treated me, making me feel small and scared of not only her but I was afraid of everything and everyone eventually, it seemed. I was the kid who would be the one with the constant red face, the tears running down it more than they should have, the one who would not say boo to save her own life. I did not know how to stand up for myself, and I did not ever learn how, or even want to! I never became that fighter they thought I could or should be. I never told anyone how truly afraid I was!

So it begins…

Chapter 3

Starting Out

I have been told we had been traveling from one state to another with a particular destination in my parents' minds. Apparently, my mother had a different plan though. We had to stop along the way at the nearest hospital. Mom's water had broken, and she quickly went into labor. In the back seat were my brother and sister. I would become the third oldest of seven. My mother had lost her second baby at the young age of only sixteen. Sadly, my brother had only lived a few hours. I could never even imagine the kind of pain or loss it must have caused them both. How heartbreaking it would have been for anyone, let alone someone as young as my parents had been.

Always a worry, I am sure, thinking about the dangers it carried for them throughout their beginning years. What a tragedy. I cannot imagine what my mom especially went through at such a young age. Crushing news to us all when we learned of it. My parents were incredibly young newlyweds too. What a devastating way to have to start their new lives together, then to be so inexperienced besides, so I had been told by my mother later in life. I am not sure how many adults would handle this kind of overwhelming life event. How do two probably immature, young adolescents themselves go about handling it? This must have been an extremely challenging time for my parents to lose a child.

Then having to worry about the next child and the next. I am sure they would be curious as to whether the next would be healthy or not. Do I dare have more children? Having another one a year apart, every year for the next four years! I wonder now, how did they dare do it? Primarily for my mother, young and grief-stricken, is the only thing she would say about that day. Otherwise, she would never talk about what had happened on this day. Even though we all have asked her, we childishly thought we understood and knew how she felt. No one knows how they themselves would handle such a tragedy. I was truly sorry for all our loss. I could never have imagined getting married at the naive age of only fifteen, with my father being only eighteen, going through such heartache.

Just babies themselves is what they would have been called these days. I could not have done it. I was so immature at that age, still thinking about running outside, playing childish games at Mom's age, still climbing trees, crying over scraped knees and cuts. I believe I still played with dolls at this age and the many other adolescent things I did! No, I was just a child in every sense of the word, never imagining going through what my parents had been through. I assume because of the childhood I began to have that started out my life with such pain while being so young, I became very immature and stayed that way for a very long time, not really knowing how to grow up.

I was not taught how to change from one stage to the next, but I sure was shown what horror was, starting at the age of about three, as I now begin to dream about that time. We will get into those stories as we go along. I just know I would not have made a very adult wife or mother though and thought I still wanted to be at home. I would not have stood a chance at trying to become an adult at that age. But some kids are just determined to do what they want and think they always know what is best for themselves, especially a lot of kids nowadays. Because we know nothing could be worse than living at home with our parents! At least that is what many of us tell ourselves when we are young and know everything, isn't it?

Although I believe a lot of us would agree that fifteen would be an age that would be far too young to be married in any era. I only know I was not even close to being ready to be. Say nothing about having a baby of my own at that age. But things sure were different back in the fifties and sixties, Mom and Dad told us. I guess many understood it to be okay to marry so young back then, and so many did. My parents told tales of extreme hush-hush shotgun weddings, ones that they themselves did not witness but one of their friends were forced to do.

That many parents also gave their blessings for their young teenagers to get married back in the earlier days! Some were even younger than my parents. My dad and mom sure did something right though. You just do not hear about a lot of couples staying married for all the years my parents did nowadays. Sixty-three years with one partner without killing one another is amazing. Although I am sure they came close a few times. I have witnessed a few of their fights myself, not just arguments and I can say with confidence, so have my siblings. Now let's get back to the story we began with and see just what happens with our starting out memories as we move on.

All went well this time, I am assuming, for this quick layover and delivery we had made. Mother and daughter were safely released from the hospital a couple days later, and off we went again to new horizons. How things happened back in those days still to this day amazes me, to hear them talk about it all. Were our moving memories happy or not? We are about to find out while they tell their stories through my eyes. Though I could never imagine traveling like they have told, with everything you own, two toddlers and just have given birth, like Mom did. How she ever did what she went through back in those days I will never know. It seems so funny to me to hear them tell how they moved back then and how much it has changed these days since.

Thinking people back then could load up a vehicle, maybe a trailer if they had one. Fill their vehicles with their children in it. Pack it so tight there is no room for another thing, except maybe the family dog. Hoping nothing falls on your children. Strap things on the top of their vehicle. Head on down the road, dreaming that maybe there will be a new job, hopefully a friendly neighborhood with good kids for yours to grow up with. While hearing the children play games in the back of the vehicle—games they make up as they ride along—listening to them being hopeful, maybe happy and quite possibly just being excited to be with their family. Never hearing anyone saying, "Are we there yet!" So the story goes. All while watching to make sure nothing falls off your vehicle or trailer while riding down the road.

Probably praying your vehicle makes it, as my parents tell it. Hopefully heading for a better life than the one you have just left behind and not think a thing about it. Because people have done it so often back then, it appeared to be no big thing. How many times had people done that in the earlier days without thinking twice about it? What about people nowadays? Most would never move like that. They would move with convenience. Big vans and huge box trucks. Maybe even hire someone to come into their home. Wrap everything up, box and package it up for you, then drive it to your new home. Don't forget to get extra insurance on everything they touch! Then pay them to unload the truck, open boxes, unpack unwrap. Some may even help set up your new home if you pay them well enough.

Moving sure has changed for people. Everything has to be as easy and convenient as can be these days, like with most things that have changed in our world today. There are not as many hard-labor jobs anymore when it comes to people getting right in there and sweating it out to get what they want. Not like back in my parents' days. The world has done some major changing since those days, and it's not stopping anytime soon. Technology sure has made a lot of us lazy. There is practically a drive-through for everything you want to do outside your home. We all seem to enjoy convenience though. It's not like back when Mom and Dad had to do it all themselves, packing and unpacking, loading and unloading, mostly Mom, I have been told so many times.

Still, it amazes me to think about all that she had to do with each and every move we made. With the number of kids that would change each year, I have been made aware of so many times. Compared to how simple they have it today when other people move their households, it must have been so difficult for her. I know she told me the kitchen was the main room when we had gotten to a new place once, the important one and the one with the most stuff to unpack. I know who had to have done the majority of it and most of all the other rooms, or so I was told. Because of the constant complaining I have always heard throughout the telling of these adventures of our starting-out memories, the majority from Mom while these tales were being told. She always seemed to spoil it when the stories were mentioned. She would blame Dad for something. They would begin arguing, and we hardly ever were able to hear the end of one of our adventures. Still, I am sure it was a lot of back breaking work by herself. If all the stories she told were true, that is. We never got an answer from Dad either when we asked him.

Nothing from him about Mom's tales of her doing all the work every time we moved, that she possibly did it all alone. Dad never said one way or the other. So I guess Mom could have been right about this part of their stories. Though I am sure, while watching a newborn and two toddlers and setting up a house all at once must have been extremely hard to do, especially right after she had given birth. Mom certainly must have been an unusually strong woman to do all she had done at her young age. It had to have been many times as much as we were told we planned to go from state to state. I was not quite sure if I had ever heard the real reason why we even began to make that first move before I was born.

"Family" was always the same answer they gave us, which to us was no answer at all, after seeing how family got along while we grew up to see it for ourselves. So we didn't think that's the only reason we moved so much. We all were curious as we grew and asked about why we left each and every home but never received an honest answer, at least not one I believed. I never understood why they couldn't tell us the truth, whether it really was to be closer to family or there was a better job opportunity where we were moving to or what it might have been. I may not have ever really gotten the real information about that very first time because my parents always told two different tales, but my parents told many of all the moves we had made while I was young.

I was told it was more than probably any of us could remember in our younger years. Obviously, I was too young to know how many times to remember most of them anyway. I still never really understood why we had moved out of the state we were moving from for that very first time, the one when I became the baby. I was told later we had many relatives in the state we had been living in, and it sounded like we had left many people behind when first hearing these stories. Then I found out the state we did move to had even more family members in it, and it is the same place where both of our parents had been born and raised, just in different towns, until they finally met, naturally, where their story began.

This is also where our grandparents were currently living. It must have been so exciting for my parents to be so close to their parents. The funny thing was, all those relatives I thought we had left behind, most of them actually followed us right to the same state we left for, eventually. Little by little, we would all be close. So we became one big happy family! Or so I thought. Until I started to hear the rest of the family tales and not from my parents as I got older. Get ready for a truly bumpy ride through the rest of these moving memories. I do not know what area we landed in for this first adventure or what it was called, but my parents said the house was close to a huge chicken farm, which is where my dad got a job picking eggs and taking care of the chickens.

The boss must have liked him because he let my dad work as many hours as he wanted on what days he wanted to work. So, unfortunately, Dad was not home very much. Sometimes Mom would bundle us up and take us all to the chicken farm with her, or she would get a babysitter for the three of us then go to the farm to pick eggs for extra money. We realized we must have had relatives in every town we ever moved to. Whenever Mom or Dad would tell a story and they needed a sitter while they were out somewhere or working, it would always be a relative who watched us.

I guess they didn't want just anyone watching their children. I'm now wishing Mom's concern could have stayed with her from way back then. Life sure would have been a whole lot easier for my childhood and that of my siblings too. My parents also told me we lived close to an ice cream stand for our very first move, that we often walked there as a family and enjoyed some afternoons and evenings together many times, sharing special moments and many times of laughter. That is what I was told later in life. It is also where I tried and liked my first taste of ice cream while I was still a baby. Unfortunately, some happy memories I was too young to remember.

I am sure there were plenty when I was just a baby, but not many that anyone has shared with me. From the stories that were collected throughout my childhood since, it does not sound like there were a lot of good memories from the time I was a baby to when I became a very small child. I was not told about any good memories or any of the bad ones until someone began to see me around the age of about three years old. I do not understand where I had been from the time I was a baby to about that age when I became three. Not one of my non-immediate family members had ever seen me, they had told me when I asked! I thought that to be very strange. Where had I been?

After that time, I was only told about bad memories they had remembered by different family members and some family friends, without me asking. Only because they told me they do not remember any good memories of me when I was a small child from about three to about six years old, and they said they were sure they would have remembered at least one good one. This, I thought, was very odd. Not as odd as I thought about the years when I had not been seen by anyone outside my house, so I was made to believe. If there were any good memories mentioned, I do not recall anyone ever sharing any of them with me, then or now. Then, of course, there were other memories that were shared too.

It was also explained to me that we had plenty of hard times just like many families did back then, just from the many other stories that have been shared with me from back when I was a young child that I now recall hearing about from family and friends. I was told by one family member that things may have been different had our family not seem to multiply each and every year. I had not been really positive what they were talking about at the time. I was not sure if they were just joking about our family multiplying or if they were being serious. I never asked them until later. The children did not seem to mind though. More kids to play with seemed to be okay with us.

Although it really did seem to multiply every year for eight years. So I guess they were right about it, joking or not. Still, as a child, I never did think that being such a big family could be the reason Dad had to work so many hours or spend so much time away from home. When you're a kid, you do not think of those kinds of things nor should you have to be reminded or be put in the position

Entertaining Mommy?

of feeling guilty for possibly being the reason why. But there are some parents who make you aware that you may have become a thorn in their side throughout your childhood. I did realize later on that having so many kids did put a strain on my parents' pocketbook and their marriage; at the time, I thought it was our fault.

I thought also we were never asked to be in this family, always telling myself as I grew older. It was fate that we were even put here. I do believe we were reminded at many stages of our lives growing up that we might just be a burden to one of our parents. I just wasn't sure yet if that were true or not. I kept hoping not! I am sure, as I keep exploring my memories, the truth will be revealed. Keep in mind, I thought we were having a great life so far! I guess I did forget! My dad always found a fairly good-paying job, no matter where we moved to or what the economy was like. We were living pretty well for a growing family, I thought, always keeping a roof over our heads and as much food on the table as we needed.

Although there were times when there were no extras for anyone. But none of us ever went to bed hungry, unless we were being punished for something bad we had done (it appearing to happen to me a lot). I even remember now, as my memories come to light, of my mother working hard, taking care of things that always needed to be done, always having something to do. She seemed to never rest either. Still, as I am reminded, we appeared to be healthy and what seemed to be happy kids at that time. I was told that for a long time, there were not a lot of jobs to come by with a growing family like ours. Yet Dad was always determined to keep his family together and fed, so he always had a job of some kind because that was the kind of husband and father he had become, always there for his family when he was needed, as was my mother for her hand in the household and extra money she would bring home from odd jobs here and there. I am not sure how old I had come to be before we made our next move. It was not a very long time, and Dad received a better-paying job offer again. So they packed up, and to another town we moved. Onward we went again.

The memories of our family stories are beginning to form now, starting out as a normal, smallish, loving family. Or so I thought. I am not sure when it started or what went wrong…but something is brewing behind closed doors! I was told that Mom was, at this time, just starting to become a bit angry after this second move we had made. Let's find out what it is all about. No one was quite certain what was happening with mom yet, but hold on, we are about to find out a lot of things going on within these walls and with this family. I never could get the true story from her, though she had been asked many times. She would never have freely given out information about herself to anyone, especially if it was anything negative about herself! No, she didn't like anyone talking about her. Unless, of course, they were bragging to someone about her or something good she had done. You will come to find this out as you read on about our dear mother.

As I grew up, other family members and family friends would tell me that she started acting strange. That was about all they would tell me at first. *Acting strange*, I kept thinking. Then I began asking more questions. What did I miss as much as I thought I studied my mother, trying to keep tabs on her and her moods as much as I dared? Finally, after asking over and over, some gave in when I asked in what way they thought she was acting strange.

They finally said they thought she might have been drinking. That is all they could come up with for her strange behavior. Are you being serious? I just burst out laughing. My mom? Drinking! That is what they had truly thought it had been way back then? I knew it was wrong after knowing my mom the way I knew Mom, or did I really know her? No! I do not believe it. This can't be true! Unless someone had seen Mom drinking, I will never believe that is what changed her. There is no way! Just about everyone in our family who knew Mom would know she would not do that. She just had never been a drinker of any kind. She always told us she did not even like the taste or smell of any kind of alcohol.

But was that the truth, or was that a cover-up? Could she have been lying to all of us all these years? Now I was not so certain. I would have guessed quicker that it had to do maybe with prescription drugs, not alcohol. She did seem to like to go to the doctors a lot. It appeared she had a lot of prescription bottles filled many times a month. So that would have been my guess. It would be something Mom would do before she would drink alcohol all the time, especially with the kinds of jobs that she had later on in her life. That is just my opinion. This would be a more-logical explanation if you ask me, I told them. Besides, alcohol you can usually smell on a person. You can see it hidden in different areas of the house, can't you? We should have at least caught Mom once in a while with a bottle of alcohol or a drink in her hand had she been a closet drinker, couldn't we? We would have maybe found a bottle or two in all those years, even seen an empty bottle once in a while in the trash? I have asked everyone. Not one of us has ever seen our mother drinking, with the exception of occasionally one of her relatives getting married.

Later on, one of her children or grandchildren would be married. Even then she did not drink at every wedding that she attended. She also did not drink a lot at weddings or any kinds of parties. I have never seen her drink to the extreme of getting drunk. I have never seen her like that ever that I can recall. Neither has any of my siblings. As with other stories and tales she has told myself and our family, we may never know the truth of any of her parts in these particular adventures of our lives. I may never know the answers to any of the questions I have had that would follow after this shocking news!

I should have asked so many different things that might have been explained to me, answers to questions I have had throughout this process, even ones to other parts of my life that concern my mom that have never even been commented on—things that have impacted my life with not one reason as to why. It may have given me some kind of peace just to have even one of my questions answered by my mother or anyone who knew the answers! I know from experience that is never going to happen. If it was alcohol, it would be an answer for me that it was not that she just hated her child or that she could not stand to look at me. If it had been alcohol, it would have given me some kind of doubt, that it was not just me she had been seeking out just to punish because she did not love me. I wanted it to be alcohol that made her do all those bad things to me. It would have been justification at least. Had it been the alcohol, it meant that I was not a bad girl all the time like she said I was and that she really knew it had been alcohol and not me or that she did not mean to hurt me all those times. Still, I do not think anyone is that good to cover up drinking for all of these years without one person discovering it. I just can't believe it! I still believe someone can just be evil! I am going to stick with that. Evil she is!

We made a couple more moves after this, but of course, I was still young and do not remember those either. I did not hear many things about these moves, as if they did not happen, so we will just call them a couple more of our starting-out memories. However, the beginning of our early family stories really is beginning to start out with a bang, and I was told that they began just like this. Hold on to your hats. I think we are in for one bumpy ride! We are again movin' on!

A Mom Should Be...

The beauty of
a child's new life.
Their breath upon
your cheek

Should make a mom
cry out with joy.
It may just make
you weep.

If you're the type
of mom to be
that shows it
in your smile

It won't be long,
you'll share a bond.
It should just
take a while.

The love a mom
and child
could share
should be eternity.

The first of many
special times
brings love.
Just wait and see.

Gemma

Mom will love,
no matter what.
She's nurturing and kind.
What "could have" happened
to the mom,
the one that I call mine…

Chapter 4

Being Selfish

I understood my parents' next story told was that our very next move was to a place that was some type of big apartment we were about to move into. Some baby memories, yay! While there, they said I grew from a baby to a toddler fairly fast, standing quickly, trying to learn to walk early. From this home, I also learned an awful bad habit I would carry with me for many years to come. I also believe this changed a very big part of my childhood because of it! Maybe why mom made such a big change also. I am not really sure how, but we are about to find out why. This time in my life is when I learned to suck my thumb, a habit my mom did not mind at first. Most children my age may form this brief habit, as well as some other types of habits, the doctor explained to my mother when she told him it was a concern she had. So she thought nothing of it when it first began. Until I did not stop, unfortunately! This is when Mom began to get angry at me, beginning with hollering at me now and then. Her hollering increased with each peak of anger as the weeks passed, and I did not stop. When that did nothing, she started lightly slapping my thumb out of my mouth after the age of two had passed. At this point, I had not become scared of her yet. Not that I remember anyway. When that did nothing, she began giving me regular spankings on the butt. Later on, she found out this was not going to work at all either.

So I believe she became frustrated. At her wit's end, she used to say. After a while, Mom told me she began telling everyone that knew us of all the bad things I did, that I was sucking my thumb because I had become selfish. Yes, she said I was selfish! Back then, I never would have known what that word meant. She looked at me all the time and called me selfish! How could a child be selfish if they were sucking their own thumb, and why be so angry toward me about it? I really did not understand what I was doing wrong. I had another sibling who sucked their thumb all the time. Nothing was said about that. What was wrong with me doing it? When I became an adult, I thought, *How does a mother say sucking your thumb was being selfish?* I didn't understand! Was she just picking on me again?

I did not get it at all! Why did she have to tell everyone that? I would ask myself over and over. I still could not come up with a logical answer. Her description of a child doing something for attention, yes, I could almost see that a bit better. I could even see Mom telling friends or family because she was so frustrated with me. Though that was not the case at all! Attention I was not after, or was it? At least I did not want the kind of attention she gave me. I did not understand then or now. That, however, is certainly my mom never being wrong, as you will soon enough find out throughout this story. I thought I was not doing anything wrong at the time while I was younger, so I never stopped myself or wanted to.

Although I'm not ever going to agree with mom that would have been the reason in my later years either. I could not stop myself from sucking my thumb because I didn't want to. Even though I did try a few times, I just did not want to stop. So I guess you could call not wanting to stop as being selfish! Yes, that was pretty selfish of me! I just did not stop no matter what the punishment turned out to be, and there became a lot of them. I just knew that it always felt to me like I was only doing it because there was something I was missing in my unhappy little space, something lost that I felt I was needing in my life, something I was not getting. Yet I couldn't have known what that would be if I never felt it.

I truly believed I used sucking my thumb as some kind of security. Okay, security for almost thirteen years may have been pushing it a little too far! Yes, I sucked my thumb for almost thirteen years, but…wait and observe. This part of the story you just may find an interest in once you find out a few facts. It gets very enlightening, surprisingly interesting, but truly sad, especially for one small, innocent child, one who naturally would blame herself throughout her story. How could she not blame herself? She thought so many different things. There was no one to explain what she was being punished for.

Why would she also not think herself an ugly child if called one constantly? Was she really being selfish? What could she possibly be doing wrong to be in so much trouble all the time? I now remember asking myself, *Why does Mommy look at me that way? I will never be able to understand any of this if she does not tell me why or what to do to be good. How am I going to fix it? There is something wrong with me if I am the only one she comes to find for no specific reason to punish me for doing nothing but always just waiting for me to do something wrong.* Then again, I do not even have to do anything wrong. I was always the one she chose when she was angered. I will never understand why my mother singled me out so many times to take her punishments out on when she would become so mad!

Although she sure knew when to holler my name when it came time to ask who did this or who did that. Which is why I never understood why she even asked in the first place. She should have just called my name. My name was the one she seemed to like to holler best. It usually seemed to end up being my fault anyway. Do not get me wrong, my sisters took a good share of punishments also. But no one took them like I took them! For as long or as many times as I took them, ever! I think my mom personally had something against me. I could not quite describe it. I think it was the way she looked at me! It is something I might never find out! No matter who asks or how we ask.

It may just be a secret she may take to her last resting place, without me ever finding out the truth. The possibility could have been because Mom was furious through each and every year, with good reason, about the thumb-sucking. I am honestly not sure but sincerely wish that I knew. I guess I shouldn't speculate. No matter what the reason was, it was truthfully not a good-enough reason to do what she has done to me all these years. I am sure most mothers would have been almost as upset to have any of their children sucking their thumb for as long as I had. But I don't think anyone would have gone to the extreme my mother did. Some moms might have at least tried to find out why their child could possibly be doing it for this long! Not my mom though, oh no.

My mom became angrier and meaner toward me for the thumb-sucking without giving it a thought. My mom did not seem to be very logical when it came to her children, especially with me. She would just seem to lose herself in any kind of spanking or beating she felt like giving me on that particular day. I am hating that it is all coming back to me. This is feeling so painful to tell this now. I began to realize even at such a young age, I did not recognize my own mother as I had known her. Or did I ever really know her? Could it be that I only imagined what she was like when I saw the way she loved some of my siblings? The boys in particular? Was I just imagining a mother I wanted her to be and not who I saw?

She looked like a monster in one of my nightmares I would have at night if I were to describe the real mom I knew and could see, which made me even more afraid of her every time she came near me. Whether she had something to beat me with or not, it never mattered. Her fists and open hands did some fairly good damage to my body at times. She no longer was my mom to me anymore after a certain amount of time. I think this is when I realized she had been the selfish one, taking all her frustration and anger out on a child starting at the age of about three! That is as far back as I can remember. How could she be so selfish and cruel. She was now someone who has been just scary to me, and I thought it best for me to just stay far away from her as best I can.

I now remember always running or hiding from her every chance I got. Mom getting scary and angrier did not stop me though. That thumb seemed to find its way to my mouth, no matter what! The things my mother tried! How I can laugh about it now. Back then, I felt rage toward my mom. Things were building inside; I couldn't stop it because of all that she put on my thumb to stop me: the hot sauces she made me suck on my thumb, the hot peppers she taped to that thing, the tape she would try to keep taped on my it. So many different things. Nothing seemed to stop me. I kept that thumb stuck in my mouth so much it was now as much a habit as it was a source of security for me. I may have vomited a lot from the hot stuff and other things, but it still did not make me quit just yet. She would even tape gloves and mittens on my hands. Apparently, I would get those off my hands without any problems, as well as anything else she put on them. When Mom was not watching, it was off! I can see it being frustrating for Mom, but nothing she had come up with seemed to stop me so far. You would have thought she'd have just given up already. Nothing had been working at all for Mom or for me!

The spankings had begun to get out of hand though. So much worse than I could have imagined. I remember then Mom began hurting me badly. I began to be hit with rulers, sticks, and broom handles. Wooden spoons were used to slap my thumb out of my mouth, with it beginning to hit my face, sometimes leaving marks. Yes, I can recall a few selfish things Mom has done to me, and this is just the beginning of the selfish person she had become. I will not let you know what all of them are. That could take a while! As they say, actions speak louder than words, and she had a lot of action in this story. Perhaps when she withheld her love from me is one of the most selfish things she could have done to me. Is this really being selfish, or is it something altogether different? I do not think I am the selfish one here, but let's read on and find out.

Chapter 5

More Ways to Hurt Me

The spankings began to leave bruises and marks on other places of my body. I began to wonder sometimes if she was going to ever stop hitting me. Anything within her reach was not off limits to hit me with. If something broke while hitting me, she would reach for whatever she could get her hands on. As long as it hurt me, she would use it to hit or beat my hands and bottom with. Then it got to be my legs. Then she did not care where she hit me or with what. She just went all out of control. This is when she also began a new trick with my hair, using it as a new form of punishment to hurt me even more. She always loved her new ideas to hurt me, laughing as she enjoyed inflicting a new kind of pain onto me. How miserable and worthless I began to feel even as a young child.

Then she thought her idea of keeping meals from me would stop me from sucking that thumb, but it did not. I didn't seem to care what punishment she thought of. I could not seem to keep my thumb out of my mouth for any reason, at least not for her intent. We seemed to be in a war of some kind, neither of us letting the other win. She had made me just not care anymore, and the resentment began! I am not really sure what age I had been when this all started taking place. I know now that any age is not good to be hit or beaten by anyone, no matter what the reasoning or excuse would be because there is none. I know that now! I would begin to realize that as I got to be older.

Sometimes if I were to become hungry at mealtime and she was withholding food from me, I would still have kept that thumb in my

Entertaining Mommy?

mouth. I didn't care what her punishment was going to be and told her so. "That's okay, Mommy. I am not hungry today," I would tell her. That would make her even angrier if that were possible. Then she would try to start bribing me with food, thinking I would be hungry after a while, or that my favorite foods might entice me into stopping. But sadly, this did not work for either of us, with Mom usually ending up throwing the food at me when I would not eat it or her thinking I am saying I am not hungry just to make her mad, no matter how hungry I had become.

Even then, I wouldn't let her win! (Who was being selfish now?) Swearing and name-calling then beating me, as if that still did her or me any good. Both of us were getting very frustrated by now, I felt pretty sure of that. Even though at the time I didn't know what frustration was, I sure felt it. Then she tried scaring me into stopping. Mom, knowing how terrified of mice I had become, worked in her favor. All throughout many years, she would tell me my thumb was turning into a mouse. She would go into great detail about how my thumb was changing and growing daily. "I see a tail forming. It is starting to grow out of the end of your thumb. Do you see it?" she would ask me.

It would always make me panic, even though I did not know that is what I was doing at the time. "There is dark fur starting to grow on your thumb. Doesn't that taste funny to you?" I always took my thumb out of my mouth long enough to check for those kinds of things, then it would instantly go back into my mouth, making Mom scream and swear at me harder and louder, looking at me like I was some evil child. I thought I felt this feeling, not knowing what it was then, whenever she looked at me like that. She became even more scary to me if that were possible as she began to tell me of her mouse fairy tales.

She started to sound more and more like an ugly, creepy witch I had once seen at a movie theater when I was taken once. I was more terrified of that voice of hers than I was of the mouse, but I was always looking for something growing on my thumb even so. I also remember a nightmare I had several times of a witch laughing loudly, always flying on a broom and carrying a big stick, trying to hit me as

I ran. Although I could never see the face, I always knew it was my mother. There was always something in that nightmare that terrified me. I also repeatedly looked to see anything growing on my thumb, just watching and waiting, because mice did always scare me, so she was winning, a tiny bit.

Not that it did not affect me in other ways because it did. It kept my thumb out of my mouth a bit longer than usual. But only because I had to take it out to keep checking and make sure there was no tail growing or any fur to see, and I kept having those nightmares about mice and a scary witch. But nothing ever happened to my thumb. So it remained in my mouth, and even all of that still never stopped me. Some days the spankings for my thumb-sucking would get so out of control I felt like I would not be able to breathe again. That if I did, could it possibly kill me? It would hurt so badly for me to breathe in. Hey, I was very young. I did not know what was happening to me.

There was really no one to ask, so I just believed what went on in my mind—bad things, mostly all bad things. Nonetheless, I still sucked my thumb. She could not control it, so she remained angry about it and continued to get angrier as time passed! The spankings were becoming so much worse I knew they were not just spankings anymore. I knew they were much worse than any old spanking. So I began calling them just what they were, beatings. I was still spanked, but hit gentler in the face with a wooden spoon when my dad was around, which was not often. Those had become minor to me. I barely felt them. I think Mom made up for them later in the day when Dad was not around, which always appeared to make her angrier. It always seemed to take more of an effort when she had to be gentler with her milder spankings because Daddy was there.

I was so used to the fierce blows, the brutal slaps, the punches, the whippings with things. Still, that pat on the britches he was witnessing was nothing compared to what I received many days in my young life. I just kept doing whatever it was I was doing without looking up at her when she used those taps and little spankings on me in front of Daddy. I bet that had to have made her angry too. But they were that lightly felt! Still, my dad was concerned about all the marks I was getting on my face, which were the only ones he could see, and Mom knew that. With her not letting the girls be around Daddy much, he would never find out!

Knowing that is all he would ever see, Mom told him, "Do not be concerned." They were from trying to knock that stupid thumb out of my mouth with a wooden spoon! Mom said she was going to break me of sucking my thumb if it was the last thing she ever did (she told him). I truly did try to not put my thumb in my mouth as much while Mom was around. Dad must have told her of his worry because, for some time, Mom stopped hitting me in the face altogether and almost stopped with all the spankings and beatings for a while. I was one happy child for a bit! Just a very short while though. It was a breather for me so I could heal some. I was so happy! If only it could have stayed that way.

My life may have possibly become bearable to me. The spankings and beatings were really beginning to wear me down at that time. Instead of Mom bruising up my body again, she began screaming at the top of her lungs at me all the time! When she was not hitting me in the face, she was putting her face as close to mine as she could get it then screaming swear words and names at me, making me cry from her loud voice being so scary; making me so frightened I would pee my pants, and then I would get punished for that! I was not really sure which was worse, her beating on me or if it were her scaring me whenever she felt like it, which she was doing more of than the beatings, I think, at that time!

I was getting more frightened every day, it seemed. I knew now that was her goal because she constantly did so for no reasons at all, only making me wonder more what I had done to deserve all of this. Obviously, I was always going to blame myself because moms just did not stop loving their children for no reason. I had to have done something truly bad. If she would just tell me what it was so I could fix it, but she would not! Mom began actually jumping me as soon as I would start to relax, even if I was hiding and she found me. If I was asleep at night, she would scare me. I really think she was doing it to make me a jumpy, scared person…but why? I still always wondered what it is I have done!

If I could have known why, I could have made it better, and she would possibly stop! I always got scared how it made me feel when she was done taking her anger out on me with her yelling. I felt so nervous inside, so sick to my stomach. I wanted to vomit most of the time throughout most of my childhood. I guess that could be why I vomited so much when I was an adult whenever I got nervous. I finally know now that is how she wanted me: frightened, jumpy, feeling alone, scared, nervous, and feeling worthless. If that was her goal, she had met it several times over. People do not call moms like that a good person. I think they call those monsters.

At times, I thought Mom was trying to keep me from wanting to live anymore. Why would a mom do that to her own child, make them feel all these bad things? It scared me so much to think my mom would keep me from wanting to live anymore. I thought that was pretty bad for such a young child to be thinking that way all the time, and I did. It seemed the more terror I showed on my face, the more she got an evil smile on hers. Never enough to stop me with my bad habit though. I did want the pain to stop, always wishing that Mommy would just wake up one day and realize how sorry she is for all she has been doing to me and how much she will make it up to me by showing me her love!

I guess I would forget at times I was even trying to find ways for me to stop sucking my thumb on my own just to get her to stop hurting me! Sometimes I wish I had done more than just try because if you think it got any better for me as I grew older, think again. It would only seem to get worse as time passed. So to move ahead a bit in my story… I will come back to this part of my journey soon. You do not need to hear about every one of my battles with my mom beating me because of a silly habit I started. I know, if I had only stopped, maybe she would have too. Who am I kidding? She was enjoying this way too much! I did always wonder how many moms did this kind of thing to their children.

I am not so sure about any of this though. There were so many things I could have done differently and changed the course of my life possibly, but I did not, and these are some pieces of my shambled story.

Entertaining Mommy?

I am now six. My sister was in the same class with me in kindergarten. Mom even tried to embarrass me into stopping with my thumb-sucking. Anything to keep that thumb out of my mouth! One day Mom put just a shirt and diaper on me for school and nothing else, explaining to everyone that they were not to worry, I am very clumsy, always falling down and bumping into things, in case they looked at my battered and marked-up body. Mom got a baby stroller, brought my sister and I to school, putting me into the stroller when we arrived. Mom made my sister push me around the hallways and classrooms to see if it would embarrass me enough to stop the thumb-sucking. It did not seem to bother me in the least.

I stuck my thumb in my mouth and with the other hand waved to everyone we saw like we were just walking in a parade, smiling and waving to the crowd. Mom came to pick me up early after finding out this plan also had not worked, beating me as soon as we got home because, apparently, she was the one who had been embarrassed, so she told me. I think she beat me longer because no one was around to calm her down or stop her. No, I had to wait until she had no more energy to beat on me, and of course, I might have passed out at some point, waking up in a heap on the floor, probably a few minutes or so later. I really was not sure of the time I had laid there. I always dragged myself to a hiding spot, knowing if Mom saw me moving, she might start all over again because she had before.

I was lucky, I guess; at least she didn't go as far as ever trying to kill me! The beatings and spankings were not working either, but secretly, I think my Mom was beginning to really enjoy them. As I grew older, I was still spanked and severely mistreated. Me, unfortunately being too young to realize, I could have told on my mom, and it would not be tattling or get me into any kind of trouble if I had!

Mom also was really good about not breaking bones or doing very much noticeable damage because I do not ever remember being taken to a hospital or doctor that I recall. She might not have only because she probably knew she would not have had any kids after one of those kind of "stuttering" explanations. Mom began using her hand to slap my thumb out of my mouth after a while. I was so used to my thumb being in my mouth I would forget to keep it out of my mouth when Mom was around and be in shock when she would find it there while I would not be paying attention. I know now, she knew her hand hit my whole face and stung more, unlike the spoon. The beatings also never stopped, unless, of course, Dad was home. This was when she also began keeping me still by holding on to my hair with one hand to keep me in better place while she was beating on me or reaching for something to hit me with, and I remember how hard she twisted it tightly around her hand. I wondered at times where she came up with these ideas to cause me more pain! I think she laid in bed and thought of ways to hurt me without anyone else knowing it. The hairpulling would hurt every time so bad when she pulled on it, or even if I tried to move to get away from her hitting me. I always checked for bleeding when she was done. She liked that though. Even though I could not see her, I would hear her with her low chuckle every time I would wince when it pulled and I would reach up to grab her hand to try to ease up on the tightness.

She would then smash my hand with whatever she was beating me with and really laugh loud like she enjoyed that so much and seemed to pull harder on my hair than before, hoping I would keep putting my hand on top of my head when it would hurt the worse. She seemed to enjoy that a lot! I know, quite the mom, right? Well, I knew that, but she was the only one I had and the only one I knew, no matter what she did to me. At the time, I thought, I still needed her to love me. So I kept on trying, day after day, no matter how much pain she caused me. What! Don't think I didn't hate myself for even thinking that way because I did every time I thought of it!

Even way back when, I thought like that at three years old! I guess I would forget about the pain she caused me, the names she called me. At the time, I did not know what all those names meant anyway, like when she called me a loser or telling me I would never amount to anything when I grew up. I did not know what that meant, but once I remembered my memories, I remembered all those mean words she screamed at me throughout my lifetime. Mom swearing at me and calling me bad names, like those really affected me anymore. Oh, the times she would seek me out to come find me doing anything wrong! She seemed to enjoy our little game of hide-and-seek, but I did not!

No matter where I hid to get away from her to suck my thumb, it was like she had nothing else to do but come find me then always start beating me when she would catch me with my thumb in my mouth, but not before she scared me half to death first! Laughing that evil witch laugh that she must have known frightened me terribly. But then a great thing happened! Just before my thirteenth birthday, I quit! Yes, I stopped sucking my thumb all on my own. No threats, no spankings. I just stopped. Coincidentally, around this exact time, something else in my life stopped. You can find out just what that was when you continue. So be my guest and read on.

Although I can tell you that after a few years, what started as a child's poor habit, as with many children, and after many years of nightmares and silence, I knew I was not being selfish as my mother had always thought it had to be and told everyone. There were times in my life I am sure I did a few selfish things. Except there is one sounding a little selfish I was reminded of often and made fun of many times for it throughout my lifetime. It has always been my mother who started making fun of me because of it, having other children join in with her to tease me about this unkindness (she thought) I did. But at the time, I was only three when this horrid act took place. As I am sure my mother would have thought. Just one more way to hurt me, I guess, because it still did, like everything else she has done to me! She told me everything I did was so horrible that it was punishable! Also, after a while of retrieving flashes of my past, I recall being just barely able to stand and always placed in a corner. With Mom keeping a watchful eye, I am sure. I would stick my thumb into my mouth while being punished for sticking my thumb into my mouth. I do remember now how furious that made Mom to know I did that while standing in the corner. I remember that mouth of hers and how angry it looked.

I also remember I did not get away with it for long. You would think after a while from the scars, the bruises, and the objects I have been hit with, that I would have learned by now not to stick my thumb in my mouth in front of my mother at all! I was just a child! I forgot a lot! I think I was a very nervous child, even at such a young age, and kept this habit at that time due to nerves, stress, and maybe anxiety. This may have played a role in it; I am not sure. I am not a doctor but have been told by a couple doctors, this may have been the case. I have done a selfish thing or two as a young child, though, I will admit to them. I did not know at three I would have to, though. Kids have habits! At least some children do!

But Mom, only because it happened to be me, I am sure she was thinking it a sin or something. Maybe at three I was thinking I wanted something to be just mine or I could have just been selfish at three. My mother has told this story so many times. I know it word for word. The story of my bag of toys. Of course, this is the kind of story she would repeat over and over and, let's not forget, tell everyone she knew or that knew me while I was a child or even when I became an adult how selfish this was. At the age of about (again) three years old, I had a bag I dragged around everywhere. I picked up all small toys that I liked the looks of, putting them into my bag that I would not let go of.

It did not matter to me if they were my toys or not. If they went into my bag, they became mine. If they were little, they were in my bag. If the bag became too heavy and pulled me forward or knocked me over, I never let go of my bag of toys. Being very determined, I was told if anyone came close to them, it was explained to me, I would scream bloody murder. That is what Mom has told me repeatedly. If anyone tried to play with them while I was taking them out of the bag to look at them, the same thing would happen. Everyone around knew when I was not happy. I would hardly even touch these toys, I was told, hardly look at many of them myself. Though I did not want anyone else to either.

I am sure I was afraid of having someone take some of them, but I could still have them all be mine this way. I did ask Mom if she ever thought anything that I ever did seem adorable to her at any time when I was a child. I wish I had never asked. I knew I should have known better! She only looked at me and laughed, making me hurt once again. This is the story, Mom told me. So, of course, this all just had to be truthful if Mom kept repeating it! Yes, this was selfish! If the story told to me time and again were true, Mom would also tell me that everyone thought the world was coming to an end the way I would scream if my bag happened to break open or get a hole worn into it and toys began to fall out.

Mom told of how she would laugh when she would encourage one or more of my siblings to go help their sister out. "Please help her pick up her toys just to shut her up!" Mom knew that if anyone tried to help me pick them up even, I screamed and cried louder. All the time my mom would be laughing and joking with someone about what a brat I am, only doing it for a way to hurt me once again. After a while of hearing me screaming and crying, she would spank my ass good, she told me, just because she could. But doing that just made it look good once in a while. It gave her a reason to spank me in front of someone.

But she told me later, she did not need a reason to beat on me. She only did it every once in a while in case Daddy heard about it. Wanting to make it look good every so often, she said. Well, I did not think anything made up or real would be a good-enough reason to beat on anyone mother. Again, you look like a fool and a cruel, mean mother. I do not think anyone is laughing with you now! But that is the story she has told over and over. Still not funny, Mom! My punishable, selfish act of unkindness, yes, I did that! A fresh memory of when I was three.

Retrieving a Memory

Growing up in a house like ours,
what can I say?
It is a story worth telling.
A childhood I could not recall,
and honestly thought I'd never know.
But as an adult,
getting help from someone
skillfully experienced,
who began retrieving my,
deepest, darkest secrets.
Thoughts of my childhood
memories
that I once had concealed.
Until one reflection
began to unveil
my past
of distressing nightmares.
I became a child once more.
A memory came to life.
A thought of my mother,
and I began to cry…

Chapter 6

Remembering Three

I woke up to yelling and loud crying. Daddy was yelling, and Mommy was crying. I was laying in the back seat of a car. I remember feeling really warm, almost too warm. I brought my head up to look. There was a blanket wrapped all around me. I tried to move. I couldn't! Wait. Something felt funny. I forgot what I was thinking because all of a sudden, I heard my mother cry out.

"It was an accident I tell you!"

My father was incredibly angry at her. I was not sure what they were hollering about, but Mommy was crying a lot, and Daddy did not seem to be listening very well. I wanted to say something, but Daddy sounded too angry. *I will just wait and listen. Maybe I will find out what is wrong and where we are going.*

I wondered what they were talking about, then I felt so puzzled. My thoughts came back to me. *Why am I in the back seat laying down? Why am I covered with a blanket? Why can't I move!* I looked at my legs. They were straight out on the seat. Daddy yelled something again, jumping me. Mommy was looking at him. I could see her face. It looked so sad. Mommy was making me feel sad. I wondered why Daddy was so angry at her. I looked up again, and Mommy looked into the back seat at me. Now she looked really scared, but I did not know what she did wrong. I wished just once Mommy would smile at me, and we could bond with a little smile. I knew we could not; that was not something that confused me at all!

She turned back around, with tears running down her cheeks. Poor Mommy. I wished she would like a hug from me, but she wouldn't let me hug her. Mommy didn't like me to touch her, I did remember that. I was hoping that Daddy would stop being mad at Mommy. I'm sure she was sorry! I heard her tell him. *I will tell daddy later she really is sorry, and maybe he will stop being angry at her.* They still argued while I fell back to sleep again. Then I felt the car stop. It jolted me awake again. My dad got out of the car first, reaching into the back seat. He asked me if I was okay and called me sweetheart, making me smile.

"Yes, Daddy, I am fine," I told him.

I wondered why I would not be fine. I was only sleeping. Still, why was I in the back seat sleeping? I began to ask him when Mommy asked him if he needed help with me. *Why would he need help? I am a big girl, aren't I? Why can't I think of anything on my own?* Daddy lifted me off the back seat like I was a small sack of potatoes, carrying me all the way to where Mommy was standing. When we got to a house, Daddy stood me up beside Mommy. She put her hands on my shoulders. He unwrapped the blanket from around me. I looked around, yet something felt so strange to me. What was it?

Then I looked at the door we were standing in front of. Was I supposed to remember where we were? Then I realized I really did not know where we were. Something still felt really funny to me. All of a sudden, my cousin opened the door to where we were standing in front of. My siblings were all standing in a room I can hardly see into. They all ran to the door, hollering my name, looking out at us. Everyone was talking at the same time. Then I noticed the jacket I was wearing and realized I also felt something on my head after I touched it. I pulled it off, and it was a matching hat. It was so beautiful, I thought, but I did not recognize it. Where did it come from? I tried to put the hat back on my head, leaning against Mommy.

I couldn't stand because something was making me feel so strange. *Where have we been again?* I tried to think... I looked up. We were standing in front of a house I did not recognize. I saw all my siblings, my cousin, my mom, and dad. I knew all of them, but where were we right now? It was so loud. Why couldn't we get in the house where my siblings were? Everyone was standing in the door. No one could get in. No one could get out. For some reason, I wanted to scream, "Everyone, quiet!" I wanted to think. I was so confused. I wished someone could understand my words more. I needed to ask someone so many questions, but it was so loud.

I felt like I was going to cry. I did not know where I was, and I felt so confused! What was all this loudness about anyway? My brother said something to me that I couldn't hear, and then he pointed down at my legs. I looked down. Oh, that was what felt so weird. I had something on my leg. My siblings were all talking about whatever it was they saw on my leg. My parents were trying to tell my cousin something about where we had been, but no one could hear anything. I was trying to listen to my parents talking, but I couldn't hear over all this noise! I was still trying to hear, so I said, "Shh," to my siblings to try and quiet them down. It did not work. They couldn't hear me because it was too loud. I still couldn't hear anyone.

Everyone was trying to get a look at my leg, and Mommy was trying to hold me up. I was not very steady with my legs; I began to get it now.

"I cannot understand any of you," I hollered back at them. "You're all talking at the same time."

They didn't understand me. I looked down; even the baby was jabbering. I began to smile, feeling special that they all wanted to talk to me. It was cold out here, and I wanted to go inside. Daddy must have read my thoughts. He began pushing everyone aside, enough for us three to get through. I hobbled with mommy's help into a house I'm not sure I recognized. What was wrong with me? I knew everyone here. I was sure we must live here, but I did not know where I was standing.

It was scaring me that I did not know things. *What is happening to me?* I thought to myself. *Should I tell someone? Am I going to sound a little silly to them? Will they all make fun of me, laugh at me?* Daddy and Mommy were discussing a doctor or hospital visit we had been to with my cousin, but I didn't remember that either. Maybe that was where I got this thing on my leg. My siblings were still being loud, so I couldn't hear anything they were saying. While Mommy took off my coat and hat, I hugged the coat up against me. I did not remember it before, but it was so pretty. I looked down at my brother. He said he was signing his name on my cast—what he called that thing on my leg.

He was so funny.

"Why you doing that?" I asked him.

"That's what people are supposed to do when you get a cast on anything," he said.

"Oh," I said, like I knew what he was talking about. Why couldn't I think?

"Mommy." I tugged on her coat. "Where did I get this cast thingy on my leg?" I asked.

"At the doctor's, honey," she said.

Before I could ask her why or any other things, she ran off, and I almost fell over. She must have forgotten she was holding me up. How come I did not know where I had this cast thing put on my leg or when or even how it happened! Or what a cast was even for. I didn't even remember how old I was. I must have said the last part out loud.

My brother told me I was three. He was smiling at me as he walked away, knowing I had more than one question! Though nothing else, no one else, would tell me anything.

"Please, someone tell me!" I screamed out loud.

Of course, they still didn't understand me. *What is going on?* I thought to myself. They were acting so weird! Everyone seemed to run the other way! I again did not know what to think about everyone acting so silly. I was not really upset that I could not think a lot of things about the cast because I knew something bad must have happened, but no one would tell me what. So maybe it was good not to remember just yet; maybe it would scare me too much, the way everyone was acting just now.

I did wish I could remember my house, which was where we lived for a while, my brother told me, and the many other things I could not think of. I began trying to hobble everywhere and needed lots of help. I got to sleep on the couch so I would not have to climb the stairs, which I didn't think I could have even tried to do. Everyone helped with whatever I needed. I did love that! I felt so special, and I did not have to do very many things for myself for a long time. Still, no one would tell me what happened. I asked everyone, but no one else seemed to know either.

They would say, "I don't know." So I stopped asking. The only time I had to get up was to use the bathroom. Mommy brought me food on trays, drinks with straws in them, and as many fruits and snacks as I wanted. I felt truly special. Still, I knew nothing that happened, and it made me kind of sad. Everyone ignored me whenever I had asked any kind of question about it. Mommy would ask me all the time if I needed anything to just ask her. I did not dare to at first, but she was being so nice to me. I really did like her soup, so I said, "More soup please." You know! Mommy went right out and made me a new pot of chicken noodle soup she told me was especially for me! Mommy took such good, loving care of me.

I don't know what was happening to her. *It's got to be one of those miracle things I was thinking about before.* We were getting along so well. Maybe I was finally being good for once, and she did not have to be mad at me for anything anymore! Mommy even gave me sponge baths because I could not take a bath yet, and she talked really sweet to me all the time she was washing me. While I had the cast thing on, she never once yelled at me or spanked me for sucking my thumb. So I thought maybe she had sort of stopped being angry at me, but I soon found out I was wrong about that! I did really like sleeping on the couch though.

My siblings would come sit on the floor in front of me, just talking to me. Other times, they would sit on the arm of the chair or couch. My baby sister would crawl all over me while I sat or laid on the couch. Lots of times my brother would read me stories. That was one of the best parts. I liked playing games with them too. I also got to sleep on the couch for a really long time. I liked that a lot. I slept right next to my parents' bedroom. The walls must have been pretty thin because I could hear just about everything they talked about. I did not like that part of it! A few nights after we came home with the cast on my leg, I could hear them once again arguing about the same thing, like they had done in the car. I woke up because my leg hurt, and I had to pee. *Oh, please hurry up and stop fighting. It is time for bed, isn't it?*

I tried to hum so I would not hear them again. But I was too tired. I just wanted to pee. I almost fell back to sleep, but a scream jolted me, and I got really scared. I thought I would just ask to sleep upstairs in my own bed after tonight was over. This was too scary for me. I didn't like hearing Daddy angry. I was already used to Mommy's anger and her loud voice, but I did not like to hear Daddy mad at anyone. He sounded really loud when he yelled at mommy. He was much bigger than Mommy too. I was just glad I was not scared of him like I was of her. I did not want bad dreams of my daddy too. I was thinking now, *I know my brother could help me up and down the stairs. I am sure he won't mind.*

It might be hard for me to do, but anything was better than listening to Mommy and Daddy fighting all the time! They were yelling bad words to each other again. I looked at the ceiling, wishing they would stop so I could holler to them that my leg hurt and I had to pee. I needed help! I closed my eyes once again. Then I heard Daddy yell at Mommy for breaking my leg. My eyes opened wide! What? I sat straight up in bed, and my heart began to race for some reason I did not know. I thought to myself, *Why would Daddy... I don't have a broken... Breaking my leg, but that is not... Mommy would not...* Then a huge flash came back to me. I remembered the night it happened! *Oh no, Daddy is right.*

Mommy's scary face. Mommy yelling and swearing at me. I tried to hold her face so she could listen to me talk to her as I begged her! "Please, Mommy, listen to me!" Holding her angry face, I begin to cry out loud again. No wonder no one would talk to me about what had happened to me that night, why I could not remember why, or how I got this thing on my leg. That I really did get a broken leg and that my mommy did it! Everyone did know what happened.

They were all there. They all saw it happen but told me nothing about it. For some reason, they wanted me to remember on my own, but why? Now I did remember everything as I began to cry myself to sleep. Then I started having this dream of Mommy, a footstool, and a fly swatter, Mommy's frightening words she began to holler, as I cried, trying to hold her face in my hands again so she could see it was me and not someone she did not know. She slapped my hands away from her face, screaming those bad words.

"Please, Mommy. Please, let me tell you!" I screamed back… then I remembered nothing.

Chapter 7

What Really Happened?

It all started a few nights before. My parents had gone out for the evening. I'm not sure where they had gone, but they left us with an older cousin to babysit. We were in the living room, raising hell. Yes, they told me, hell! Being loud and misbehaving. I kept smelling something coming from the kitchen. I quietly snuck to the door, peeking my head through, asking my cousin, "What you doing?" He said he was making us a special snack (thinking about it now, it probably contained some kind of sleep potion if he were a smart babysitter). He told me to go on along and tell everyone in the living room to settle down. Or there would be no snack for anyone. I smiled, thinking I was very grown up.

I went back to the living room, saying in my best three-year-old voice so everyone could understand the words my cousin wanted me to say: "Everybody, settle down."

I hollered, "Ebbery buddy, seddle down."

They didn't even turn my way. I hollered again. No one heard. They were being so loud how could they ever hear me? I looked around and saw a fly swatter on a table by my daddy's chair. I ran over, grabbing it. Then, having what I thought was a great idea, I threw myself across my daddy's footstool and began pushing it with my feet and body. I looked up. *This might take a while*, I thought to myself. *It's really heavy*. I knew I wanted to get it pushed until I thought it might be in the middle of the room.

I had to lay across it and rest to catch my breath before I could finish out the rest of my plan. This was more work than I have ever done, and I was tired! Still, my siblings paid no attention to me. I finally had the footstool to where I thought was the middle of the room, then I slowly climbed onto it and began trying to stand up. When I thought I had my balance, I began waving the fly swatter all around me like I was casting a spell over my siblings. In my loudest voice, I screamed again what my cousin wanted me to tell them.

"Ebbery buddy, seddle down!" I was going to tell them about not having a snack and was excited to be the one to be able to tell someone a secret finally. But...

At that very moment, my parents walked into the living room. I turned my head a little bit to look at them. My mother had the scariest look I had ever seen on her face. It was so scary I almost fell off the footstool. I felt my face getting really red, and before anyone said anything, I knew I was in trouble. My siblings looked up too and stopped what they were doing, turning their heads to look at me, then wondered what I looked so frightened about. Then they also saw Mommy standing with that same scary look. The room went completely silent. Out of the corner of my eye, I saw my cousin come into the living room.

I barely heard him say, "What are you doing up there, young lady? Get down right now!"

Then he stopped when he, too, saw my mother's face. I lowered the fly swatter. I had the feeling Mommy saw only me in the room as I stood on the foot stool. I heard Daddy start to say a word to her, then Mommy's voice filled the whole room with words I had never heard before, drowning out whatever my daddy was going to say. It was so loud I almost fell off the footstool again. Her words sounded so angry I just knew I was in for something bad just from the sound of that voice. When Mommy began screaming, she ran toward me, grabbing me so hard, pulling me up in the air. Then she shook me while still hollering all those angry swear words.

I was crying really loud as she shook me, and I was trying to tell her I was supposed to be telling them they would not get a snack if they were not quiet, but no matter how loud I yelled, Mommy yelled even louder and never cared what my answer would be. I tried putting her face between my hands so she would look and see that it was me while I cried. Mommy did not care who I was, slapping my hands away. She picked me up like I was a big ball again, throwing me toward the couch. (I think.) Her aim was not so good because I ended up hitting the wall hard, crumbling into a heap on the floor. I was told later, Daddy ran to me, picking me up, and said, "Maybe she is just sleeping."

They said Daddy began making this awful noise, a cry and a mumble sound at the same time. Daddy laid me on the couch, crouching down beside me, waiting for me to move.

When I did not, he stood up and yelled, "You've killed her!" Daddy sat on the couch beside me, picking up my head and holding it to his. Then he began to cry out loud. He sat there, sobbing, while the room was way too quiet, except for the low whimpering of my siblings, who were scared also, just hoping to hear the sounds of me waking up. At least that was what they had been praying for, they told me later. I was also told my cousin and mother had stood there in total shock. My mother's face had turned almost white.

All of a sudden, Daddy stood up and shouted, "She's breathing! Get her coat, hat, and a blanket. We are going to the hospital!" Daddy had to scream twice at Mommy before she realized he had been talking to her. "Get her coat, hat, and a blanket, damn it! Get the car keys and go warm up the car! She is breathing. We are taking her to the hospital now. MOVE YOUR ASS!"

Mommy did as he had asked, putting her coat on, and ran out. Daddy gave my cousin a few quick instructions while putting on my coat and bundling me up warm then carried me out the door. I did not know any part of this accident until someone told me this story, how it all took place after I had become older.

How could I forget something so tragic? Oh yes, now I remember… I was unconscious, they had told me later. That must be how I forgot. Maybe that is also how I lost my memory, or it is such a tragedy I just wanted to forget! What could have happened to my mother on that day? To lose it in front of everyone? I always wonder if she had just been angry once again or if she really was just mean and wanted to hurt me for an unknown reason! I will never be able to find out. She will never talk about what happened, and as far as I know, she never had anyone she confided in. We moved out of this house shortly after this incident, I was told.

If informed correctly, we moved out of this town for a time then moved back some time later, again making me wonder if we moved so many times for being closer to family, job opportunities, or someone thought she may be found out mistreating her children. I believe, in the beginning of all this, my daddy thought these incidents were really accidents, as my mother had probably told him they were. I wonder how much covering up my mom had to do to keep my father thinking they were just horrible accidents. She must have spent a lot of time and energy trying to convince people that her children were all accident-prone and that is why we all (me especially) always had marks and bruises covering our bodies. How sad that anyone could ignore what was right in front of their eyes. They did not see or hear our pain.

A Note to My Mother

To my dear mother!

I remember you took care of me
out of guilt, not love.
I am still unsure what made you so angry.
You did not have to throw me!
Another beating I could have forgotten.
I assumed you had a hard life
growing up.
Many of us did.
That is never an excuse
to take it out on
your own children.
I was not asked to be born.
You did not give me a choice!
I did not get one again when you chose
to abuse me.
I never deserved your anger.
I was innocent too.
You should have broken that chain,
that vicious cycle,
the way I learned to do!
Your story is not mine to tell.
"This" is a reminder of mine.
I am getting through this
without your help.
You did not yet say,
I'M SORRY.
Never mind though… I would never
forgive you anyway!

Your daughter

Chapter 8

The Moving Memories

I was told we moved quite a few times before we found the right place for our growing family. It just took several moves before it happened. This time, Mom told us we would be living very close to a park and that we would be able to do fun things there. But only when we were good. So we got to go there a lot because we tried really hard to be good. We just loved the park. Mom would bring us many times, and we would bring a picnic for lunch. My older cousin would bring us a lot too, or there were family friends that we would go with sometimes. There was a girl there that I would notice who seemed to be about as tall as me. I noticed she was there as much as I was. I would never dare to say anything to her.

I was very shy, and it seemed that she was also. We both just looked and smiled every time we walked by each other. This happened for several days as we both decided to be shy for a while. One day, when I was on the swing, I was very nervous when she came over and said hi to me and told me her name. Even though my face turned many shades of red, I was so happy she was not as shy as me. The rest of the day, we played together and talked about our parents, where we lived, and our siblings. She was an only child and stayed with her grandparents most of the time because her parents were in the service, but I did not know what that meant, and I did not want to ask at that time.

Her grandparents had to explain what this had meant to me later. She introduced me to her grandparents the following day. I thought they seemed really nice. My mom even came over and sat with my new friend's grandparents. Mom said she liked them and that they did seem really nice. We played together almost every day for a few weeks before we really got to know one another. We became like sisters, spending every day together we could at the park, getting to know one another very well. After we had talked about her grandparents some more, we found out they only lived two houses down from our house. We were both so excited, hoping we could visit each other. When we finally did get to, it was so much fun!

We began to visit each other at our houses almost every day. But I liked her grandparents' place better. It was just the two of us, and it was really quiet there. No one spanked me for being naughty or when I sucked my thumb either. My friend had some really nice things her grandfather made for her, some beautiful dolls and this really huge doll house with all the furniture in it. That was my favorite thing to play with, so we played with it a lot. My friend said it was her favorite thing too. We also did crafts and baked with her grandmother. Her grandmother did not even get mad at us if we spilled something or made a mess. She would say, "Do not be silly. Everything cleans up."

I wished my mom would say that, I thought to myself. I loved it there and secretly wished they could be my grandparents too. But I knew I could never tell anyone that. I would get into big trouble, especially if my mom knew I was even thinking that. My mom was beginning to be nicer to me, and that really surprised me. I still got my share of spankings and hit with a wooden spoon if I was caught with my thumb in my mouth, but I did not care. Things seemed to be going well for me and my little part of the world. I was just so happy to be spending time at my friends as much as I did. Mom did not seem to be hitting me hard with things for a while.

Little did I know, it was not because she was being nice to me; it was that she was getting rid of me for all those hours and that someone might see the marks on me if she left any. Thanks a lot, Mom! It sure changed fast when my friend gave me my own doll to take home with me and keep for my own one day. That made Mommy so angry again, and I did not know why. When I brought it home, I was so happy and excited. I skipped to the kitchen to show her. She turned around and saw the doll I held up so proudly.

Entertaining Mommy?

Her face became so furious-looking. Her mouth made those straight, angry lines that I instantly started to cry.

"You little bitch," she screamed at me. "You can march your ass right on over there and give it back! Now! Who do you think you are anyway?"

I blinked! Not knowing what I had done wrong this time either. *Why does this keep happening to me all the time? I do not understand what it is I am doing wrong.* I became frightened and hid my face behind the doll, also forgetting about my thumb and sticking that in my mouth. Mom stomped up to me quickly, grabbed the doll out of my hands, throwing it to the floor. I cried out, sorry for the doll, trying to bend over to pick her up.

When my mom slapped me so hard across the face it knocked me over backward. She yelled, "And keep that damn thumb out of that damn mouth of yours! You are going to pick up that stupid doll and take it back over to those snooty people. Do you understand?"

No, I did not! I thought to myself.

"Who do they think they are anyway? Don't they know I have more than one brat over here? What are they trying to do, start something? Get you all fighting over one stupid doll, is that what they want? Do they not think your father and I can provide you with your own doll? I have a good mind to go over there and give them old coots a piece of my mind! Now you go on back over there and you say, 'Thank you, but I have sisters that would be upset if I had a doll like this when they do not have one!'"

I got up off the floor, wiping my tears and the blood of my nose onto my sleeve while still crying. Then I tried to rub my face, but it felt too sore. Instead, I just kept wiping gently at my nose. Mother began screaming again, so I did not dare to pick up the doll yet.

"What, do you think you are going to become a snotty little brat like your friend?" my mom yelled at me, still not knowing what she meant. "You'll never be nothing, you hear me? You will end up just as I did. All of my girls will! Barefoot and pregnant!"

I waited for her to get done being mad. I picked up the doll finally, walked over to my mother, and said, "I am sorry, Mommy." I did not know what I was sorry for, but I was.

"Just get your ass back over there and give it back," she said angrily again.

I went out crying, walked back over, knocked on the door, still crying, and said, "I'm sorry I have to give this doll back." Then I told them the reason as my mother instructed. "Thank you for giving it to me. I am grateful to have such a great friend to trust me with such a beautiful doll. It will just have to be mine when I come here."

My friend and her grandparents were so sorry and said they did not mean to upset anyone, asked if maybe they should come over and talk to my mom.

"No!" I said a little too loudly. My little friend was crying too.

She touched my face and asked, "Did your mom hit you?"

"No," I said, also as instructed in the past. "My face gets red when I'm upset. You know that!"

But I did not know that they were already angry because they knew my mother had hit me in the face and had seen the blood on my sleeve. My friend hollered to me and ran to me to hug me as I started to walk away. We both sobbed onto each other's shoulders. Somehow, we both knew that she knew the truth! We did not want to stop hugging one another. I finally did let go and patted her back. I told them I would see them all later, thanking them again. I turned and ran all the way home, crying all the way. I did not know then that I would never see them again. Mom would not allow me to, and I did try to ask why, which was another wrong thing to do.

I got a spanking a few times or hit somewhere for asking. So I stopped asking. I cried all by myself, not knowing why for a very long time. I truly missed my best friend. I thought Mom was trying to be cruel to me once again just because she could. After a while, my friend had gotten another of her friends to get me a secret note. I kept it safe and hidden because at the time, I could not read yet, and when I could, it was too late.

Soon after that, we moved away, and I never saw them again. I felt so alone and really began to be this shy little girl that did not understand things about adults. A couple years after I could read, my heart broke. The grandparents had written the letter, and it said, "We believe you are being abused. If you or your siblings need our help, we are here for any one of you. You can come over right now, and we can get you help. Or wait until you think it is safe. Your mom will not hurt you anymore, we promise."

I wish I had read back then or given the letter to someone who could read. After I became an adult, I always wished those grandparents had just taken it upon themselves to get involved, especially suspecting like they did. They could have done so much for me and possibly helped my life to turn out in a much different way, but I do not blame them in any way. Until I grew up, I did not know what my mother had done, but we both know I did not deserve what I received, especially on that day when I returned home with that doll that could have been mine that I would have shared. I also did not even know what being snotty was.

That was not what made you angry, Mother! But your anger caused my pain once again. Thank you for making me move without thanking them properly or saying goodbye. Thank you again for being so cruel to me and controlling my life yet again when you had no right to! You did a great job of belittling your own child. I hope you're proud.

When I grew up to be a teenager, I always wondered if we moved so many times because of job opportunities for my dad, as it was explained to us, or because of being closer to family or if it really was because Mom did not want to explain the marks on her children's bodies! There were plenty of them for her to have to explain if anyone ever asked! Just another thing I will never find the answers to I would like to have resolved. It was, after all, something against my mom, and she would never talk about such things. I did feel that the way my mom treated me and the things she made me feel were the reasons I grew into a very shy, frightened, nervous child, and then an adult who did not know how to deal with many things in my life at any age.

Even as an adult, I was still a nervous, anxious person who has a lot of scars not only on her body but on her heart as well! What pain you have caused that poor, innocent child who did nothing to you but beg for your trust and love. You should feel shame, but I know it is yet another emotion I know you have never and will never

Gemma

feel! You are not capable of a lot of feelings, are you, Mother? I could name a few that you are capable of, though, but I think they are in the highlights to some of my other pages, so we will skip it for now! Just know that I am aware that a lot of my nervousness and anxiety I still carry with me today, I blame on you for most of it. For all the things you put me through, all that you tortured me about, that is on you, but still "with me." So thank you for that!

Let us move the memories along, shall we?

Chapter 9

A Scary Place

I did not like our new house. So many things about it scared me. I did not like where we moved to at all. There were no houses that I could see anywhere near us and no park to go to either. I am sure this means I will not be making any new friends this time. I was still not in school yet, so I would only have my siblings to play with for friends. That part was okay. I began to feel strange, jumpy, and shaky-like. I had started to feel scared of everything again. My face would get really red when I would get shy or embarrassed, worse than it ever did before. It seemed like I have been shy about everything lately. I didn't know why! I tried stopping myself from doing it, but it was no use; it just kept getting worse.

My heart felt like it was racing all the time. Beating so fast, it drummed in my ears. It felt like I was shaking inside and outside all the time. I did not understand it, and I did not dare to ask anyone what it could possibly be. I thought they would laugh at me, and I did not know if it was just me, thinking it was happening to me, or if it really was happening. I was so confused at times; I did not know what was real or what was not. It really scared me though. I wondered if I could be dying once in a while. That is how much it scared me. I felt like a ticking time bomb all the time as it was without this feeling. The ticking time bomb came from a cartoon I had remembered, and that is what I felt like. I was going to explode!

I knew I was still missing my friend and her grandparents. That was the only part of my life that had changed, except for this stupid move. The happy part of my life had been taken from me. They had become like part of my family, and I felt like a part of my family was missing. I would never, ever dare to tell anyone that! Mom might hear it, and it would make her mad at me again. She was already mad enough now! Still not understanding any of these things of life did not help me either. I wondered secretly if I could get an illness from missing someone. Hey, I was four. What did I know at that innocent age? If only I had the courage even then to ask questions.

I found out later in life, it was probably due to anxiety and stress. Then I remembered how anxious I really started getting when my brother talked me into taking the training wheels off my bike so I could really learn how to ride, he said! Naturally, in a driveway that went all downhill from our house, ending into the road. Great! Then there became an even bigger hill. You sure better know how to stop there if you are going down that driveway. I just had to learn to use my brakes, something I have never done before. Scared does not come close to what I felt! There were times when my heart raced so fast I thought I was going to die; it beat so hard. My face stayed red the whole time we were practicing. I felt it.

Either I was forgetting the brakes or taking more skin off my knees, legs, and hands when I flipped the bike, making me so angry when forgetting to use those brakes! I would always get scared and put both my feet down on the dirt before I got to the end, flipping it every time. I kept screaming at him and throwing my bike, "I can't do this!" Over and over, I kept screaming this at my poor brother, who was only trying to help me. My brother encouraged me well, running beside me, holding on the whole time, just like he promised. He showed me how to use the brakes. So many times, we practiced together.

Still, knowing I was too scared, my brother said, "I am going to let go. Use your brakes to slow down. I'll run right beside you. I promise."

I was too nervous. I knew I could not do it, I kept telling myself. My brother would run ahead just before I would reach the bottom, and every time, I would slam my feet to the ground. Always flipping me over my bike, always taking more skin off.

I would scream, "I can't do it!"

"Yes, you can," my brother would always say right back. He would not let me quit until I used the brakes on my own, always the good brother that he has always been, staying right with me to encourage me.

Love my brother! The first time I finally did it on my own, I got off my bike, throwing it to the ground, screaming, "There! I did it! Now I am done!"

That is how I learned to ride my bike. Scared to death, but I did it. Thanks to my big patient brother. He was so good to all his siblings, always helping out.

In this same house, I was introduced to bats, finding out I was also very afraid of them, or making myself believe I was. My parents were out. My brother was in the kitchen with us, and a neighbor who was babysitting was outside. I do not know what we were all doing in the kitchen, but a bat appeared. The bat began flying all around the kitchen. I had never seen one before, but I could tell I did not like them. They looked ugly and very scary. It sounded like everyone was screaming. It got to be so loud. I thought that was what we were supposed to be doing. The bat began to fly around us, and I began to scream as loud as I could. It did not take me long to take my screaming lungs under the table, hoping this bat thingy did not know how to fly under tables.

I did not get a real good look at it, but from what I saw, the bat looked ugly and gross, knowing I did not want it near me. I had lost my voice for the first time from screaming that night. My brother finally caught it and put it outside. I just knew then I was not going to like creatures. I like bats today, as long as I do not have to touch them, or even see them! I know they like mosquitos. Those are not very likable either. As for the bats, they stay away from you if you leave them alone. They fly around also. I do not like things that fly around. I still seem scared of everything. Geez, I wonder to this day what made me that way. Maybe we will find out if we read on. I know bats do good things. I just do not want them on me.

In this same house is also where I became afraid of the dark, not because of my siblings this time or my mom. Had she known I was afraid of the dark, though, she would have terrorized me, I just know it. I tried to make sure she never found out about that part of my many phobias. Mom did like to see the look on my face when I am scared!

The house was the kind of house that gave you that scary kind of feeling. I am so thankful my siblings did not start scaring me in this house. I probably would have jumped at everything that moved. Oh, I am certain I just about did anyway. It seemed no matter what room we were in, the lights would flicker on and off constantly. They also went completely out many times. I know I was not the only one who was afraid of the dark. I could hear others scream and would always try to find someone to be with until the lights came back on. I was probably just the only one who would not stop screaming until the lights came on, driving everyone away from being near me unless I stopped.

Unless Mom was near, then I only went into panic mode, so she would not find out this new fear I felt. I knew I did not like the dark and knew something was going to get me. I just felt it, I told myself anyway. I know the screaming never helped any of us. I know now it made it worse, but I did not know what else to do when I became scared. I had no one to comfort me really. I was so glad my siblings never told my mom I am scared of the dark. I was never so happy when my mom told us we were moving again soon. I could not wait to get out of that scary place.

Moving on…

Chapter 10

Finding the Right Place

Our next move was next to a fire station. For some reason, I do not remember a whole lot about this house. I can tell you the things I do remember and the stories that my siblings have reminded me of. Although a story someone told reminded me of a not-so-funny (then) story that I can truly laugh about today. It was a Christmas we had at this house. I remember it mostly because we were all so excited about the biggest, tallest present under the tree that we had ever seen. It was for our big brother. We were all so excited and could not wait to see what it was. I was not sure who was more excited, him or the rest of us.

None of us knew what it could be. My brother did not even guess it right as he opened it slowly to tease us all, obviously. The waiting time was so hard for the rest of us, and he knew we wanted to just jump right in and help him. He finally got it opened enough so we could see that it was a huge racetrack set. We all wanted to touch the box. We were all as excited as our brother seemed to be. My brother was so happy, and we were all happy for him. I do remember him hugging and thanking Mom and Dad many times. He had wanted that race track set for so long, he had told us later. It must have cost a lot back then.

Dad must have worked a lot of extra hours to be able to get it for him. He began jumping and dancing around, asking Daddy where he could set it up, and I knew one day he would let us all try it out. He was a good brother like that. We all played with our things we got, and brother kept his racetrack in the box for days. One day our parents went out, leaving our brother in charge to babysit. He asked us if he took the racetrack out of the box if we would help set it up. Then we would all be able to have our turn at it. Naturally, we wanted to help! We could not wait for him to open it up.

Once he got all the pieces out, he decided the box was too big, and it was just going to be in our way. He would do this the smart way and get rid of this thing all at once. He tried to roll it up; that did not work. He was going to cut it up but did not want to use a knife while our parents were out. So he stood it up in the fireplace. It stuck out a lot at the top, but he looked like he knew what he was doing. He lit that box at the bottom. It went out the first try. That should have told him something. He tried it three times more before he got it lit. After it caught on fire, which only took about a minute.

Up the box that fire went, so quickly, then the wall then up toward the ceiling. It scared us all. We didn't know what to do at first. I began screaming as I watched the fire go higher, so did my sisters. My brother rushed us all out of there quickly and over to the fire station right next door, telling them our house was on fire. They came with their big truck, putting the fire out really fast before it burned the house down. We had a lot of smoke and water damage, and I do not remember what was done about that, but I am almost sure my brother got into some major trouble for that one. Very responsible, big brother! This is the same house, I am told, where two of my sisters were either upset about something or just being brats.

They were not old enough to be out all night, that's for sure. What were they thinking, running away at their ages? They were searched for throughout the night, being found cold and scared the next morning. I heard they got warmed up extremely fast when they got their behinds beat good for that one, I am sure mainly because my parents were scared to death, not knowing all night where they were or what was happening while they were gone. I was afraid of everything, so that is probably why I was not with them. There was no way I was going to be out in the dark at night. I did not need any extra attention, at least not that kind.

This is the same house where the same two sisters were involved in my older sister shutting my younger sister's hand in the door, causing her to have a cast on her hand. Just the start of many accidents for my younger sister, who has probably had more broken bones, stitches, and more surgeries than all of the rest of us kids added together. All accidents. Don't worry, she is safe. Way to go, sister!

While at this house, there was also a really wonderful place to go and play whenever we wanted. We just had to walk across the street. We really enjoyed the park next to our house. We seemed to always be there when Mom would call us in for a meal. Everyone seemed to like walking their dogs there. So we were able to see several types of dogs in many sizes and colors, all of us picking out our favorite one each day. We would sit on the grass or the benches in that park for hours. I do not think we owned our own dog at that time yet. Then we moved on again just before I started school, but how we missed that dog-walking park. Then to our next home. This one I think I hated the most.

Probably not because of the house but it was my first memory of school, and it was not a good one. I did not enjoy kindergarten that year, except the first day possibly. It started out good. Later we were all sitting in a circle, holding hands. I remember the teacher was reading us a really happy story. I keep going back to that moment when I heard the teacher calling my name. It got louder. I heard it again. I felt my head pop up. Everyone began laughing as I felt my face getting red.

She settled the class down and said, "Nap time is over."

Everyone laughed again, only louder, as my face got even redder and hotter feeling. I felt sick to my stomach, like I was going to throw up, then I began to suck my thumb. The teacher quieted the other kids down like before, but not before I began crying and running out of the room.

The teacher came and found me quietly sobbing in a corner. She was kind and tried to tell me it was okay, that the children did not mean to laugh. She rubbed my shoulders until I stopped crying, and when we went back in, some of the kids were making noises as my face stayed red. When we went outside to play, none of the teachers heard the other kids making snoring noises at me or watched any of them sticking their thumbs in their own mouths and making sucking sounds, making me feel even worse all that day. So I became much shyer and stayed that way as the kids made fun of me throughout that year while no one noticed. I never told anyone about it. I just stayed away from them as much as I could.

I cried, suffering all alone, and continued being embarrassed throughout that first horrible experience during my first year of school. While not one person helped me. I was told we would be moving after this school year was finished. It could not come fast enough for me. I did not like this school one bit, and becoming shyer and more anxious all the time was not helping me at all. I was always feeling like I was going to throw up, and the kids seemed to like to embarrass me, keeping my face as red as it could get. They just liked to laugh at how red my face got, and I did not dare to tell anyone. I was afraid my mom would get angry at me. She already spanked me enough and called me names for silly things that I did.

There was no way she would know about this! So I remained silent and was fearful all year, not telling anyone. I was so happy to be packing up all our stuff to move again. No one heard me complain. I even helped with my sister's packing to help move it along faster. The next move we did make, Mom made me take kindergarten all over again. This did not make me happy at all. I thought Mom was being cruel again! Mom made me stay back because she was concerned for my sister going to school by herself; she thought she would be afraid and that she was shy. Shy! That sister. You are kidding me! That is funny!

Where was her concern for me when I was in kindergarten all alone? When I am sure the teacher must have said something to my mom about what was happening to me while I was alone! How shy I was whenever people were near me. How mean I had been treated by others. Teachers usually do that sort of thing. Not once did my mother show concern for me! It made me so mad! I got a bit too angry about it one day, and I stupidly said something.

"No one cared about me being shy when I went by myself," I said in a not-so-nice voice! The concern I received was a backhand in the mouth with a split lip. My being shy was of no concern of hers, I guess, and it was not talked about again ever.

I started to get a bad feeling about my mother and me, for a different reason, but wondered also what I had done to make her not like me again. She had not been hitting me as much. I wondered why. Could I be a good girl now and not need spankings as much? I tried to think if possibly it could have been one thing I did when I was really young or a lot of things to make my mom feel this way about me while I was younger. Those kinds of things stayed in my mind back then when I was in my early grades of school. But I did not remember those kinds of little details on my own. I had to have help. I had to have lots of help. The school year for my second time around for kindergarten was so much better. I do not know if it was the kids at this school were nicer or if it was my very shy sister who made friends as fast as she made a bowl of cereal.

I was not upset with my sister. I was upset with my mother for keeping me back a year for no reason. My sister was not even half as shy as I was. Heck, she was not shy at all! What was Mom trying to do to me? I guess it was a good thing also. I got to have lots of friends that year. I had never seen anything like it. The kids were coming up to her. The wonderful thing was, her friends all wanted to be my friends too. At least that is what they said. I suppose they knew if they did not, my sister would give them a good what-for. I did still have some kids embarrass me to see how red they could make my face if I went to the bathroom alone or was on the bus alone. I did not always tell my sister. So some of them got away with it, but not very many. The next year did not work out so well for either of us.

My sister ended up staying back in kindergarten for misbehaving (the shy kid that she was) while I moved on all alone, again. Here I was, being kept back for that! Then my sister had to stay by herself anyway. I'm sure my mother knew she was not shy. Not sure the reason she wanted me to stay back though. I just never knew any of the reasons my mother did any of the things she did when it came to me. Then throughout the rest of my school years, I was always older than everyone else. I did not like it until I got in high school and found out I could get my driver's license a year before my other classmates. Guess who was the most popular and coolest for at least that year! Ride, anyone?

I guess it is time for us to go do some of the things we moved here for, or so I was told! To be closer to family. Not that I was looking forward to it. I was very shy and did not like meeting new people. My face always stays red when I am around someone new, and I never know what to say to them or how to act around them. Most of them tease me when they see my red face too. I usually end up not liking them right away when they do that. But I guess it's time... I really wish people would not find the need to feed off from someone else's misery. Kids can be the cruelest, but they have to learn it from somewhere. Keep your eyes on your kids, how they interact with others and how they treat people in general.

Do not let them be bullies in any way. Who knows, it may be someone you know who is being bullied at this moment. It is not a good feeling at all, believe me!

Let's get to meeting our new family and friends, if we must!

Maybe, for our next move, we will finally find the right place!

Chapter 11

I Was Seven

That summer we were told we were moving again. I had a really good feeling this time deep down in my belly. We packed all our stuff once again, waiting for the school year to be finished, and we finally moved. I cannot believe where we moved to. We all began thinking we had finally found the right house—the house where we would all finish growing up together. No one was more excited than I was! We were told we moved here because we had so many families and friends in surrounding towns. This area was supposed to have even more of our relatives in it. I did not really care. I didn't want to go meet any of them! Some we had met before. Some we already knew. Some we had met when we were very young, Mom told us. We started getting settled in first, getting our bedrooms, and other rooms all organized. When we were finally done, my parents decided it was time for us kids to go meet some new family members.

"This soon?" I complained.

Obviously, there was never changing my parent's minds once they were made up! The first place we stopped was at a new aunt and uncles we had not met yet. They seemed really nice. They had a daughter who had special needs that I liked very much and a son who lived with them that I thought was much too old to be living at home with his parents.

He seemed to be older than my cousin who was always babysitting for us. For some reason, he made me feel weird right off! Just looking at him, the way he looked back at me, made my face really red. Right away I knew I was not going to like him! He made me feel so strange. I think he started giving me the creeps even before he asked to shake all our hands. I did not want to shake his hand, but my mom made me. Then she went right back to talking. No one paid attention when he first gave me this funny-looking smile, making me have the reddest face ever, and that made him smile more, which made me angry! Then he tried taking my hand again as I tried to pull away. He put a tight squeeze on it, hurting me, and I cried out.

"Oh, so sorry," he said when my siblings looked at me. Then he politely asked how old I was.

I did not give him a polite answer. "Seven," I said as I made a face at him.

He held my hand then took his middle finger, rubbing back and forth between our hands, across the palm of my hand, while he shook it. How weird is this guy?

As I looked up at him, I don't know why I felt like throwing up all over him. I wish I had now.

"I like seven," he said as I looked up at him again. His eyebrows were moving up and down, and he licked his lips.

For some reason I did not know why, but that, too, making me sick to my stomach. I was pulling my hand away as fast as I could, but he held on to it. My face turned the reddest I know it has ever gotten because I could feel myself burning with anger. I got the most sickening feeling when I ripped my hand from his.

He put his finger to his lips after looking at everyone to make sure no one was looking, I assume now, and said, "Shh."

I looked at him and quietly said, "Creep," for a reason I do not know, but he did give me the creeps, and I wished I never saw him again. I thought, *What is this guy's problem?* I could not wait to ask my sisters what they thought of this creepy old jerk!

Of course, not one person looked our way, and only I saw him. I did not like the evil grin he kept on his face every time I looked his way. I did not like the way my face stayed red the whole time we were there either. I did not like this cousin one bit and glad we did not stay there long. When I asked two of my sisters what they thought of him, naturally, they both thought he was funny. Not once did I tell what he did. Maybe because I had forgotten all about him and truly thought I would never see him again! Never was I more wrong...

We knew this house was going to be big enough for all of us: lots of bedrooms; an attic that was as long as the huge kitchen and summer kitchen combined; a huge dining room, living room, parents' room, and another bedroom downstairs; closets that would start in one bedroom and end in another; huge rooms downstairs with three fireplaces; a summer kitchen.

I did not know what that was, but we had one and only one small bathroom. That might cause a problem with ten people, but we worked it all out so that it was not too bad. Outside was a garage with a huge woodshed attached to it. The biggest barn I have ever seen was on the other side of the driveway. We had some exploring to do in many places. When we went out to the barn to have a look, when we looked up, there were three stories high of beams to climb. Storage for hay, stalls for horses, a place for pigs and chickens, and this huge storage room above one whole side. Under the barn was places to store other stuff; you could fit a couple of cars in it. The barn was going to be an especially wonderful place to explore. We finally found the right place to fit everyone. I hope my parents thought so too.

I did not ever want to move again. At least I thought for our family, this was the best place we have ever lived! I had not even given it a thought yet about my new school. I was afraid when I did. The red face and anxiety would start. I really was not looking forward to going at all if there were going to be bullies on the bus and then on the playground too, or even one of those places would make it hard for me. I had the whole summer; I will try to worry about it when it gets closer. I just hope the summer is fun and never ends. I would not worry about anything until the time came to worry; only then would I start to panic.

We were having the greatest summer ever because we tried to stay outside and did not bother our mother very much. I was still wondering why mom did not like me very much, but I do not know when I started to feel that way or what made me believe she disliked her own daughter. I tried staying out of her way as much as I could and did a fairly good job of it. Before I knew it, summer was almost half over by now, and I began to panic already about school coming up on us too fast. I should not be thinking about how my mother is feeling about me also. I do not know why we always wish to be older when we are kids.

If we only knew the truth. For me, though, I did not like my childhood so far and wanted to be a teenager in the worst way. I thought if I was a teenager, bad things would not happen to me. I found out it did not matter what age I was; bad things can happen at any age. I had guessed if I got to be bigger, no one would want to bother with me. We all got settled into the house really well. There was a huge wood cook stove in the middle of our big kitchen. Not only did it keep us warm in the winter, Mom did lots of cooking and baking on that big stove. There was still a lot to do after we were all unpacked.

There was wood to cut for winter and stack in the woodshed. Even though I was still only seven, I was strong enough to help stack wood. I thought it was better than housework, and occasionally, I got to suck my thumb without any kind of punishment from Mom. Summer was going much too fast, but it was finally going to be my birthday. I would no longer be seven. I would be going into the second grade soon. I began to get a little nervous already. I still had plenty of summer left, but my nerves began to creep up on me. I just knew this was it. Whatever happened in the second grade would be the start of my school life, I told myself. I was thinking positive thoughts, but my stomach had other ideas.

I had never felt this nervous in my life, and I could not stop all the bad thoughts of things that could happen to me—from the bus ride to entering the classroom that first day. Here we go. Summer is over. I knew my face would be red, and the kids would make fun of me on the bus and in the classroom. But there was not a thing I could do about it. I just said a little prayer while I dressed that first day. Mom surprised me though. At least I did not have the bus ride to school. She thought it would be best if she took me to school and introduced herself to my teacher. She had registered me but not met my teacher. I was so thankful for at least no bus ride that morning. When we walked into the classroom, the room went silent.

Entertaining Mommy?

I really did not know what to do but close my eyes and say a little prayer for myself. I opened my eyes and tried to put a smile on my face as I looked out over the classroom. My face was red, and I wanted to cry, but I waited to see what was going to happen. What a surprise I got! The kids were all smiling. They said hi to me, asked my name. Some girls came up to me and said hi. They were all so nice. Even the boys were nice to me. I was never so happy to be in school. I was finally going to be excited to go to school every day; I had hoped anyway. I was crossing my fingers. My teacher was so nice too. I even saw a girl sucking her thumb, and I did not hear anyone making fun of her or laughing.

I stuck mine in my mouth, looking at her, and we smiled at each other. I would have to take it out if my mouth before my mother turned around though. I don't know what she would have done! When someone looked up and saw me sucking my thumb, they did not tease me or call me any names. I did not do it all the time, and I was still kind of nervous about the bus ride home. I had no idea what kind of kids would be on the bus, but I sure had a great first day. After school, I found out there were bullies on the bus that I was eventually introduced to. But for a while, they did not see me, or ignored me. I did not care which it was back then. A lot of the time, my sisters would be on the bus to stick up for me.

I never understood this though. My sisters were brave and tough, yet not once did I hear or see them bullying anyone. I didn't understand why other kids did it. All the bus rides I prayed one of my siblings would be on, but it didn't always happen that way. At least I had some time to adjust to my new school before I sadly met any of them. For now, I loved our new house and my new school. I made many new friends, and my teacher was super nice. It was all good for now. I even handled the amount of physical abuse I would receive that year without much thought. But soon I found out I would not like being the age of eight at all, and I still had never told anyone why!

I was just too afraid, feeling all alone, without using my strength, my power, my only weapon. I thought there was no help for me and no one to turn to. I had a voice. That was my help! I only had to learn how to use it. I was frightened at that age. I was not taught about how to be safe. There was no stranger-danger in my younger years. Back then, people seemed to trust one another. If they didn't, could they have just not seemed to say so? Some may have not cared whether they could trust others or not! My mother did not seem to care! People may have turned a blind eye to some things they should not have. There have been some parents who just do not care what their children are doing or where they are.

Even back then, they left them out to play all day without checking on them until it was time to come in to eat a meal. There were even times when a parent could do that and it could have been safe, I am sure. I never would have done it! Anything could happen to a child when they are left unattended. I would want to know my children are safe rather than leave it to fate. So many bad things could happen in our world today. You may feel like you cannot trust hardly anyone with your children nowadays. It has gotten that bad. It has made everyone so afraid they do not trust strangers. That is so sad. I have heard many stories back in the day when kids were out all day.

Parents did not worry about other people taking them or hurting them. If only things could have stayed that way, when we could have trusted our own neighbors and cared about who they are.

Chapter 12

The Gravel Pit

In the back of our new house, we found a whole other world. What a playground we had to explore. This place was huge. It had a road leading down into it, starting from behind our barn. We called it the gravel pit. We spent most of our days there when we were not doing chores. After we looked the whole place over, we picked out the best tree we could find and decided to build us a tree house. First, we stole a whole bunch of boards from our dad's pile of scrap boards that he told us not to touch. I know, we listened really well. Then we borrowed many of his tools we would need after him telling us to leave his tools alone. We took nails and screws from wherever we could get them.

It is amazing the barn is still standing after the nails we took from it to build our tree house. Just kidding! We did take them from Dad though. Dad would always be so mad if he found out about us using his tools. He constantly told us we would lose them or forget to put them back, leave them outside and let them get all rusty. He was totally serious when it came to his tools. We would get caught a lot taking them because one of us would be in charge of putting them back and forget many times or put them back in the wrong place, and he would know we put a saw or hammer or even a screwdriver back in the wrong place. Yes, he knew exactly where everything was.

It drove us all crazy that Dad would always know when it was not there or it was put back wrong. Sometimes we would get a spanking from him, but not often. He usually just hollered the same thing every time. I can still hear him now.

"You goddamn kids leave my tools alone, or I'm goanna warm your asses!" he would repeatedly say every time. I would give anything to hear him say that one more time. If he was in a bad mood, he would use some foul language, but we thought it was better than a spanking. But we never listened to him. We took them time and time again! Still, sometimes forgetting to put them back, but it was always worth it. We thought we were building this grand tree house in that gravel pit.

It was the biggest tree any of us had ever seen, and we wanted the neighborhood kids to all say, "Wow," when it was done, and they all did! My siblings did not yet know I was also afraid of heights also. So for a while, I got away with just passing them boards and tools. Then I made up all kinds of excuses why I could not climb up. We also built a fort, which I liked a lot better. It was on the ground, and I spent as much time there as I possibly could. I knew eventually I would have to go up in the tree house or tell everyone the truth, but really not wanting to because I was such a sissy (as my mother called me) already. At times, what she thought didn't matter to me.

I do not know what Mom truly thought of me. She had so many names for me. None that were good, so it could not have been anything nice she thought of me. The neighborhood kids were there a lot too, and they were the ones I was worried that would make fun of me. Mom even walked down to the pit a few times to see what we were up to. We had a huge brook right at the beginning of the gravel pit that ran down behind our house. It was a good-sized brook. Someone had built a small bridge to go over it so you could drive down through the road with a vehicle. We fished on both sides and secretly swam on the smaller side. Dad caught plenty of fish out of that old brook too. Once my sister caught a huge eel. I can remember when Dad fried that eel and ate it. How gross.

Mom always told us, "Don't you kids swim in that dirty water. You don't know what's in there."

We did not listen. We swam on sizzling summer days. We got caught a lot too. One of us would get cut on a piece of glass or something at the bottom of that dirty brook. We would have to go to the house and have Mom clean it up and bandage it while we all heard her wrath.

"You goddamn kids never listen. What is wrong with you? Now look what's happened." She would beat our butts one by one for not listening. Apparently not hard enough because the very next sweltering day, we would be right back swimming again. Those truly were the days.

There was also a huge pond of water that did not flow anywhere, so we did not dare to swim in it, but we had plenty of bomb fires and ice-skating parties with family and the neighbor kids every winter on it. That pit was so big. The road that led from the brook up to the big pond, had a fairly good-sized hill that we would have sledding parties on. It made a good hill to ride four-wheelers, dirt bikes, and snowmobiles on. We had this little, what we called a minibike. I do not remember how big it was, but if two kids got on at the same time, it would have been pushing it, someone always falling off the back of it, especially when they took off. We had this trail made for this minibike that went all through that gravel pit.

There was this one huge hill that scared me so bad. Sometimes I would close my eyes going up it and down it with that mini bike, praying I would make it up and back down, too scared to watch. It is a miracle I did not get killed on that thing. It was a very steep hill, if you went just a little to the left, you could have rolled down that big old hill, possibly getting hurt pretty bad. Then again, we all made it through those many dangerous days of crazy stunts. I remember some of my siblings not being afraid and jumping that bike over some pretty good-sized hills. Sometimes they would flip that little thing but never got hurt, besides a few bloody scrapes and bruises that Mom hardly ever knew about.

We also rode our bicycles up there, took many picnic lunches, spending whole days there, after our chores were done. Then we would sometimes sit in patches of wild strawberries and eat them for dessert. There was no better playground to have than our gravel pit. We had the best days up there. Even when it was raining, we had our fun. The number of kids that have been up in that gravel pit with us was amazing. We surely could not count them all. We sometimes found places where we did bad things there definitely. Like, as we got older, we would hide from our annoying, smaller siblings when we had friends over. I know a lot of us smoked cigarettes up there.

We also built fires in the woods. A real miracle we did not have a forest fire at least one time throughout our years there. So many trees that could have gone up in smoke in just seconds. I am fairly sure we stayed overnight up there, if I recall correctly, a few times. I remember dragging tents up there and other camping equipment. We dragged so many things up there I am surprised it did not become a dump site. I do know that we were made to go up and clean it up all the time, just like our bedrooms, or we couldn't play there anymore. Good thing Mom checked up there too; she made certain it was always picked up. The sliding parties were also so much fun, but we did have lots of hills across the road that were a lot closer to walk from our house, so we had lots of sliding parties there too.

My dad had a couple of junk cars behind our house. My oldest brother took the hoods off those cars. He would wax and wax those hoods until they were smooth, slippery, and shiny. Then he would tie pull ropes on each of them. We would pull those hoods up those hills, all getting on evenly on each one, with someone holding the ropes on the inside of the hood, then give a push, and race down the hill to see who could go faster. The neighbors would come with their kids. Some would bring hot dogs to cook on sticks over the big fire we would build. Some would bring hot cocoa, some cups, others would bring marshmallows or other treats. Everyone brought something.

We would end up with quite a big sliding party. Those were some good times, with great memories. Still, there was nothing like all four seasons in the gravel pit. It was so beautiful when it changed a season. We spent more of our outdoor time at that pit than we did anywhere else during our days of growing up there. I have even been back to visit that pit as an adult many different times. It does not look as big to me now as it did when I was a kid, but it sure brought back some fond memories to me with all my siblings. Now back to when I was young and innocent…

Chapter 13

Jealous of Her Daughters?

It was unclear. Was that me she was screaming for? I strained my neck, trying to listen. I could not tell. *Just in case, I better go and check. I do not want to be in trouble again.*

"I am here, Mom," I said just before reaching the kitchen.

Thankfully, she did not hear me. Even better, it was not me she was screaming for this time. It was Daddy. I got there the exact time as my dad did, but no one saw or heard me. I stepped back fast. Mom was incredibly angry. I did not want her to notice me, or she might think of some form of punishment for me again. *I will just hide down here. They should not be able to see me hiding here. I will just listen for a minute. Mom really scares me when she is angry, like how she sounds the way she is right now!*

She asked daddy why he must spend so much time with his daughters when he had a son right outside he could be playing ball with or taking fishing right now.

Dad told mom, "I just came in from playing ball with my son. He asked if he could please spend time with his friends. I think I should allow him that occasionally, don't you, Mother?"

"Well, I guess," Mom answered. "But what about me?" Mom said to Dad. "I am tired of housework and kids all day."

Dad smiled at her. "Let me find my beautiful daughters first. I promised them a tea party. After that, we will talk about a date this weekend."

"Oh!" Mom squealed like a child, jumping up to give Dad a kiss, wrapping her arms around his neck.

While I watched them kiss, I could feel my face getting red. *I'd better get out of here before I get caught*, I thought to myself. I did feel a little jealous that Mom could show affection to anyone else because I have never felt what I just saw, what felt like love. I ran in the opposite direction with tears filling my eyes. Why does Mommy not like her own daughters? I really wished Daddy would take Mommy on a date every day. I have never seen her looking so happy. Mommy seemed to be in a good mood for several days, and I did not seem as afraid of her as I usually am every time they went on what they called a date.

I was never sure why she seemed to give me more than my fair share of punishments, but I do know why I cried the most. She tried to hurt my feelings the most. Now that I think about it, I do stand in the corner a lot more than anyone else, but I also won't complain about that because it does not hurt like when she hits me. Was it really only because my hair was lighter or the color of my eyes being different from my siblings? I remind her of someone? I really just wanted to know! I thought back to Mommy's question to Daddy about spending so much time with his daughters. For one, it is not true. He never gets to spend any time with his daughters. Two, why would she even care if we were not bothering her?

If Daddy kept us occupied and she did not see us for an hour or so, would that not make her happy? We never got to see very much of him now; he worked all the time. When did she expect her daughters to have time with their father? I did not understand. Did Mom not want Dad to have any time with his daughters, not want him to love us? Almost made me feel like no matter what we do, she is never going to love us or want us to be loved or feel love even. It is bad enough that I think she does not love me, but are we all going to grow up feeling like she resents all her daughters and what did they do? I am the one she dislikes the most. How is this going to be for us five girls, always wondering why? Growing up, knowing our own mother will never love us? How will we feel toward her? Maybe I am just being silly. A true mother could never be that way. Love one child and not the other? Could a mom really be jealous of her own daughters? She showed us little to no love. Mom seemed to like

Entertaining Mommy?

beating on her girls. I do not remember a lot, but you would think I would remember Mom giving her boys a whipping or two, but I cannot recall. Although my older brother was super nice to me, so maybe he did not get into a lot of trouble. I really do not remember.

My baby brother, well, he was just that, the baby. Everyone wanted to carry him because he was so little. We all had our own way of handling Mom's abuse, and some got extremely good at dealing with her. I was not one of them. But my sister that was only ten months younger than me…now that girl could amaze me. I do not know how she did it, but she taught herself not to cry, sometimes even stand there with her arms to her sides, not protecting herself at all. Maybe that's why she is so tough to this day. I am not sure, but at other times, I could almost laugh because I know I remember, she would put her hands up like fighters do and make noises. I think that actually scared Mom sometimes. So Mom did not beat on her as much after she grew bigger. I wonder if that has something to do with why they had so much confrontation throughout my sister's childhood and adult years. Possibly why they no longer speak to this day.

Unlike me, the coward who lived inside me decided to take up permanent space inside my body and make me cower like a baby no matter how my sisters tried to teach me to fight. Yes, my older sister could be the same way most times; she also could amaze me. She has also stood up to our mother throughout our childhood and now through our adult years. I wish I could have been heroic like my sisters have tried to teach me to be. But again, Mom has made me completely afraid of her. I have also learned that if you cried right off, Mom likes that sometimes best and beats on you worse for it, enjoying herself like a vulture feasting on a kill! I never learned how to not cry because of how terrified of her I had become.

She was too scary for me not to cry! My sisters did not even know how bad it had gotten for me. If she didn't make you cry with her hand, that meant she was not hitting you hard enough. So she would use a stick or whatever was within her reach to finish the job. My younger sister who was like a tomboy was so tough. She did not seem to care about things like bullies, about things hurting her;

she was not afraid of anything. Including our mother, it seemed to me. It still surprised me when she did not seem to care when Mom hit her, or with what. Sometimes, when I was being hit, my sister reminded me of the times she would hoot and holler, always jumping our mother. I believe it got to a point where my mom was afraid to hit her, having that scared kind of look in her eyes sometimes.

My sister was always trying to show good ways to protect the blows with an arm, hand, or leg, always hollering when she wanted me to look while Mom would be screaming, "Get the hell out of here, or you will be next," while my sister laughed at her. My sister was something else. We laughed about it after the fact back then but really laugh about it now. My younger sister would also mock Mom's face and her moves when she was spanking or beating any one of us girls, including her. I do believe what bothered my mom the most is, she knew that my sister kept a smile on her face the whole time Mom was beating on her and that she never once got to her! That really made her angry!

Mom would tire easily with this sister. But other days, we think Mom loved the challenge, thinking she was going to break her, but Mom never did. My sister was courageous and my hero. I knew I was the weakest child, but so did our mother. I was the one who cried the most, so maybe that is why I got it the most. We all knew as we grew up, she enjoyed doing it. I do wish I could have been more like my two sisters. What made me so weak, so frightened, even to this day I get terrified quickly? They would all say, "Don't cry. Mom will leave you alone more." I did not believe that for one second! Mom had it out for me since the day it first made her angry when I sucked my thumb too long, and she held on to that, never forgetting! Because she could not break me herself, that made her angry! But I did hope that one day she would love her daughters more not just act like she loved us when other people were around, faking it.

I also never stopped hoping that one day she would see me and not want to hurt me. That never happened either, but I never gave up wanting it. All those years of needing my mom, the joke seemed to be on me. She never seemed to want or need me for anything but maybe a punching bag. I do not think I have ever felt for myself that loving, nurturing feeling a mom was supposed to give to her child. So I missed out on that. I also did miss that something I have never had before! I then remembered Dad asked once for Mom to let his girls grow our hair long, and she let us (shocking). Eventually, we were able to sit on it. Dad liked it that way, but Mom did not.

She complained it was too hard to wash; we did not keep it brushed properly. She did like to brush it for us because she was so rough, and it caused us a lot of pain. She really liked that. So I never understood what possessed her to do what she did after some time went by. Secretly, I do not think she liked Dad calling us his pretty girls. She did, however, like to grab on to it when she wanted to get our attention. Jealous of Dad's affection for us, perhaps? Yes, I believe she was! I also believe Dad had upset Mom one day for some reason. It must have been awfully bad for her to do what she did next. (Who am I kidding? She would have done it on a dare.) She chose me (go figure) to cut off my hair. Not just cut it off either. When she was done, I looked just like a little boy. She seemed to be so happy she even picked out a boy's name for everyone to call me, when Dad was not around, that is.

Dad was so furious when he saw what she had done. I know they argued, but it did not seem to bother Mom too bad because, eventually, she did the same thing to all four of the other girls that year, giving them boy's names that she called them also. Again, Dad was furious. Mom did not seem to let it bother her at all. She laughed at us when Dad was not there. Mom teased us all like she had become a kid herself, wanting everyone to call us the boy's names she had picked out. My haircut had been at the beginning of that summer, so I had the summer to grow it out some before the start of the next school year. Mom never came near me with scissors again after that haircut. I am not sure about the other girls.

We noticed after we would eat dinner that if Dad tried relaxing in his chair, the five of us girls would sometimes sit around him just to listen to him tell a story. Mom would always shoo us away, never letting us spend more than five minutes with him at a time, it seemed like, or ever hearing the end of any of his stories. The boys, however, were allowed to sit on the arm of his chair or his footstool, in his lap,

Gemma

talk or play all around him, for all the time they wanted. If Dad came up to tuck us into bed, Mom would call him downstairs for some ridiculous reason before he could say good night to us all. It was like she had him on a leash, and a lot of the time, he didn't want to argue with her, so he let her get away with it.

If we asked Dad to fix something on our bike, Mom would holler to him for something more important to do. Dad would have to do things secretly for us so Mom would not call for him. We never understood why she always did that to the girls and not the boys. Later in life, we began wondering again if Mom could have been jealous of her own daughters! From our own father? It was so hard to imagine. Could it have been something we dreamt up? It had to have been. Mothers do not get jealous of their own flesh and blood…do they? Maybe Mom hated the fact that whenever Dad had to punish us, after she insisted on it, he would always come and apologize, telling us he was sorry, that he loved us, not wanting to hurt us, but that we needed to do better next time. No matter what, we always felt Dad's love.

Love and miss you every day, Dad. Gone from our lives, never from our hearts.

Chapter 14

Only Part of My Feelings

Where I came from, you hugged, kissed the cheek, maybe even a simple smile. I have done this my entire life as far back as I can remember. For me, it all seemed fake, truly unreal to me, hurting me inside every time I was forced to do it, and I did feel like I was being forced. When deep down, it never felt real or meant anything to me. Why does it disgust me so? Why do I hate it? What can I possibly do about it? Have I created this all in my mind? I do not exactly know. I am so troubled, so confused, and not yet sure what it is that has made me feel this way. So odd, so different from all of them. Or even when this could have happened to me. Why me? There is something here, but I cannot quite decide.

Why is this bothering me so much? This is my family that I love, don't I? There is something being hidden from me. This can't be some kind of trick someone is playing on me. No one could be so cruel! I honestly do not know what this is all about. I am sincerely scared. I do not know what it is I am supposed to be fighting here or if I am supposed to fight it at all! Again, I know the feelings are there, making me feel frightened of whatever it is I cannot put my finger on. I am not pretending. This is far too real, too eerie. I do not want these feelings inside me. Why do I have to have all these feelings? I have never shared with anyone the anguish I still feel. How much I despise it all entirely.

I never thought this way of thinking or these strange feelings would lead my thoughts in any kind of direction, that anyone would ever find out; that I would keep them locked up like all the secrets I have kept for so many years. Now so many know, and my heart still feels the kind of pain it did when I was the only one with the knowledge of this pain, and it does get so painful at times. Imagine how I am feeling right about now, never having shared any of this with anyone ever before, especially the hugging; how I hate the hugging. I thought maybe I could somehow just forget these awful feelings or that they would simply disappear eventually, that I would grow out of it. They have gotten much better with my siblings. Some family members get too close to me, and it is hard not to scream when they get near me. Growing up since I was a young child, those feelings have always been there, but only *I* knew why.

Then, somehow, I did not know, that knowledge had left my mind. It was all too confusing for me. I hated myself for having these feelings, especially toward my sisters when I knew nothing about these feelings. I know they did nothing wrong. I would have known that. No, it was not something they had done. It was something that had to do with me. Even when I discovered things, I still kept them to myself, not wanting to upset anyone or hurt anyone's feeling while deep down I felt like I was being strangled to death! You see… I could not even help myself. How was I to get help? I did not know how. I did not know from where. I just never found my voice. I was always too afraid, which only made me suffer alone.

Then who could I have possibly blamed for all my cruel torment I had received once I had revealed it? Myself, my abusers, or maybe that someone who should have been protecting me but did nothing, practically closing their eyes to it all? I was so unsure, yet feelings of contempt were there…lingering. I had just become so uncomfortable at such a young, innocent age, so much I did not want anyone coming close to me or touching me in any way. The worst part of it was, I did not understand any of it. I kept asking myself, *Why? Why did I feel this way? What has happened to me? Did I do something wrong then prevent myself from ever thinking of it ever again?*

I wished somehow my struggles and fears would have surfaced on their own. Definitely, they did not. So I suffered tremendous pain, with no one I thought I could talk to. Just cowering away, doing nothing but generating extreme agony for myself. Could it have been possible for me solely to stop these kinds of family traditions from happening to me? Never allowing that deceitful feeling, that phony mistrust wash over me ever again? Have I ever tried to stop it? Obviously not… The coward inside me would not escape!

Our family is not small. There are our parents, their seven children, a foster son, all our spouses, twenty of our children, great-grandchildren, and great-greats. Just imagine the get-togethers we have had, feeling obligated to hug each and every one, not leaving anyone out. Do not forget to hug goodbye the same way. Fake that smile and kiss the cheek if you must. It sure took a lot of time and energy at Christmases and BBQs to get through all that! Along with all our other get-togethers, to put on that fake smile when it never felt good, felt real, or even felt right. Sadly, that is only a small part of how we were raised. We were also taught to lie. If people would ever ask what any marks or bruises were on our bodies or faces, we were not allowed to tell the truth.

Mom taught us how to lie very well, under pressure, about many things that happened throughout all our childhoods. We had to tell a story Mom had already made up or produce a good, believable lie of our own if we knew what was good for us. Naturally, we were raised with manners, or else! Our behavior while in public was not always as sophisticated as our parents would have wanted, but we did learn as we grew. We were also taught to respect our elders, no matter what. We knew how to be courteous, and we cared about people. Although it was extremely difficult when it came to people like our grandmother and some other hard-to-deal-with family and friends.

When we first began to know our dad's mother, Grandmother sure made it challenging. I had already resented her for giving up my dad when he was born to her mother, my great-grandmother, whom I'd never met. When my grandmother seemed to raise her other six children while fostering many others with no problems, she let my dad go. I did try to give her a chance, but she was a very harsh woman. My siblings and I found out she was a hard woman to love. She was also very mean, we quickly learned. She did not treat us like grandchildren at all. She would try to treat us like pawn pieces in a game. Well, I did not want to play, always wanting us to be against our mother, saying bad things about her, being disrespectful.

I would never understand grown-ups! Then as I grew older, I wanted nothing to do with her. Each one of my siblings ended up feeling the same way. Her loss, we decided. I really did not want my dad to know how I truly felt about his mother, but I really resented her and did not respect her as a person at all. We all ended up feeling the same way toward her. Even though he said, forget about her, we could all see how deeply it hurt him. I did try my hardest to get along with grandmother, but I just could not take any more abuse and hers was verbal. No telling what it may have ended up being if we had stayed around her much longer. I wanted no part of that or her lifestyle.

I was always terrified about sharing my thoughts and feelings with anyone even then, always too worried I would hurt someone else's outlook on their meaning of family when mine had become so damaged. I have felt like I have never fit in since about the age of eight, then getting worse as I grew older. Far too young to be alone with my reflections and fears without knowing how to reveal them. My bleak and dismal emptiness began taking its toll on my thought process, as I separated myself from most people because I did not want to think about how to communicate my past, my struggles, my unspoken truths of my childhood horrors without someone penetrating the vicious battlefield going on in my head.

I knew my thought process would never fit in with what my family would have wanted it to be. I feel no unity, strength, no bond. I must feel some kind of love, even have a perception of feelings in my own way. Though I am not yet aware of what they could be. I just seem to fight this "hair" standing on the back of my neck, feeling every time I opened that door to my family's home. I am so unsure. Is it them, or is it the place, just those memories that came crashing into my body like a wave of pain? I'm not even sure of what I'm fighting here. I think I need some help as I sit here in silence, "waiting" for something to happen without the "help" of my voice.

Chapter 15

The Good One

Then there are some of my immediate family members who do not live in the same state as the rest. I have always envied them. Some that do, do not have much to do with many family traditions because of a distrust they share. Me, I have a love-hate relationship with myself when I have to visualize my nightmares against bitter feelings of cruel deceit that I always feel rising up when certain family members get too close. If you were an outsider looking in, you could possibly think we were a close, loving family. You may even be envious. Don't be. You would be wrong! I have always had that sense of looking in every single day. I do not like what I see or what I feel. Could it still have to do with that fakeness?

I do not have that deep connection with anyone that I should probably have by now. I see such conflict, betrayal, and pain. Lots of pain. As most people already know, a big family does not mean a happy, loving one. I know we all have our own concerns, issues, and disagreements with one another at times. I seem to be having a tug-of-war with my heart, always telling me, "Let it go. Let go of your anger, your own issues, and your pain." Not easy. I cannot. I have always been afraid even remembering as a child. Scared of my own shadow, as they say. Laugh if you want, but believe me, I was! I suppose I brought some of this dreadfulness with me into adulthood. It would seem it never left me.

Because I do still have it with me unfortunately. It follows me everywhere, making me a target for everyone to shoot at. I get used easily and say yes to everyone for everything they ask me to do. I now play the game of the "good" daughter. That is what my siblings call it, the loyal one, devoted and trustworthy. That is what they always say. As if I do it on purpose, and for that reason, I am afraid I have become a doormat because of a weakness I feel. I hate being a doormat! Always hating the feeling it leaves me with, like I have really been stepped on. If only I could stop it. If I had to, I would, wouldn't I? It happens to be because the *no* word does not seem to be in my vocabulary.

I just cannot seem to say that word! I will not refuse to do something, anything, for my family or friends. I do not want to go against anyone's wishes. I do not want to see or hear anyone's disapproval of me. Which is why I get taken advantage of. Believe me, I am no saint and not pretending to be one. I just do not like the irritation of arguing with anyone, so I try to do what I am told without any kind of grief or turmoil. What is it that makes me this way? I ask myself why so many times about the things I do that are wrong for me. I seem to isolate myself from everything and everyone from time to time for a while when I get frustrated from it all then become shy and quiet once again.

I guess being accepted is more satisfying to me than being rejected, which is something I have always felt from my mother. I wonder if, one day, she will ever accept me or any of her daughters. Maybe another reason why I stay this way. I am never sure of anything these days. I know I strive for approval and love and never seem to have it, but I keep trying. You would think I'd have learned my lesson by now. Rejection is all I know, all I have ever felt from her, so why keep torturing myself? Apparently, I can withstand a lot of pain. The problem is, I have this hate for her also, this anger, this unforgiving suffering that will not let go of me. I fight it every time I see her. I feel so much rage. I did not know at this time why.

I did not want to be that person. I want to be better than her. I want to be greater than what I have felt throughout my life. I do not want to be known as a failure, and that is what I feel like when I feel those things for her. I am better than that. I have to be. It is one of my goals in life. Whenever I am around her, she makes me feel like I am a failure, like I will never be good enough for what she wanted for me. With help, I did start to remember why all the resentment, all the hate. Becoming this person would be no better than what my mother has been or what she has done. I can be a fighter with my feelings, not someone who has given up on herself. I am worthy of love; I want her to know that.

I was a good daughter and did not deserve her battering throughout my childhood. I do not know why she would think any of her children are failures or deserved what she took from us. We were strong enough to live through what she did to us. We failed... nothing! I have always wanted to be a stronger person, not knowing how to make that happen. You would never have wanted that for me—to be stronger, to be courageous, heroic, or brave. Yes, brave.

I have always liked that word *brave*, always wanting it associated with my name, for me to be known, just once, as brave, like my sisters are, just to stand up for something or stand up to someone; to be the one to help myself with all these problems I suffer with; to withstand and endure these horrors of my misery and torment when I had no courage to open up and expose the horrible monsters, the horrid secrets that my thoughts experienced happening to me; just one time to do something brave without thinking about fear, weakness, or pain; to fight that coward I am now feeling being destructive inside me; just for someone, anyone, to know, to see, to help... If only I had vocalized my darkening, violent nightmares that stayed with me night after night, just to be bold enough back then to tell. How different my life could have been if I had been brave!

If only to express the way I feel about the conflicting traditions we still carry on in our family dynamics today, for me to reveal just how wrong I have felt all these years to act like I support them. How much I hate them with certain members of my own family. To uncover the real me, especially with the disturbed family members who have already been exposed for their ruthless wrongdoings with my protector knowing of their sins (we will call them) without punishment, never being held accountable to this day when they have hurt me in some vulnerable way. I could have exposed them to everyone. That could have been something extremely brave or heroic. That would mean they may have not called me the good one any longer. I may even be hated, looked down upon, disliked by some.

Instead, I feel that coward rise within me. I become fearful once again. Just to think I would hurt another family member that I do care about by exposing some others. So I remain silent once again. It has become confusing to me why I have become so cowardly. It really concerns me that I cannot use my voice. Still afraid to make a sound as the intimidating voices still hammering in my head say, "Don't say a word." Why do I still feel so fragile? How will I ever know the answers? As the coward lurks below, laughing a devious shriek, knowing it is winning again, and I am still so afraid. But I cannot speak. The coward is choking the heroic image from my thoughts. I once again have lost my voice as I utter no sound.

Chapter 16

Always the Cynic

This is the real me! I never disappoint when it comes to anyone having ideas, any kinds of plans, or if someone is deciding things for me. I have never dared to express if I wanted anything different. I fail to let myself have a voice. For all the years of my life, I have said nothing, with something always screaming inside to let it out before I explode. I know what it is to have my own ideas, my own plans I want to share, decisions I can make for myself. I want to, yes. Yet there comes no sound; nothing will come from my mouth. I sometimes feel this mild hatred for someone, just anyone who should have really seen me, to ask, "What is wrong? Why are you so sad? Do you need to talk, or why do you always look hurt? How could I help you?"

They also speak no words, ask no questions of any kind. Not one single person looks my way while turning their heads to not see. They overlook me on purpose, avoiding my eyes, so as not to see my tears or not to see or feel my pain, especially my siblings. I am not seen once more. Even starting out as a young child, I remember always wanting to play a game I would like with my siblings, friends, or any of the neighborhood kids. When I would ask, I would always get the same answer from all or some of them. "No" would be everyone's response eventually. They would tell me, "Sorry, we will be playing this!"

Never anytime did anyone want to do what I wanted to do. It hurt, yes! Never would they try to ask if it would be okay to play something they wanted instead. They just said no, and I went along with it. Because they always knew I would never protest, say no, or even try to argue with anyone. They all knew that was who I am. It seemed to everyone I was an easy one to have a friendship with or that I was just a pushover. Either way, I said nothing. Whatever anyone wanted to do was fine with me. At least that's what I always told them, even when my feelings were hurt, which was most of the time. I let everyone tell me what to do, even how to do it, never saying a word against anything or anyone, even when I felt they were doing something wrong.

Why was it me getting treated so different from others? Oh right, the coward in me. I was always just too afraid they would not want to play with me anymore or not want to be my friend. So I always said nothing. There would be days when it would be my turn to pick what we would have for lunch. Then one of my siblings would coax me into choosing something they would like better. I always ended up agreeing, too afraid to do anything else or say what I really wanted, worried they would not like me anymore. At least that is what I always told myself. They always won because I had no voice! Even too shy to say no to my own siblings or any of my closest relatives who were around my age.

In other words, anyone who happened to ask me if I wanted to do something I really did not want to do for our day that particular day. I have often wondered what could have made me so insecure. Why couldn't I be more like my brave sisters? Why? Why did I have to be like this? Will it always be this way for me? Am I just being silly, or is it something I made up in my own imaginative mind! How did I not know? Will I ever find out? Without my voice, how will I get help from someone? Why even bother? I thought so many times. No one cared about the real me. That I was a person who had feelings. What would they do if I said no? Never want to play with me again? Hate me? Just laugh? I feel so lost.

One more reason I felt no pull at my heart when it came to real love for my family. At least not the kind of connection you should have, like resembling the kind of tie you feel when you hug a grandparent you have missed or you haven't seen in a while. I know I have always felt guilty for my feelings. I wish they were not inside me nor do I want them to be mine. I really want that happy, secure family feel, but never have I. Guilt is a feeling I feel. I have certainly had other feelings, so many kinds of feelings. Like doubt. Let us not forget the fear, lots of fear, uncertainty, and always the pain. Let's not forget loss! That is a feeling, isn't it? Again, all these feelings. Why did they have to become mine!

Never understanding any of this! I was never made to feel unloved, was I?

I still did not know yet, or did I? I know my mother wanted me to feel that. An outcast, maybe. Rejection? Oh, the rejection my mother has made me feel. The pain it has caused me. The happiness I think it has given her because of it and how sad that was for me. I wanted to matter to someone and felt I never would. This is exactly how I have felt. If only I could talk to someone, to vocalize my fears, share the grief I have sensed, just to have the ability the words, the courage. I know I cannot. I will not because I still hear silence. Could I not be allowed to fantasize about something different than what I have always known? Why do I feel so guilty? Why should I not be allowed to wish for something other than what I have right now!

Possibly a different house? A different kind of life, other than the nightmare I have lived in my brief time? Why couldn't I? Would I really wish for a different family? Perhaps…a new mother? I would like to keep the rest of them. It sure can make a person dream. I am puzzled though. I knew nothing of having anything other than what I have always had. Where does this come from? There were no influences. We did not own a television yet. So I could not have seen it. We had no telephone at the time. I could not have heard about it, and back then, there certainly was no Internet. So far, I could not have dreamt about the world yet. I didn't talk to anyone about it, that's for sure.

How could I possibly wish for something I did not know existed? I am sure I have many positive reflections of families reuniting, happy with life and strength. I could wish for that if nothing else! Anything I could wish for, to dream about, would feel like hope! Then as I became an adult, I became confused when a sibling tells a story, taking me back to my childhood, back to memories that are very few, without the help of a sound, a touch, or something I see that reminds me of a time I want to remember or one that I wish would never be revealed. How do I cope when I do not remember what they could be talking about? A reminded story sometimes makes a memory clearer for me.

Sometimes the flashbacks start. The past violently collides with my present thoughts. I become that frightened child again. I am alone, looking for someone to help me. The memories do not stay long. Often it saddens me; other times it makes me feel thankful. They are here just long enough to frighten me once more but stay only briefly, and they are gone while I am praying; they never return. I become angry many times because of the past when I cannot remember by myself what it is I cannot yet see. I still do not understand why they will not come on their own. At times, it becomes so frustrating. What is it I do not want to surface?

What is it I keep out, not wanting to see? Could I be hiding something dangerous, something that terrifying? What is it that scares me! What is it that will not escape? My memories lay below, like cowards waiting to surface. Yes, one day, but when? Will I be able to endure the suffering as I have done in the past? Could I possibly vocalize my fears this time that just wait like bad, weakening dreams? I know you are coming. I can feel you. Do not worry, I am getting ready. But then suddenly I become afraid of you all over again. I am much too afraid; I do not ever want to remember! What will I see for this reveal? What will I hear? Will there be anything good at all waiting for me this time? I wonder. I could only hope.

When someone lacks courage, it does not help anything. It is not helping me at this moment. I must become braver, bolder, even! To fight that coward waiting for me. This time, I will try not to be frightened. My voice could be heard. I can do this. I know I can because I want it to happen. If I hear no voices telling me nothing else, things could improve in my life. I have to listen to my own voice. It's the only way! Whenever I get this upset, though, things seem to deteriorate for me. I become a different person. I can do things I would not have done before; for instance, if I become angered, I change.

Entertaining Mommy?

There are things in my life that I am still angry about because of a childhood that I am still unveiling. I was not aware of the many things I was hiding yet. Once my memories started to come to life, so did my anger, my rage, even more fear. Once it started, I could not stop it, no matter how I tried! Maybe it was good to finally let it loose. It needed to come out. Be unrestricted. Just like the rest of my life and my thoughts were beginning to do. Too much anger, so much rage. It truly needed to be set free. But wait… It seemed to be all directed at my mother more than anyone or anything else. If she only could have shown me love. If only she would have noticed me, seen my tears, my pain that for once she had not caused, or had she caused it all?

Did she already know what was happening to me? Could it be true? I would not have endured so much of the torture that I have gone through within my life had she helped me. The other assaults were my abuser's doing, but I can blame my mother for not being there for me, not paying attention, couldn't I? For not helping me when she saw my pain! Not seeing me, looking through me, instead of at me? Could she not have helped her daughter? If I had not buried all the abuse I received from my mom, I may have been confused, conflicted possibly. I may have even felt hate from time to time possibly toward her. But she could have helped me, should have helped me.

If I had only received a genuine hug from her just a few times, some form of love a mother feels for a child. She would have helped me, would she not have? A mother does not really abandon her own child, right? The struggles I am having now could be her fault! Would how I feel about my own mother be confusing my thoughts? Such a conflict! Not understanding what I should be doing about them is hurtful for me and another complication I cannot handle at the moment. A conflict I do not need or want. Even not knowing that word as a child, one I did not know, could mean so many things. It certainly caused me enough problems and became a big part of my life throughout.

After realizing what it was, what it can do, I tried to avoid it at all costs. Something rising inside of me again, it seemed. A conflict with my mother? One word I would soon come to dislike. All the conflicts I have had with all the people in my life, I have always known deep down what I should have done about it. There should have been such an easy choice, but as with everything, I must make things easy for others, never for myself. That is why I can easily be used as someone's doormat. It has happened all my life. By my own hands. I have let it. Yes, shame on me for letting these things go on, even to this day.

This is when the coward comes to the surface and somehow makes me feel some type of guilt for another person, causing me my own kind of sadness, sorry for any pain they may have. Even though they have probably caused some of mine at times. Why do I still feel the need to be the one to make sure my mother is okay? Yet feel this rage, this hate for the things I now know she has done to me, to our entire family! Causing everyone so much hurt and pain. When I get away from her, I am so relieved and feel so calm. When I see her, it is instant anxiety! I sometimes feel guilt for the way I think about her, all the bad feelings I have, the rage!

The conflict can send me on an emotional roller coaster, and it has many times. I am the peacemaker, but why? Why should it be my duty when others have never tried? When Mom would never do such a thing? No, conflict is mom's thing! Still, it is unknown to anyone why I have tried, why I still try, to help someone like her. Why would I want to make things better for others, to reunite if I can, when inside me is so damaged still, so emotionally conflicted? Trying not to address it if I can avoid it, yet helping with it if needed, I must. If I had a voice then, what conflict I could have transpired. I would have developed a huge conflict had I found my voice then! That word, that emotion would come to life before my eyes, before all eyes. To speak in volumes, it would, while the conflict arises to tell all my secrets, my truths, my pain. Conflict would awaken for many. To vocalize my horror, the nightmares, my story…

If only you could hear me!

Chapter 17

Feeling Someone's Pain

This has all made me such a gullible person, a sucker. I have always felt sickness in my heart at the very thought of something or someone hurting or tortured in any capacity. My heart aches when I see others suffering. Just another reason why I do not like fighting, torment, or conflict—anything that could cause someone harm. It makes me feel vulnerable and weak. I know because I have had my share in my lifetime. I know exactly how it feels to have all this. No one deserves any kind of pain. Those who like to cause others heartache and pain are extremely sick individuals. That is just an opinion of someone who has had her share of pain, from someone who was sick! I would never want to know the mind of someone who inflicts terror and suffering onto others for selfish or pleasurable reasons.

Yes, some need psychiatric help or hospitalization. There are others who enjoy watching someone else suffer. It is like a bully. They like to pick on someone that is vulnerable—someone that cannot or will not fight back—calling someone names, laughing and humiliating someone who is innocent, usually to get someone to laugh at their bullied, innocent victim; to make themselves get some form of attention they are not getting in other places in their lives. They feed off from their victim's suffering, probably making them feel powerful. Reminds me of some bullies who terrified me on my bus for a while. I was young, alone.

My face turned red easily; bullies seem to like that sort of thing. I kept my head down, but those are the kids bullies like best, I soon found out. They wanted to evoke their vicious energy on me. I had no courage to fight back or even look up at them. For a while, I watched as they made other kids cry and knew my turn was coming eventually. I tried to mind my own business and not even look up when they picked on others, but here came those bullies! I was made to feel weak and vulnerable once again while becoming more afraid, if that was possible, of everyone around me, especially if I did not know them. Those bullies took my books. Eventually, they emptied my bag. Anything I carried they took or destroyed while I said nothing. I sat there, intimidated and frightened.

A small girl with them liked to pull my hair! One day, she pulled out a clump. I did nothing but cry and put my arm over my head to protect myself. They laughed, of course, then would push me in my seat, calling me names because of how red my face could get. They were not nice at all. Most bullies are cruel; these were no different. They hit me, calling me some more names, so others would laugh and did nothing to help me, obviously. I made no sounds, knowing they would call me worse names and stay at my seat, bullying me longer. Just from listening to them when they would be picking on others and those kids would make sounds or cry, oh how they seemed to like that. I was no fool!

My head stayed down in pure fear, as I was humiliated by a bunch of strangers who knew nothing about me! Except that I would take their bullying and remain quiet, not telling any one of my new hateful enemies. The only thing I did was stay afraid. I did not want to ride the bus ever and tried to be sick as much as possible to stay home for a day here and there. I wanted to know what made me so weak? Would I ever know? Could I ever be brave enough to tell? Would I find the courage to stand up for myself, ever? *Someday*, I told myself, *I will not be afraid.* Only time would tell. Then I screamed inside. *What about now! Be brave now!* I was happy to find out, I would not have to worry about those bullies for much longer.

I was truly shocked when this happened to me. One morning, my older brother got on the bus, finding out who every one of my bullies were, somehow, as if I had told him who each one of them were! He found every single one of them without saying a word to me! Asking them nicely to meet him at the back of the bus and talked to them all so quietly I could not hear a thing. My brother walked by me, winked at me with a huge smile, got off the bus, and was gone. Each and every one of those kids came up and apologized to me for their part in bullying me. Some even tried shaking my hand. I was still too afraid to even do that, thinking it might be a trick. But it was not.

Those bullies somehow became really sorry for what they had been doing to me, apologizing so much I had to tell them it was okay, and some of those kids became my real friends. My brother was so great. I do not know how my brother even found out. I did not tell him, and he would not tell me when I asked that night or tell me ever what he said to them. Only saying, "I promise they will not bother you again." Thanks again, big brother. I wish all your choices make great memories for you and your family! You are a terrific big brother. There are so many horrible stories we have heard throughout our lifetimes of this type of abuse or that kind of torture or suffering. It just should not be happening!

Maybe you have never heard of any type of abuse unless it was on the news. Hopefully, you have never known anyone who has been abused in any way. You are fortunate. I wish I could say those words. I certainly would help someone if anyone asked. Even if it was a stranger. I know I would help if I saw any kind of abuse happening or if I heard it. I would help because I can feel someone else's pain. I have been where they are. I have been that person in some painful way. I know what it is like to need someone else's help. I truly know how hard it is to ask! What if you were a child and did not know how to ask or who to ask?

I have often wondered how many people have said or even thought the words, *I had a terrible childhood.* Did you ever? Should you have? I'm sure there were several that thought theirs were so horrible. There are many out there that had the best childhoods and would go back to that life in a heartbeat. I would not be one of them. I am also sure some of yours were bad. Some even worse than bad. I bet what some kids went through does not compare to the minor abuse I had as a child while growing up. I say minor, considering mine could have been so much worse. Some had wonderful childhoods and would not know what it was like to even have a spanking.

I would have dreamed for that kind of childhood, even with a few spankings. Others I am sure having something so much worse than anything any of us could have imagined. I know there were even countless deaths from child abuse, many that were never discovered. I was so lucky compared to some of those children. Yes, I think lucky is the word. Because I lived. I ended up having a wonderful life after I got away from my abusers. How many abused people can say that? I always wondered about back in the day what they considered child abuse or if some even knew it existed. I had never heard the words *child abuse* while I was growing up. I do not think I have ever heard anyone discussing that word.

I guess someone would have had to explain it to me if I had heard it back then. What I received were called beatings because that's what I thought children who were bad were supposed to receive. I just wanted to be good and did not know how to do that, apparently. When I was seven or eight, I realized it might not be me. I may not be the bad one possibly! You really did not hear a lot about anything like that in my time. Abuse! Oh, it happened. Just never talked about as much as it is nowadays, if ever. Not so sure you can even spank a child on the bottom in public these days without someone thinking it child abuse. How times have changed for this day and age.

There were a lot of closed mouths years ago and beyond about child abuse. People did not want to get involved. It was someone else's problem, let them deal with it. How sad it must have been for the children who caught your eye in public, the ones being abused while you did nothing but turn your head and look the other way. You know who you are! What do you think happened to those children? Or the children who went to bed hungry, crying from the pain of starvation? What do you think they were living with? I feel their pain. It is an awful thing to know what someone else could be feeling. I have felt others' abuse when I have read about it or seen it on the news. I have felt that hurtful torture, the agonizing silence, the frustrating defeat. What about all the others? Maybe the ones you heard about who did not make it after someone heard their screams while they did absolutely nothing to help!

Entertaining Mommy?

Yes, that really did happen and much worse. If only I had known about those two words, *child abuse*, or *sexual abuse*, maybe just the word *abuse*. My life as a child may possibly have been different, maybe a happier one. How would I have known? My childhood is gone now. I have a resentment for that at times. Yes, I lost most of the one I should have enjoyed. It was traumatizing to me. So much I blocked it all out. I am living with the heartache of it all now, nothing more. When I think about someone else's feelings, what they must be going through, what they have already been through, or why they cannot find their voice. I know the fight they are fighting. Now I only pray for them in silence because I know what it is like to feel some of their pain. Yes, I even know some of their pain.

I have had enough in my life. I just hope you realize, there is help for all of us, at any age, for any type of abuse or bullying. I know what it is like to think there is no help, that there is no hope. You are so wrong. I could and should have gotten the help that I needed when I needed it. Even though I was a child, a young innocent child, I still could have done something to help myself. There is always a way out. No matter what the situation is. You fight for your life and *never* give up! If you are being abused in any way, if you are being bullied, it is wrong! You get yourself some help! Do not let someone take your dignity from you. Talk to someone you trust. Talk to someone who trusts you. Tell them everything! There is someone in your life who will help you. Just use your voice.

Do you think you would be too ashamed or humiliated to fight back? How do you think you look just letting someone take advantage of you, beat on you, do whatever they want to do! Don't let anyone do that to you. They know what they are doing is wrong! You know what they are doing is wrong! Fight back! Do not let them tell you lies or try to blackmail you with hurting one of your family members or bully you into doing things that are wrong! Take charge of your situation! Take charge of your life. Let's stop all of this abuse and bullying now! We can do it together!

Remember the national abuse hotline numbers are at the back of this book. Please! Call today if you need help!

I Am Done

When I awoke
and felt that pain
of all that you have done

You took the child
right out of me.
You thought that you had won.

When I remembered all the
torture
that you put me through

That love you'd had
repeatedly,
there's nothing I could do!

However,
I know all the truths.
You'll never have my love.

I've found such trust
and kindness.
It's something I've
dreamt of.

I am happy and at peace.
Can you say the same?
I've finally cut the chains and ties.
I'm all done with your games!

Chapter 18

Feeling Uncomfortable

Everything finally seemed to be going well for our family. The house was great. My dad had an excellent job. My mom could work part-time anytime she wanted to earn extra money at a mom-and-pop store right down the road from where we lived. We got fresh milk from a farmer a few houses away. Never tasted milk like that since. School life began to go smoothly for me for the first time. I had lots of friends, many that lived in my neighborhood. Life began to feel really good to me. My shyness and anxiety began to get better. Then I had a feeling it was too good to be true. It all seemed to come crashing down on me. That's when another very frightening time in my life started. A different nightmare began.

My anxiety was starting to build. My silence stayed unbroken. Another abuse to keep secret. As a child not knowing, I thought once again I should keep my pain and secrets hidden; live with my suffering all alone; tell no one, like the voices always told me; try to forget it all, to push everything further down past that surface, where I will not remember and where the coward would hold on tight to whatever I give; remain silent, like the good one should. Still, I was wrong, so very wrong! I know that now, too late to help my childhood anyway. I was eight years old now. I never thought a child that young would come to despise their childhood so quickly. I have always heard people say, "Don't wish your life away." If they had mine, they may want to rethink that. If I'd had to live mine again and got one wish, I'd wish to never be born! I know, unquestionably harsh. That is how much I hated my childhood. Or I possibly could go right to becoming a teenager than growing up extremely fast. No one could hurt me if I were bigger. I just wanted my childhood over.

I would not take back my childhood for all the gold and money in the world! Now here comes more of my story… Along comes that cousin back into our lives. You know, the one I did not like, the one who frightened me, gave me the creeps, held onto my hand strangely. Yeah, him, the one I thought nothing more about until he showed up at our place.

He began to stop by our house just to say a friendly hello, he told my mom. He wanted to get to know us better, he told all of us. *Great*, I thought sarcastically but kept it to myself because the whole family seemed to like him. They were giving him hugs and seemed to welcome him with open arms. All but me. I stayed far away.

Mom said to me, "You remember your cousin, don't you?"

"Not really," I replied as I stayed planted where I stood, hoping I could stay there.

"Now, do not be a smart-ass," my mom said a bit angrily.

He walked to me and gave me a hug and whispered in my ear, "This ought to be fun. You will truly enjoy me."

I jumped back as if he had slapped me, not knowing what he meant and hoping Mom heard him. Of course, she did not, but it sure made me feel worse than the handshake when I met him. They were all welcoming him into our family. *Still, he is not our family*, I thought to myself. *I have a bad feeling about this.* I looked up, and he had this smug look on his face. I bent my finger, wanting him to bend down, like I had a secret for him. I waited so I could whisper.

"I do not like you. Stay away from me, you ass," I whispered to him.

He paused a couple of seconds before standing back up straight. I looked up at him, and his face was now the one that was red! *Who is feeling uncomfortable now?* I thought to myself. *Now maybe he will leave me alone!* I suddenly felt beyond proud of myself. I put a smug look on my face then. Just before I ran out the door, my cousin began talking with my parents, ignoring us kids, so we all got ready to go to the pit to get lost for the day, which we did.

Then we got hungry and decided to go in for lunch. Oh no, my cousin was still there, and he was staying for lunch. Just perfect!

"Wash up," Mom told us.

We all lined up for the bathroom. I turned around. My cousin was looking right at me, smiling! I really wanted to stick my tongue out at him, but I did not want to get in more trouble. He smiled this evil smile, and I turned back in line to wash my hands as my face got red.

Now I was uncomfortable again. We all sat down while my cousin began to say all our names one by one, getting them all right like he had studied some test.

When he got to me, he said, "I am going to call you trouble."

Mom laughed at him and said, "She would be the very last one to call that. She is usually the quietest one in the group."

"Really?" he said. My cousin looked at me and said, "I really never would have guessed it!"

My face grew redder than usual, knowing the secret that we both knew I told from earlier.

Mom said, "See what I mean," when she looked at me and saw my face get red.

I could not eat with him sitting across the table, watching me.

So I left my plate there without finishing and went back out to play while feeling very uncomfortable again. My cousin unfortunately came back the following day, this time sucking up by bringing Mom a bag of groceries. She hugged and thanked him and, of course, asked him to stay for lunch again. I made sure he sat at the table first, so I could sit where he could not stare at me the whole time I ate. The following weekend, he was back. I saw him give my Mom money, and I thought that was kind of strange, wondering, *Why would he give her money? Would it be for eating meals with us?* Then I thought maybe he had borrowed money from my mom before and was just paying her back what he owed her. I never said anything to anyone, and I just forgot about it.

We all went to the pit for the day. We were having a great morning when who showed up but our annoying cousin. *This is not happening*, I thought to myself! I was not incredibly happy about this at all. He watched while I was handing everyone things from the ground to the tree house. All of a sudden, he picked me up and told my brother to grab me as he puts me up in the tree. I was so shocked and scared I didn't know what to do or say. I was just terrified, and it happened so fast.

What a lousy jerk! I hollered as I kicked and screamed the whole time. Not only because I am terrified of heights but also because that jerk was touching me. I tried my hardest to kick him so he would not touch me again. But he was too fast. I began to cry out loud as my brother sat me down in the tree house.

He whispered, "I know you don't like heights, but it will be our little secret. Just stay here and watch me. Do not look down. I will help you down in a few minutes. We do not have to tell anyone else you do not like heights, okay?"

I shook my head yes, and I did as he asked, but not without crying first! When my cousin climbed up, I hollered at him, "Don't you ever touch me again, you jerk!"

He said, "Or what!"

I just knew right then that we were not going to be getting along very well. I just did not know why.

Everyone was showing him all the secrets we had around the gravel pit, and I was getting so angry because of it. My brother even told him we swam in the brook on hot days, but not to tell our parents. It was giving me a very bad feeling, making me feel uncomfortable.

"Geez, you guys do not even know him. Our parents don't really know him, not that well. Why do you think you can trust him with all of our secrets?" I asked them all later.

"Why, what is wrong with him?" they wanted know.

I wanted to tell them how uncomfortable he made me, but that was not a good-enough reason nor would any one of my excuses be. They would not agree with any of my reasons since they all liked him so much.

I told them, "He buys Mom groceries, and I saw him give her money."

They didn't seem to care!

"He is an adult. He will tell on us for sure!"

I kept quiet about the rest, thinking maybe I was wrong, but I felt so weird around him. It was something I had never felt, and I did not like it. Instead of saying something I felt, which made me sound stupid, I just kept quiet and tried to follow their lead, which did not last an especially long time for me. My siblings were okay with him hanging out with us, which really seemed to be bothering me. He creeped me out, but why? For him to do whatever it is we do and to know what we know.

All our secrets only kids should know. They trusted him, and I would just have to keep my eye on him to make sure he would not tell on any of us. Just see what it was he was really up to. I still had this weird feeling about him. Not really sure of what it was yet, but I knew I was not making it up. Because I knew I had never felt this way about anyone before. There was nothing wrong with me keeping my guard up! I would try to be nice to him if he was trying to be nice to me. We would see how long our game of being uncomfortable around one another would last.

Chapter 19

Being Bribed

I still did not like him spending all kinds of time together with us. My face turned red whenever I was around him. No matter what he did, I always kept this weird feeling about him, making me jumpy and nervous around him all the time, more than I usually was. He tried being nice to me sometimes. He also tried talking to me like I was his friend or something. I just could not stand the man, and that was one of the things that bothered me—he was a man! He did not belong hanging with a bunch of kids. I did not understand why Mom was letting him. She didn't think there was something odd about him playing and hanging out with young kids? She did not wonder what he was doing it for?

Mom did not want to know if there could be a reason a grown man wanted to hang out with a bunch of kids, play their games, have picnics, in a tree house with them, spend all day with them, then stand in line to wash up for dinner, laughing and joking as if he was one of Mom's children! Also, didn't anyone else notice the way he looked at me or smiled at me? It was too creepy. Then he started going to the tree house to eat lunch with us for all his afternoon meals when we went, never wanting to eat with the adults! Something else that I thought was strange, yet no one else did? I also noticed he always tried to aggravate, tease, and usually upset only me.

I think he figured out how scared I was of heights. He was always trying to pick me up to pass me to my brother, putting me higher in the tree house, no matter what level they were on. Why pick on only me? There were many more girls around other than me, and so many of our friends were girls that were there. No one but me would notice him smiling at me, his eyebrows moving. Why, he tried to whisper to me! It was all too noticeable for only me to see it! I would kick him and scream whenever he tried putting me up high in the tree house, even swearing at him. My brother let me know he did not like me to swear. Every time my cousin touched me anywhere though, I swear my skin would burn.

I cried really hard this last time he put me up because he put his hand between my legs to lift me up, and that made me feel fear for some reason I did not know why, and my brother finally told my cousin to knock it off! I did not like him putting me in the tree house or putting me up higher. For him to not touch me again. I always loved my brother so much; he was always standing up for me, looking out for me. Another sibling who was my hero. My cousin did stop, then he finally just smiled strangely at me all the time, still giving me the creeps. I told him more than once he was too old to be playing and hanging out with a bunch of kids. He was a lot older than my oldest brother, and he had a job he went to every day like my daddy did.

Then he would come out to play with us on the weekends, even sometimes after he got done working on a weekday. No one thought that to be strange but me? I just thought he was too weird. He also followed me around like he was my pet dog. Again, no one thought that to be a little obnoxious like I did? I should start a list of all the strange things he did around me. Then one day my sisters and I could laugh and joke about it! The oddest thing was, I couldn't get over my mom not thinking it strange he wanted to play with a bunch of kids. Why? I didn't get it at all! He ate a lot of lunches with us; that wasn't enough. He soon began staying for dinners too. I guess he must have been bribing Mom somehow with all the groceries he brought to the house. He began doing that a lot too

Oh, and how much he praised her cooking. Mom loved that. They would hug, and she would giggle like a little girl. It sure made me sick to my stomach for some unknown reason. It was like he had cast a spell over her and he could do whatever the heck he wanted to do. It did not matter how strange it was. I thought to myself, *How far could this bribery eventually go! Would she let him do whatever he asked her? Let him get away with anything he wanted to do?*

I wondered if he was tempting her with groceries for some reason and possibly giving her money also. I did see that once, but why? Just to eat with us, to play in the pit with us? It did not make sense to me. I knew he was not doing it to be a nice guy because I didn't think he was very nice. I would still keep an eye out for anything different about him! For weeks, he hung out with us, going swimming with us; and the other kids were right, he did not tell any of our secrets so far. But I still did not trust him. I thought that was what he was doing, trying to win all our trust! But why? He started to play hide-and-seek with us. Although I only played a few of the games because he spoiled that game for me.

He always found my hiding spots and tried to hide with me, no matter where I hid. When I would try to run from him, he would grab me under my arms, twirl me around, touching my skin, always making it feel like it was on fire and giving me that creepy feeling again, making me dizzy as I kicked and screamed every time until someone came to find out why I was screaming.

No one understood why I acted this way around him. But what I could not figure out was why no one realized he did nothing like these kinds of things with the other girls. Only me! Why did I notice and no one else could? Was I just imagining this? Being silly? I said nothing because I would just look stupid, again.

It was not enough to go get groceries for the house. He began going to the store, wanting to take all of us with him. The first time he asked, I said, "No, thanks. Mom would not let that happen."

"Oh no!" she said. "You are going! He is trying to be nice to you go for a ride do something different."

So I went unwillingly. I had a feeling he was doing this for a certain reason; I just did not know why yet. When we got to the store, he told everyone to go in, but I refused. My siblings came out with bags of candy and treats. I did not want his candy. Mom made me go several times, and every time I refused to get out of the truck. I could tell it was making him angry that I did not go in. I kind of liked that.

Entertaining Mommy?

I also knew he was trying to think of a way he could bribe me along with the rest of my family. Nothing he said changed my mind. I just knew that he was up to something! I just had not figured out what that something was yet. I may have been young, but I was not going to let him bribe me in any way.

One time he came out of the store with this big smile on his face and said, "Look what I have for you."

Being polite as I can be without looking at him, I said, "No, thanks."

It must have made him angry because he told Mom. The big crybaby, and a little while after we got back, Mom took me into the summer kitchen, closing the door. I knew this could not be good.

Mom said, "What is your problem!"

I acted like I had no clue what she was talking about and straightened right up in fear.

She asked me why I would not take the candy or anything he offered. I told her I just did not want any candy. Then she got angry and said she wanted a good reason. I tried telling her my belly hurt, that I knew if I ate candy, I really would not feel good. I began to cry then did not say anything, knowing the truth would make her even more angry. Apparently, she did not like my answer.

Mom asked again in a much-angrier voice, "Why don't you want any of his candy, goddamn you!"

What do I say to a woman who is on someone else's side no matter what? I looked up at her through my tears, and I knew there was no pleading with those angry eyes and enraged-looking mouth of hers.

I began to scream as she grabbed me by the hair then produced an orange rubber racetrack strip. I wondered then if she had one standing in every corner of the house. *I would have to look later*, I thought as the strap came across my butt and legs. I screamed for her to please stop, that I would take his candy. I sobbed through my hiccups I now had. My sister and I would have to check through the house and find all her hidden weapons and destroy them, especially those orange strips from the racetrack. Those hurt extremely bad on bare legs and arms. We would have to find them all and burn them at the pit. Just like we did all her other weapons when we found them.

Funny that she never asked or accused us of taking them when she could not find them whenever she wanted one. We just could never find out where she hid her stash of them. We knew she had to have one somewhere in the house or maybe the barn. We were looking to destroy them all as soon as we could locate the stupid things. She always seemed to get them stood up in parts of the house again where we could not find them. Mom always had an abundance of orange racetrack strips to whip us with. I don't think she ever ran out of those hurtful things.

After a few more hits across my bare skin, she stopped, without letting go of my hair, and screamed into my face, "The next time he offers you something, you be polite and take it. Be thankful someone's willing to buy something for your stupid ass!"

"Okay, Mom," I told her through my sobs again as I tried to grab my hair she was pulling.

She gave me one hard swat across my legs, leaving them stinging bad, before she let go of me. When I walked through the kitchen, my cousin was leaning against the woodstove. I looked up with a red face, and that jerk was actually smiling at me like he was saying, "I won." I turned around to see if my mother came out yet. She had not.

I turned back around and said through my sobs, "I hate you! I wish you would never come here again, and if you think I am going to eat your stupid treats, you are crazy!"

The next weekend, my cousin asked Mom if he could take all the kids to get an ice cream.

Everyone squealed but me. I knew it was just another bribe for something. Maybe he wanted to move in with us because he did not like his own family, I thought. I had no idea yet. I just knew I was keeping my eye out. I would never trust him. I knew he had something in mind, and I had a feeling my mother was in on the bribe! Again, I was made to go, not wanting to get an ice cream or help him scheme and plot his bribe. We all had to line up to get an ice cream.

Entertaining Mommy?

My siblings were all thanking him when he told them to get whatever they wanted, except me! I was not thanking him!

He smiled at me walked over, bent down so only I could hear and whispered, "Well I guess you are just going to have to get an ice cream now, aren't you!"

I could feel my face burning hot, knowing it was beet red from anger this time. It was my turn. I was looking at the menu, and as I stood there, I decided to get the biggest most expensive ice cream I could get. Everyone was incredibly surprised when I turned around, especially my cousin. I know he knew I got the most expensive ice cream for getting even with him for the beating I got when he tattled on me the other day, but I didn't, not really! He turned around like it did not bother him, sat down watching, and smiled at me like he won again. Until I turned and tipped the ice cream upside down and dumped it into the trash without taking one taste.

Then I smiled at him. Some of my siblings who saw just sat there with their mouths open, but my cousin's face was priceless. I wish I had a camera to capture that moment! That was the very best! If I did get another beating, it would be worth seeing his face at this very second, and I would never forget the look of defeat I got to see in his eyes if only for a brief moment! He did tell on me again. I knew something was coming when I walked through the door. Mom slapped me across the face hard, knocking me on my back, in front of everyone. When I sat up, my cousin, of course, was smiling, and I wanted so bad to attack him.

Mom said, "To your room. No supper!"

I did not care; it was well worth it!

I did not play into this bribe this time either. I had this good feeling that being bribed did not work on me at all. Why could not one person see anything that was going on here? Nothing was strange to anyone but me? All this trouble I was getting into, only me, was because of our stupid cousin. Could anyone please see what I was seeing? They could not yet see that all these things he was doing was somehow leading to some kind of bribe? Did no one care they were being used in some kind of sick game? A game I had an idea that my mom was in on. Those two always seemed to be up to something, always in a corner, whispering and laughing, looking like a couple of teenagers instead of two grown adults! I still would not be bribed, no matter what they thought up or what they would do! Hopefully, someone else would open their eyes, and very soon.

Chapter 20

Getting Even

I did not go hungry that night. I knew I could count on two of my sisters. They always snuck me food. We always looked out for each other when we could. They asked me what was up between me and our cousin.

I told them, "Nothing. He just irritates me sometimes. Tries to be funny, and I do not think he is at all."

They looked at me funny, but they did not ask any more questions, seeing how angry-looking I had become. The following weekend, my cousin showed up, only eating dinner with us. He sat across the table from me as usual, now always waiting for me to be the one to sit down first. I didn't know why he was doing this to me, pretending to be always watching Mom preparing things and complimenting her.

When he did sit across from me almost every time, he was always smiling at me the whole time he was eating or talking. I wanted to scream, "Does anyone else notice him staring at me? How he smiles at only me!" Of course, no one noticed how red my face stayed through supper either or how my head stayed down while I ate, or even how I no longer talked at the dinner table to anyone; and again, I told no one…while no one was aware. He was beginning to get on my nerves! My cousin showed up the next day in the early afternoon. He told us we were going to the store first thing then informed us that Mom told him he could take us swimming for the day.

"Get your bathing suits and towels."

I looked at him and said, "No, I am not going."

He bent down and said, "Oh, but you are."

"Not either," I said as I stomped off.

I went to my parent's bedroom, knocked on the door.

Mom said, "Come in."

Mom was getting all dressed up. No, no, no!

"What are you doing?" I asked in a panic.

"Your dad is taking me out while your cousin takes you all swimming for the day. Go-go get your things together."

"But I am sick," I told her. "My stomach is making funny noises, and I think I have a fever."

"Then you can lay down in his vehicle with the doors open while your siblings enjoy the day. Either way, you are going!" she said with that mean stare. "I packed a cooler. Make sure your cousin remembers it."

Damn him, I thought. He had already known I had to go, again getting even with me by making an idiot out of me.

I did not like going swimming mainly because I was so afraid of going over my head and drowning—a fear I've had since my feet hit the water. I never really learned how to swim very well, and I panic if my feet cannot touch. Just another secret I have never shared with anyone. I may as well just say I am afraid of everything. Of course, unless something makes me really mad. Then my face gets really red, and I don't seem to care what I'm afraid of. I do things then out of pure anxiety and anger! I got my bathing suit and towel. He made some snorting sound as I walked by. So he got even this time! I did end up swimming without going over my head.

He kept his eyes right on me the whole time. I swear I could feel it. But I did not pay any attention to him. When we got back, I believe I got even with him. Just a little too loudly is all. When we returned home from swimming, my sister and I made sandwiches for everyone. He came in from doing something in the barn since he was all greasy. Unfortunately, I did not see him come in. I was standing on a step stool, with my back to the door, helping to make lunch, when my cousin came up behind me, putting both his greasy hands on my sides, squeezing hard. It felt like steam was coming out of my ears. I thought I had never felt so mad! It made me feel like I just jumped out of my own skin before it caught on fire.

Entertaining Mommy?

Then he whispered in my ear, "Can I have a couple of those?"

I threw my knife down, making it fly across the counter, turned around, stepping off the step stool as I pushed him away with my sticky hands, saying a little too loudly, "Make the damn things yourself!"

The room went completely silent. Everyone looked at me like, "How could you be so mean!"

I just looked at everyone and said, "What, he is a grown-up. He can make his own stupid sandwiches."

I walked to the table, sat down while everyone stared at me like I was the mean one, of course.

I looked around the table and said, "WHAT!"

No one said a word to me after that. I knew what they really wanted to say though. How mean I was! I just did not care.

No one thought of him as I did, so they would not understand. My other sister must have felt bad. She got up and made him sandwiches, looking at me like I had lost my mind when she walked by me. Everyone was looking at me like I was the bad guy. Later my sister asked me what was up. Did I not like our cousin?

I wished now I had told the truth, but I lied instead, saying, "He is okay, but he annoys me. Now let's go to the pit."

Our cousin walked out and said, "Not so fast, girls. We will have to go to the store first. I promised your mom I would pick up something for dinner."

"Why do you buy food for our house?" I asked. "Do you think we are going to run out or that you are going to move in?" I said in as rude a voice as I dared while my sister nudged me.

"Just being nice," he answered in the same kind of rude voice.

I rolled my eyes at him as I began to walk away.

"Get in the car," he said like he was mad.

"No!" I told him.

He reached for me, and I jumped back but he caught my arm quickly and roughly. It felt like he was going to pull my arm off; he was being so rough!

"Ouch," I yelled. "Let go of me, you ass!"

He tried pulling me toward the car, but I kicked him hard.

"Let me go, you animal."

He was strong. We started to wrestle. I started to cry. He was hurting me, being so mean. He tried forcing me into the front seat of the car. I kept kicking as he slapped my bottom hard, telling me to knock it off.

"Keep your filthy hands off me, you uncivil idiot," I screamed, kicking and crying. Then he opened the back door and tried shoving me in there. "Let go of me, you jerk," I hollered.

I knew he was much stronger and that I would be getting in the car, but not without a fight. He smacked my head on the doorframe while trying to push me in. I stopped fighting instantly, screaming in pain. He shoved me into the car anyway.

My older sister hollered at him, "Don't you think she gets enough of this crap already? You did not have to handle her that way."

I stopped crying and put my hands up to feel my head. There was a huge bump on my forehead.

"She asked for it this time," he said in a voice that was all out of air.

I thought, when we got to the store, I would get out and get some candy this time. I had a real sweet tooth, and he was buying. I suddenly forgot all about the pain and the bump on my head.

I went in the store I grabbed one of the biggest paper bags they had for candy to get my treats.

While filling my bag, my cousin walked up behind me and whispered, "That a girl. Get anything you want. I truly am sorry for hurting you back there."

"I do not care," I said in a loud enough voice for everyone in the store to hear it. "That is what I am used to! You did not even hurt me!"

I filled my bag over the top with candy. My cousin seemed pleased with that. I knew it was going to cost a lot. He did not seem to care. He sure thought he had won this battle and gotten even with me! Not yet, he had not! I waited until all my siblings were out the door before I headed for the car. I made sure I was the last one to leave the store.

My cousin was standing there with this huge smile on his face, like he had won a grand prize or something. He was standing by the car, holding the door open for me to get in. I was going to the trash can like I was going to throw away a wrapper or something. I lifted the cover off the trash can. The flies that swarmed out and all around it were disgusting, and I did not like them. Still, I was not showing I was scared, and I had to keep my eyes on the prize. I turned my bag of candy upside down so every single piece went into the trash before he could stumble toward me to stop me. Oh, the look on his face! Talk about getting even! I looked up at him with this huge smile on my face as I dropped the paper bag in.

He turned to walk back to the car and looked very stiff like he was walking like a robot does. Then I made this face and stuck my tongue out before I walked past. I could not help myself. I began to laugh really loud! I saw his fists doubling up a couple of times as he stood there. It scared me a little, so I walked slowly then stood a little way away from him, but I tried not to show anything but my red face, which happened all the time. I could not help showing that, but I did not move one bit.

"Get in the car now," he said in the strangest voice as I stood there, waiting to get in the car.

He repeated, "Get in the car now," and I didn't want to push it, so I did. He slammed the door hard, almost before I got all the way into the car! I tried sitting where he could not see me in the rearview mirror, but my siblings would not move over. I did laugh all the way home! I saw him in the rearview mirror. I looked up at him a couple of times while I knew he was looking at me. I could feel it.

I said in a loud voice, "Keep your eyes on the road," like I had heard Mom say to Dad so many times.

All that I could see now was how angry he had become. I knew he was only trying to scare me. I was trying to show him I did not scare so easily, so I glared right back at him. I did not care; he better not touch me again. I thought I had become fairly good at getting even too. Maybe now he would leave me alone!

The rest of the ride home was so quiet you could have heard a stick snap in the woods if you stepped on it. No one had told my mother about him trying to get me in the car or him hurting me or even what happened at the store. I was surprised because I knew he liked seeing me punished, and in a way that gave him the perfect way for him to get even with me, but not this time! So I prayed that this was the end of my battles with the weirdo. For now, I felt super smart that I beat him at his own getting-even game. Finally, he would not like me anymore. That night, it was getting extremely late. I heard my parents talking to my cousin still. *Go home, you jerk*, I thought to myself as I fell asleep.

I began to dream of a witch and a broom. The witch was chasing me while I ran. I did nothing but scream and cry. I was so frightened because I had never seen this ugly witch before. She had a scarier and louder evil laugh than when my mom was a witch in my dreams. I couldn't get away from her.

"Please, someone help me!" What do I do now? I had nowhere to run. There was no path to take, and there was no light. Everything was pitch black. All of a sudden, the witch was back, chasing me and screeching an evil laugh then telling me to run to the left, run to the left! I did not know what to do. There was no one here but me and the witch.

Should I believe her as I ran around in circles, crying and screaming for someone to please help? I guess I would do as she told me.

What did I have to lose? I couldn't see anything anyways. I ran to the left, and the witch vanished. She was not playing a trick on me. *Thanks, evil witch*, I thought. Then I heard something ahead of me, and I started to run the other way when all of a sudden, I began falling into a black hole! I saw nothing but black darkness all around me. I was screaming my head off. An arm reached out to grab me, and I was so relieved to stop falling. I was standing up straight, and who was standing in front of me but my strange, weirdo cousin. He reached for me with his other hand as I started to scream, then I woke up.

Chapter 21

The Nightmares Start

It was a Saturday night. I knew Dad was not working tonight. I fell asleep to voices and laughter downstairs. I was awakened by a hand covering my mouth. There was extremely hard pressure, and I began to choke as I started to panic and cry into the big, smelly hand. I tried to look through the darkness to see if this was some kind of joke that I did not think was very funny. The blankets lifted as someone laid down beside me.

"Please, someone help me," he cried, mocking me as I woke from my nightmare that he said I was having as he tried to pull the covers over us both.

What is that smell! I looked again, and there, lying beside me, covering my mouth tightly, was my crazy, weird cousin.

Okay, if this was payback and he was trying to scare me, it worked. I was done trying to get even with him, I thought as I sobbed and shook my head no. His hand smelled like urine. That was what I was smelling. I began to gag against his hand. He got too close to me and began to whisper, sending horrible chills up my back, and making the hair on the back of my neck stand. His hot, smelly breath on my ear and neck made me gag even more. I could do nothing but cry and try to breath. I was trying to get out from under his strength, but his legs had me pinned down also, and my struggles were doing me no good.

I realized at that moment that the vomit was coming, but I could not throw up, that I was now swallowing my own vomit because he was holding my mouth so tightly with that smelly hand. So I stopped struggling, knowing it was taking up the only air I had left.

He whispered, "I am going to take my hand off your mouth. If you cry out or if you try to scream, I will have some fun with one of your little sisters. Do you want that to happen?"

I did not know what that meant but did not want him touching my sisters or going anywhere near them. So I shook my head yes, as if I understood. He slowly took his hand off my mouth, and I finally was able to breath.

He said again, "Do not scream, or you will be sorry, I promise you."

He took his leg off the top of mine, and I began to kick him as fast and as hard as I could without saying a word.

He never said I could not be physical.

"STOP!" he said into my ear with clenched teeth as his leg went back over mine and his hand covered my mouth again.

I must have gotten him good because he was bent over and acted like he was in severe pain, which I was happy about. His breathing sounded funny, and he could hardly talk.

"Do not make a sound. Do not speak. Do not say a word."

He put one of his arms under my back and tried to roll me over as I struggled with him. He removed his hand from my mouth again.

"I do not know what you are doing" I whispered, "but you win! You scared me good. Now we are even. I promise I will not do anything else to annoy you ever again. Just leave, and I will not tell anyone."

"I am not leaving," he whispered in a very strange voice still, "and you will not tell anyone anything ever."

I wanted to scream as he rolled me toward him, facing him. He must have known because his hand slammed down on my mouth hard again, and he said, "Don't." It made me begin to cry harder. "I am going to take my hand off your mouth," he whispered. "Don't scream. Don't cry. Don't say a word. I'm not going to hurt you." Suddenly his whispering also was making me sick. "Do you want to be in big trouble?" he asked me.

I did not move as the tears flowed worse down my face and I began to shake. I did not know what he was doing here, but I knew there was something bad about him, just like I thought.

He shook my head with the hand that still covered my mouth. "Do you hear me?" he said again, shaking my head even harder!

I shook my head yes, not thinking or knowing what he just asked me. My body just trembled.

"I do not know what's happening," I whispered to him through my sobs as he removed his smelly hand.

He put that arm around me, wrapping both arms around me in a hug.

Oh no, I hate this feeling. I cannot let him hug me. I cried a little too loudly as I pushed on him hard. He rolled very close to the edge. I did not care! I didn't want him touching me, and I really hated him hugging me. That was supposed to be a moment when you feel good toward a person, not the hate I feel toward this jerk! I could not let him spoil hugging for me. It's the only kind of love I feel or get from the rest of my family. He caught himself before he fell off the bed, almost bringing me down with him.

"That was not incredibly wise," he told me.

"I don't care. I do not want you to hug me!" I told him.

"Well, too bad!" he fired right back. "Now be quiet, I told you."

"I do not care," I said again just as loud. "You will not be hugging me!"

He clamped his smelly hand back on my mouth, hard. My tears would not stop falling.

I could feel how angry he was with the strength he was using.

I said, "Stop it," as he pushed my face down toward my pillow, making it hard for me to breathe again.

My tears begin running over his hand, making the urine smell twice as strong. I gagged again, then I wondered if he ever washed his hands. Oh no, I truly could not breathe! I tried to struggle again, but that was only taking up more of my air.

"Do you hear me?" he said, bringing me back to making me gag once more as I once again swallowed my own vomit.

"No, I did not hear you." I shook my head no, hoping it did not make him angry again, that he would stop scaring me and get out of my bed and let me breath again. He had proven his point! He won! He got even with me, way better than I did him. He turned me back around, and I thought to myself, *I won't go near him. I will just stay away from him.*

I tried to blink so I could see him in the dark, but I could not see him hardly at all. I already knew he was a monster. He shook me again.

"Do you want to be in trouble?" he said through angry, clenched teeth (is what it sounded like when he talked).

I shook my head no, not understanding any of this. Again, he removed his hand as I gagged. I did not know what had kept it down for yet the second time. My stomach felt so weak. He began to try to hug me again.

"No, I can't let you hug me!"

I hate this feeling. It is making my skin crawl, sick-to-my-stomach feeling, I think to myself. Something also felt really weird when he tried to hug me. He tried to pull me to him, making me feel really sick again. I felt it coming back up!

"Please, I don't want to throw up right now."

I did nothing but sob and fight him the whole time. I cried out, "Please don't hug me. I hate hugging."

He began to hum. *What is he doing!*

"What are you doing?" I asked. He said nothing. "Please don't hurt me." He was too strong. I couldn't get him off me. I did not want to feel something weird he kept pushing into me when he hugged me. I did not stop pushing him away. I did not understand. He won. Why was he still here?

"Okay, you won. Now go away," I told him.

He only laughed at me! I began to cry out again as I pushed him away. He told me to shut up, and his arm squeezed around me, cutting off my breath again, hurting me more.

"Shut up! Don't you know what that means?" That weird feeling is pushing up against me hard.

"Stop," I said a bit too loud for him because I was so scared. I did not know what was happening to me. What did I do that was so bad?

"I promise I will not throw away anything else you buy for me," I said through my sobs. "Please stop hugging me."

Entertaining Mommy?

He finally let me go as I tried to move away from him fast. He removed his other arm out from under me. But he did not let go, pulling me even closer and began rubbing my back, making a cooing sound as if rocking a baby. It did not feel the same as when Mom or Dad rubbed my back when I was sick. I suddenly started feeling sick again.

"Don't," he whispered, "or you will be in big trouble. Don't say a word."

"Why is this happening? Why won't you stop?" I sobbed.

He continued rubbing my back, then with his other hand, he began to rub my chest area over my pajamas.

"What are you doing?" I whimpered through my tears.

"Shh," he said, "I'm not hurting you."

"Yes! You are!"

I am terrified! What is happening? Should I scream? Should I wake up my sister? What should I do?

I knew he was a monster, and I hated him! I told him to go again. He kept rubbing through my pajamas. *Please make it stop, please, somebody, please!*

"If you do not want to be in big trouble, then don't say a word. Never tell anyone," he said in an angry voice. "Unless you want big trouble. Do you like trouble, little girl?" he asked.

Then all of a sudden, he was gone. I laid here sobbing for such a long time. I was too scared to go to sleep, too scared to move. I didn't know what to do. So I asked myself all kinds of questions as I cried. *Why me? What did I do that was so wrong? Would I really be in trouble? Please make this be the one and only time! I do not want to ever feel this way again. I never want him touching me again. Please, I beg you. Amen!*

I could not sleep. I didn't know how I could. I had to keep asking myself questions. *What just happened? What was that? What did that stupid monster do that for? Why would I get into trouble anyway? What did I do wrong? How am I ever going to sleep now? What am I going to do about this? I don't know what to think or do! Could someone please help me? Who do I trust enough to tell?*

I know, even if I told someone, I doubt anyone would believe me over him. I knew how much everyone loves him! Mom really would not believe me. If she truly loved him and not me! Who do you think she would believe? She and everyone else, who thought he was so great! Or should I say, he had everyone fooled into thinking that!

I know I cannot say anything! I doubt I will even want to sleep at all tonight, and if I do, what will be in my dreams? Or will they be those horrible nightmares again? I am so afraid, confused. What do I do? I have to stop crying first and just quietly think. I am too young to be going through something so terrible and being all alone. No, I can do this. I am smart.

As I cried about the horrible things I did not understand, I began to fall asleep. I fought it… I kept fighting it… I was too scared. No, I couldn't sleep. I was too afraid to sleep. The last time I was this afraid, I had a horrible nightmare about a witch trying to chase me and hurt me.

Now I was afraid again after a real monster came to visit me in my bed. What would happen if I fell asleep now? The last thing I needed was to have another bad night of horrors to think about for days. I was getting sleepy. I couldn't seem to fight it any longer.

Please let me have a nice dream tonight. I need a good night's sleep. Then came my very first bad nightmares that tortured and terrified me. Okay, I was scared! *Now, how do I get them to stop? Who can help me now? How do I do this? What will my sisters say to me? My parents… oh no, what will they think?*

Chapter 22

I Had My Chance

I guess I did fall asleep. Why was it that I could remember my nightmares so well the next morning? Or when I woke scared to death from something or someone chasing me. I really wish I couldn't remember. I truly wish I could stop having all my nightmares. The beating in my body had slowly stopped banging as I began to wake. I thought again about last night, the way my breathing began to slow as my heart stopped beating so wildly. But I still could not stop myself from crying. For so long, I cried thinking about what that monster did. Why me? Why did he hate me? Too scared to go to sleep for a very long time last night, I tried to think about what to do. Why did I have to dream so much, have so many nightmares?

Could it have been something I dreamt? No, it was too real. My body knew I was touched. I could still feel his legs on mine, holding me down, trying to stop me from breathing. I had never felt this way, and I really did not know what to do. I didn't even know what it was called what he did, or why. What would I tell someone if I were to tell? It was a different kind of horror than from the nightmares I got when Mom beat me. I could not sleep for hours, thinking, wondering. Why could I not stop shaking! Though I did stop eventually. Then I thought about him touching and rubbing and hugging me again! Oh, how I hated that hugging. I could throw up right now just thinking about it.

My body felt like it burned everywhere that he touched me. It still burned. Oh great, I felt vomit coming up again. *Please, I don't want to throw up now. I cannot stop thinking about what it is that I did that was so wrong. I am sorry, I am so deeply sorry, whatever it was I did.* Was whatever I did that terrible that the monster was allowed to get in my bed and do that to me and scare me like that? Did I really deserve what I just went through last night because I was mean to that monster? I would just have to stay away from him as much as I possibly could. No more getting even, no more being mean, I promised. *No matter what he does to me, please accept my forgiveness!* I really must have fallen asleep after that.

I felt my younger sister waking up beside me. Yes, she had been in the same bed the whole time, right beside me throughout my whole ordeal. Another reason why I did as the monster told me to do. I do not know what I would have done if she had woken up to that monster. She would have been so scared. I'm so very thankful she slept through it all. She got up and began jumping up and down.

"Come on, sis. Let's go get breakfast," she yelled.

Suddenly I wondered again if maybe it really was just a nightmare. Maybe it did not happen to me at all. It was all in my imagination! Was it a dream? Then the smell of urine hit my nose, and I knew it had been real. It made me gag all over again.

It really did happen. Oh no! Now I could smell his breath and feel his gross hands on me. I can still remember him trying to hug me. Why hug me? I never wanted to be hugged again. I began to shake again, then I started to cry. I threw the covers over my head so my sister could not see my tears.

I told her, "I am sorry, but I have a tummy ache, and I have to stay in bed for a while."

"Awe, really? All right, but hurry and get up. I want to hurry to the pit before Mommy gets up."

She must have told Mom because I hear her coming up the stairs about an hour or so later. I took the covers off my head and looked out the door. I saw that Mom was carrying an empty laundry basket as she began gathering dirty clothes.

I could hear her talking to herself, but not what she was saying! She hollered toward my room.

"What is wrong with you this time?"

My heart started beating so fast. *Tell her I was screaming inside! Say something. Don't say a word.* The voices were telling me, *Tell her what happened to you! You will be in trouble. This is your chance. She will not believe you. She never believes her daughters. She will think I did something wrong. I will get another beating. Don't tell. You'll be in trouble.* I had no courage, of course, saying nothing.

There was a coward just beginning to build its walls up. It was very weak for now, but they would become walls nothing could get through!

Instead, I said, "I have a tummy ache." That was what came out of my mouth as his words kept ringing in my ears, "Don't say a word."

I asked if I could please, please stay in bed for a while. She only let me lay there while she gathered laundry and dirty dishes. Mom told me to get up, get dressed, then try to eat something. Maybe that would make my belly feel better, she said. I knew I would not feel better, whether I ate or not. I also knew it was best not to argue with Mom. Then after a thought, I asked if my cousin was still here.

"No, he left early this morning. Why?" she said.

"I was just wondering if he was going to the pit with us today, that is all," I lied.

I decided I better get good at telling fibs; it was better than getting a beating. Mom was about to head downstairs, and I was about to lose my only chance to come forward and tell what happened to me. I thought more about being in trouble.

I have had enough trouble in my life already, as my chance just walked down and over the stairs. *You coward! You just blew your only chance to tell!* When I finally went downstairs, Mom was in the summer kitchen, doing laundry. Everyone else was outside already. I got some cereal that I did not think I could eat. Mom came out and began wiping off the table.

"Are you sure it is just a tummy ache?" she asked.

My face turned red, I knew. *Another chance, you little coward,* but I heard, *Tell her. This is your chance. Don't blow it! You can still tell her.* Then a voice rang in my head, *Be quiet.* Then a louder voice roared, *Don't say a word. You'll be in trouble. What if she blames me?*

"I think I might be getting a fever," I told her.

"Hmm," she said then went to the bathroom to find a thermometer.

It is your last chance. You have to do this. Tell her, you coward! I could hear her now. *You're such a little sissy. Why would you make up such a lie like that about someone so kind?* Then the beating would start. That was all I saw, all I felt. She came out of the bathroom and stuck the thermometer under my tongue then put her hand on my forehead. *Last chance. Speak up. Tell her now, or you will be in trouble,* the voice screamed louder.

"You do not feel warm at all," she told me.

Tell her! Don't say a word.

"Really? I thought I was burning up, ready to explode," I told her.

She would not believe me.

I did not believe me. I could not do it. I already knew what she would do, slap my face and say, "How dare you." Then I would hear, "I know you have not liked him since you met him, but this is taking it too far." I knew it had happened, but was it my fault?

"Well, there is nothing wrong with you now. Maybe you had a dream you were sick, or it could be something else possibly! You can go play with your siblings now. What, is it your turn to clean the tree house and you do not want to because you are afraid of heights?" she asked. I looked at her as if she had slapped me. "Yes, I know. You are such a little sissy."

I knew it had to be that monster that told her I was afraid of heights.

My brother would not have said anything to Mom. I truly hate that troublemaker. I started to eat my cereal so I would not have to talk or answer any questions. But I did not feel like eating. I had lost my appetite way before I got my cereal. I ate a couple more bites.

"Finish your cereal and go catch up with your sisters before you cannot find them," she said as she started to leave the kitchen.

"Okay," I said. That was it. I blew it. I would not be able to tell now! No one was ever going to believe it now.

"Unless, of course, you want to help with the chores," she said sarcastically.

I grabbed my bowl, dumped the rest of the cereal in the trash, threw the bowl in the sink, and ran out of there before she could say another word, leaving my last chance sitting right there in my chair. Then I hear her laughing, the witch. My mom sure knew how to play my tune when she wanted to. Whether she thought it was funny or she was only joking or just wanting to terrorize me, she always seemed to scare me in one way or another. With the way she smiled at me, she truly enjoyed what she did to me, how she made me feel. It stayed that way for so very long! I did not go to find my siblings right away. I took a detour so I could sit and think by myself for a while.

I just had to figure out if there was another way for someone to know without me getting into trouble. I sat there and thought but could not come up with any explanation that would not get me into trouble along with that monster. I know he told me not to say a word, and if I did not think of something soon, it looked like he was going to get his wish. I had to come up with something fast. *No one will believe me after today*, I figured. My head hurt. I would think more later. Time to find those siblings of mine!

Chapter 23

Wanting to Be Alone

I was on my own. I never did think of any way to tell on the monster without getting myself in trouble too. So I began to be that very shy girl again, and I made myself believe this whole thing to be my fault. I did not want to be in trouble. I just wanted to forget it ever happened. I thought I had. No one knew; I never told anyone. I was safe. But my nightmares just would not stop. I could not forget any of it. The nightmares would not let me! I have tried, truly I have. I did not know what else to do. I had changed drastically, and not for the better. I was trying to be an eight-year-old, but the way my life was headed, I would not be able to be a child at all.

I went to school. I stayed by myself. I did not want anyone near me. I did not want anyone touching me. I hurt my friends' feelings, even my best friend! They were all upset, of course. They did not understand why I wanted to be alone. I could not explain it, except that I was sick, which was not lying to them. I felt sick all the time. I thought if anyone got near me, they would somehow be able to tell what had happened to me, that someone would somehow find out. I would be made fun of; I just knew it would happen. I could not take that kind of hurting right now. I just had to do everything alone, not because I wanted to. Because I felt I needed to for now. I needed to figure this out on my own. There was no one to help and no one I trusted that was an adult.

I was so afraid someone could somehow tell just by the way I had become, that I knew I was different and I felt like some kind of freak. I was only glad it was over. I never wanted to go through this again. I needed to sleep without nightmares terrifying me or waking me up, too scared to go back to sleep. Everything would go back to normal. I started to play some outside at home again, after school, but always by myself. My siblings did not understand either. One sister I did a lot with asked me constantly to please do something with her. Then I would always hurt her feelings, telling her I couldn't, using the same lie that I was sick. I hated myself for the look in her eyes when she would walk away, not understanding.

My siblings asked me over and over why I could not play, sounding worried about me. I just kept saying I couldn't. I did not know it would get me into trouble just by wanting to be alone though. Mom called me in the bathroom one afternoon. I was so scared. I knew this would not be good.

"Why won't you play with your siblings?" she asked in an angry voice. "What is wrong with you?" she practically screamed. I looked at the floor and said nothing. Mom slapped me hard in the mouth. "I'm talking to you!" I put my hand to my mouth to feel for blood as I cried. "I will beat your ass raw if you do not tell me what is wrong with you. Now talk!" she yelled. Mom had caught me off guard.

I did not have a good lie thought up for this one. *You will be in trouble. Do not say a word*, a voice screamed in my head. I knew the trouble I would get in for telling the truth would be far worse than what I thought I was going to get now.

So I stupidly said, "What makes you think there is something wrong with me?" I said through my sobs and hiccups.

She grabbed my hair in a tight fist, wrapping it around one hand, then began beating me with her other hand nonstop! She held my hair in a tight grip the whole time, pulling and tugging.

I finally screamed, "Okay, okay. I'll tell you. There are some bullies on the playground at school picking on me, pushing me around, and told me not to tell or it would get far worse for me. I am scared of them all. I just get scared, and I want to be alone sometimes."

Phew, she must have believed me. She did not hit me again but kept a tight grip on my hair. She pulled my face right up to hers by pulling on my hair and said, "You better get your ass outside and play with your siblings, and quit acting like a little sissy, or I will give you something to be scared of. Do you hear me?"

When I left the bathroom, my younger sister was standing by the bathroom door, crying. I told her, "I'm sorry," when she tried to hug me. I ran by her and out the door to find a hiding spot, away from everybody where I could be alone. I was hurting so badly, physically and emotionally.

My head from her pulling my hair so hard was throbbing with pain, and my butt and legs where she spanked them were stinging. I laid on the ground. *Ouch, that hurt*, as I began rubbing my head to feel for any blood where she pulled my hair so hard. I did not find any then began swearing under my breath. I must have fallen asleep. Next thing I knew, my sister was waking me up, asking if I was all right. I smiled at her with my now swollen lip, and it made it hurt worse.

"Let's run away," she said as I stood up.

"Did you not get an ass-whoopin' for that once already when you were younger?" I asked and smiled at her, making my lip hurt even worse as I reached up to try to relieve some of the pain by touching it. That was not such a smart move, it really did hurt.

"Besides, where would we go?" I asked.

"Anywhere is better than here," she told me. "Does it hurt bad?"

"Nah," I said. "I have had much worse."

She tried to hug me, but I cried out and stepped back. Thankfully, she thought it was from my injuries and not because I did not want to be touched. I was glad I did not have to hurt her feelings again.

"I will get some ice for your lip. Be right back." Off she ran.

I thought about how close we were and how much I really wanted to tell her about my nightmares, then about the monster. But I was too afraid she might think it was somehow my fault or would hate me, and I didn't want her looking at me the way I was looking at myself all the time.

So I stayed quiet once again because the coward inside me knew I had become a very weak possibility for its lively future. She came back quickly with ice. Wow, that felt so much better as soon as the ice touched my lip.

"Thanks, sis."

She did ask why I did not play anymore then asked if she did something wrong.

"Oh no, you did not, I promise. I have not been feeling very well," I lied again. Still, I really wanted to tell her my secret, but that damn voice again, "Do not say a word." I just could not. What if she told? Then I would be in so much trouble. She asked if I wanted to go for a walk.

I told her, "No, not right now. I am too sore. I was going to the bedroom to read a book and relax." As I walked off, I saw the tears in her eyes.

I felt like the worst sister ever. I stayed alone even more in the next few days, mostly when Mom was not around. I thought I had become a different person. I felt very ashamed and doubtful about everything I did. Very unsure of myself, if that makes any sense. I also became much more bashful. I tried to be normal as much as I could. I began playing on the playground. Then I had slowly begun to calm down some as time passed. It was so hard to concentrate. I began to slowly play with some of my friends again, but alone was always better for me, I thought. My friends looked so funny at me when they tried to touch me or hug me like they were able to do before.

Now when I would cry out or jump back, they did not know what to do. I felt stupid. That was why I wanted to be alone! It got easier with my friends and siblings. They tried to understand, or they just ignored it. Although I still felt I would get shaken if someone tried touching me, or especially tried to hug me. I felt so bad, but I could never explain something I did not understand myself. I did try. I thought of things to help me forget my frightening nightmares before going to sleep. There was nothing I could do. It did not help that I thought my mother found joy in spanking and beating me, especially calling me names and making me cry. Then I began having nightmares of my mother.

I made a prayer to never see my cousin again and for my mom to never hit me again before I went to sleep every night after that. It did not work! I should have prayed to get the courage to talk to someone who would listen to me about my nightmares. Just how terrified of my own mother I am. The prayers never came true for me, and no matter how scared I got, I never told anyone. Maybe if I would have gotten help, what happened to me next might never have taken place. If only I had found my voice. Suffering from any kind of abuse is hard for anyone, physical or sexual—both a couple of hard ones to adjust to alone. Just imagine being a child of eight and receiving both continuously at the same time. Imagine what an innocent child is thinking when she can't trust. Just when I thought things were getting better, my nightmares were back, and during the daytime too.

Chapter 24

What Can I Do?

I began having nightmares that would not stop. They were not just about beatings anymore. I even had what I called daytime terrors: flashes of that monster touching me, hugging me over and over, making me jumpy, then something strange pushing against me—that terrified me for some reason. The hatred I felt for that monster, how much hate I felt building inside of me day by day. I did not like me anymore. I did not like who I had become inside. I felt like such a bad person, and I had no one, only me and the voices to talk to!

I know it is not healthy for an eight-year-old to be having the bad thoughts I was beginning to have. Plus, the things I was worried about should not be in my head, and suffering through it all alone made it hurt even worse. Everything began to make me restless. When someone hollered or touched me, I screamed and ran from it as fast as I could. I must have seemed so strange to everyone. I could not stop being so jumpy whenever a noise would be made. I would jump. Mom would love me to be this way again. I couldn't tell her. What would I say? That something was terrifying me in my dreams? I had a monster that wouldn't let me sleep? He even climbed into my bed. He was touching me, rubbing me, making me feel so strange!

That coward was lurking once again. Seems I could not get rid of it! The truth after all these days had passed. The chances I had to tell her were gone. She would never believe me now, so I told her nothing! Mom thought I am keeping a secret from her. How would she know that? Then when my sister tried to hug me and I jumped away from her and make a scared-of-you noise, seeing tears in her eyes then usually running away, that made me hurt the worst.

My other sister also, the same thing. Only she was older and got mad at me for things I did not do anymore. I did a lot of crying myself, crying and shaking never knowing what to do. I wanted to tell them, but that voice in my head just would not allow me to. It was stronger than my own voice, stronger than my will to want to fight, to want to help myself! What could I say to make anyone understand without telling on myself? I did not want to be in trouble more than I was now. Every night I did not want to sleep, always dreaming of someone hurting me or someone hugging and rubbing me. Witches or monsters. Nothing good anymore.

It seemed to get worse with each night, each dream. They became nightmares. I would repeat to myself as I closed my eyes every night, "It's only my sister in my bed. No one's going to hurt me." Over and over, I would say that as I fall asleep, but the nightmares never stopped. They just became more intense. A big arm always pulled me into the darkness, deeper into the depths of the night, as each night passed. Then there was whispering all around me. Loud laughter! Someone beat on me, dragging me all the way into the darkest place. I hate the dark. I am frightened…going further down. I tried to push away. I was trying to block the punches, trying to cover my ears at the same time to stop all that whispering. I could not do it all by myself. I needed help.

"Mom, is that you?" Yes, it was my mom. "Mommy, I need your help. I am scared! Please help me!"

She was the evil laughter I heard. She was scaring me. I ran from her. *Why is Mommy not helping me?* Something was chasing me again.

"Someone help me!" I screamed.

Then I suddenly woke. I was in a pool of sweat. My heart was beating too fast. I had to calm down. Too scared to close my eyes but too tired not to. This was wearing me down. It was hard to stay awake during school, even dinner, but hard to close my eyes at night. I was so afraid. I did not know what to do. Great! The school sent home a letter to complain. I could not be falling asleep in class. Was I having some kind of problem at home? My mother repeated to me as she beat me because she was embarrassed again, "How dare I do such a thing! I just can't seem to catch a break!"

I was so confused! What do I do?

"I will give you a problem," she yelled, not trying to find out why I was having nightmares.

Not that I would have told her, but she didn't even ask. I embarrassed her was all she cared about. I still fought to stay awake the rest of the week at school, still too afraid of what I would see when I closed my eyes at night. Thankfully, I had a very nice teacher I could talk to. She did not seem like she was trying to just get information; she sounded like she truly cared. The school did not write again because I finally told my teacher that I was having nightmares. Only I did not tell her what about and asked if she would not tell anyone.

She said, "It will be our little secret."

The teacher was so nice. She let me take naps instead of going to recess the following couple of weeks without telling anyone, and I never got in trouble about it again. Things started getting better. I thought it was over, so I began to relax, and the nightmares began to ease up a little bit. I slept better anyway. I found out later, this was only the beginning for me. The beginning of my real suffering came next. Relief? Yes, I felt like I had gotten relief from my hellish horrors. Two whole weeks had passed. No one had seen our cousin. I think Mom was beginning to worry about him. Why, I don't know! She began talking about him, asking about him, wondering where he had been.

Mom even went over to his place. Only his parents said he was working a lot and just that he had been really busy. I was so happy when Mom told us that. Maybe it was because he felt so bad about scaring me and getting under the covers with me. Maybe he would never come back over again. I could only hope it was my prayer that came true, and I would never see him again. Unfortunately, it turned out to be two very short weeks! The monster was back the very next Friday. He asked if he could spend the night just before we ate dinner. I told Mom just before dinner was ready, I was not feeling well and had better not eat anything.

Mom looked at me and said, "Again? What is it this time?"

I said, "My tummy hurts."

Mom said, "All right, but there may be nothing left if you get hungry later."

"That is okay. I'm not hungry," I told her.

"Straight up to bed. No dessert and no playing."

"Okay. Night, everyone," I said without looking at the monster, who I knew was looking at me!

I went to my room and did nothing but cry. I did not know what to do, what to think. *What exactly could I do?* I thought. *Run away! No, I cannot do that. If I'm not here, the monster might try to get under the covers with my little sister, trying to hug her, then she would hate hugging too.*

I would not let him near her! *Think*, I told myself. Nothing! There was nothing I could do. Unless I marched down and told Mom in front of everyone right now. How stupid would I look to everyone? I knew they would all laugh at me, or even worse, they might hate me. If I pulled Mom aside and told her, she would probably beat me then tell everyone at the table how stupid I was for making something like this up! Then the voice I had not heard in a while said, *Do not tell. You will be in trouble.* I couldn't tell! Who would believe me after this long anyway? I had lost my chance more than once; I was the stupid one. My own fault.

I had over two weeks without him there. Why didn't I tell then? Why would they believe me over him? Mom loved him, not me. She would convince everyone I was lying. So would the monster. How did I get in this bad spot in my life? Better yet, how was I ever going to get out of it? As I always did, I stuck my thumb in my mouth to think. Mostly because I was alone, and no one could tell me to stop! What could I do? I was just going to have worse nightmares if he could not stay in his own bed. Maybe it was just that one time to scare me and get even. He was just showing me who the big winner here was, who ruled. Okay, he won. He sure did scare me! *It will not happen again. Yeah, that's it. He was just scaring me. I am worrying for nothing. Maybe he will not even spend the night, that he asked to spend the night in front of me to upset me. He's not really staying. Yes, that's it. He's going back to his own house. He wanted me to be frightened.*

Entertaining Mommy?

Just then I heard my siblings playing. I looked out the window but could not see anyone. I still knew they were close by; I could hear them. All of a sudden, my cousin came out from under the porch, looking straight up at my window, smiling an evil smile and waving. I quickly stepped back in fear. What the heck! How could he have possibly known at that moment I would be looking out my window? He was just so creepy! *What am I going to do?* I began to sob again.

My older sister walked in at that moment with some food, asking, "Are you okay? Do you want me to get Mom?"

"No!" I practically screamed at her. "I do not need Mom. She is the last person I want to talk to."

"Well, talk to me then."

"I just have a bad tummy ache, I told you. I'm sorry." I sobbed when looking at her.

"Want some medicine?" she asked.

"No, it's all right. I am going to try to eat some of this food, thank you. Then I will lay down and go to sleep early. I'm sure that will make me feel better. I knew you would come through for me. Love you so much, sis."

"Love you back." She said, "Okay, if you need anything, holler out the window."

"Okay, I will. Thanks."

Just then I heard my cousin laughing with my mom. I wished the jerk would go home! After I ate the food my sister brought, I laid down to read. Next thing I knew, my little sister was waking me, saying it was time for bed. I knew I was dreaming of monsters chasing me when she woke me because I was shaking.

"You were crying when you were sleeping," she said.

"I am all right," I told her. "Good night."

"Night," she said.

I could not believe I slept that long. Maybe I could stay awake all night now, and the monster wouldn't get me. I laid there for what I thought felt like hours. I could hear two of my siblings in their rooms, snoring. Well, it seemed that the monster was not going home! I could still hear them downstairs. I truly began to feel sick to my stomach. He must be staying. What could I possibly do? *That's it! I can be sick*. I hurried downstairs, feeling so proud of myself. Mom and my cousin were whispering. I hate whispering! Now they laughed. I watched quietly for a while. He puts his hand over my mother's on the table. No wonder Mom loved him. He was so nice to her. If only I could show her he wasn't! He almost looked like a kind person, only I knew he was not.

I stomped into the kitchen like I was mad, not even looking at him. I started to cry. I learned this from my beatings. Mom mostly liked it if she hurt you right at first. That meant she hit you hard, and on to the next child. Other times, she liked you to cry. It made her feel powerful, and she would hit you harder! Then say, "You want some more?" You would take a chance on what kind of mood she was in every time. To me, it would not seem to matter what kind of mood she was in. She enjoyed it! I looked right at Mom while I cried as I put my hand over my ear. I pleaded very well, I thought.

"Mom, I need some medicine in my ear. I have an earache. It really hurts." I began hopping up and down, holding my ear, crying. "Can I please have medicine and sleep with you?" I hopped up and down again then put my hand over my ear once more.

I knew she would mostly let us sleep with her if we had an earache and if Daddy was working the night shift. *This just might work*, I thought.

"Nice try," I heard her saying, then told me to run along to bed. If my ear felt worse later, she would put medicine in it. That did not help me right now! I stood in front of her, still crying and trying to pout.

"Bed!" she said.

"But what about my earache?" I became angry!

Mom said, "If you had an earache, you would have kept your same hand covering the same ear, but you switched from your left hand to your right. I do not know what is going on with you, young lady, but I am all done playing these games with you."

I was so mad at myself. How stupid of me to forget!

"Now go to bed."

All of a sudden, my cousin patted me on the head like a dog and said, "Scoot along, little girl."

I turned to look at him, still being so angry at him, and said, "Why don't you shut up! You are not my father!"

Forgetting Mom was right there in front of me, she slapped me hard across the face, almost knocking me over, and said, "You apologize. That was not very nice!"

I did not care how many beatings I was given. I was not apologizing to him! I rubbed my cheek, turned around, and stuck my tongue out at him, making sure mom could not see.

He was smiling and said, "That is okay. She didn't mean it," patting my head again!

I pushed his hand off me, running to the stairs, and yelled, "Yes, I did! I hate you!"

I meant every word. I stomped all the way up the stairs while hearing Mom apologize for me, then I thought I would push it and slam my bedroom door. If only there was a lock on it. I wished I was strong enough to push the dresser against it so no one could enter!

Then I saw my sister sleeping, surprised I did not wake her. I started to cry harder and began being mad at myself once again. *What were you thinking!* If I had slept with Mom, the monster might have gotten her. I hated myself for being so selfish. How could I sleep now! I started to panic, and then I began to shake, and I could not stop. I felt so cold. I climbed under the covers, wondering what I could do. My head started to nod off while the motion would keep waking me up quickly. I knew I would be falling asleep soon. I could feel it. I decided to sleep in my clothes. At least it was not doing nothing at all, and I was too tired to change into pajamas anyway. I could barely hear Mom's voice with the door shut. Then the monster laughed.

Go home, you stupid monster. No one wants you here, most of all me! Please go home and never come back. I promise to not be in trouble anymore, not let Mom be angry at me all the time, try my very hardest to be the best little girl I can, if you just let the monster stay away tonight. Amen. What else could I possibly do? I wished I could think of something else that would truly keep that monster away, but what? Besides getting myself into trouble by telling, I could not think of another thing I could do. I could feel my eyes getting heavier. I sat straight up in bed. The monster would get me if I slept. He would be in my dreams too, I know. Better in my dreams than touching me. I heard complete silence. Then came the creaking of the stairs. Oh no, he was coming! The monster! He was coming to get me! I had to stay awake so I could scream when he walked through my door.

I kept fighting sleep. I just could not go to sleep. Then all of a sudden, my nightmares begin. Why was it so dark. Where was the moon? There was not one star in the sky either! I dreamt of witches and monsters always after me, always wanting to hurt me. Why would this night be any different? And there she was, the one witch who looked like someone I knew. She was the only one who had not hurt me yet. She had such an evil laugh though. I was still very afraid. I tried to walk up behind her to see if she was possibly someone to help me in my nightmare. She always flew off before I got too close. Why did she look like I knew her, and why couldn't I see her face?

I hollered after her, "Please do not be afraid. I want to be your friend."

Then that shrill scream rang out through the pitch-black night, and I was frightened all over once again. The witch vanished. I was all alone. What could I do?

Chapter 25
This Would Get Me in Trouble?

I wake in a pool of sweat. Nothing happened! It was over! He just tried to scare me. He did his job. *I will never do anything bad to him again. I will stay away from him as much as I possibly can. I will eat his stupid treats and be as nice as I possibly can.* I kicked the covers off to try and cool off and look out the window. It still looked like nighttime. I decided to cover my whole body with my covers after I had cooled off just in case from head to toe for protection. I must have fallen asleep. I smelled that urine smell. How gross. I will never forget that smell. I wanted to throw up again, but his hand was once again covering my mouth, so tightly this time, tighter than I remembered. I had to swallow it back down but began gagging worse. I tried to see him again. I knew who it was; it smelled like him!

I began to fight the monster and tried to kick and scream as before, but this time, I could hardly move. He had me pinned down with most of his body across mine.

"You got a smart mouth, don't you? Ya little brat!"

Fear, pure fear was all I could feel. Too young to know that was what it was, but that was exactly what I was feeling, and I knew now the monster was here for real. He was not going to leave me alone as I had thought. He was not here just to scare me! Well, he was going to have a fight on his hands this time! I could not move anything or any way to fight him as I began to sob louder and shake more than I had ever done. The smell of urine was worse than I remembered it being from last time. Then he burped right near my ear.

What is that gross smell! It was making me even sicker. He began to whisper in my ear, and I slammed my head into his, causing him to cry out in pain, even though it hurt my head too.

"You are going to pay for that," he whispered.

Even though my head throbbed, I didn't care. I tried pushing his head away from mine with my own head as he whispered again, but he was too strong.

"I am going to take my hand off your mouth. Don't scream. Don't cry. Don't make a sound, or I will reach over and cover your sister's mouth with my other hand. Do you want that to happen?" he whispered.

I shook my head no as I cried in fear. *Don't you touch, her you jerk*, I thought to myself. Tears would not stop; my body wouldn't stop shaking.

So what, he scared me again. He won! Why keep doing it? I won't do anything else, I thought to myself.

He took his hand off my mouth and said very angrily, "Don't you ever sleep in your clothes again, or I will make you sorry. Do you hear me?"

I shook my head yes, and I did not move but did not understand. The only thing I could hear was my loud breathing. Was that me? No, that was him breathing like that. He burped again. There was that disgusting smell again. *What is that!* He somehow got both arms around me even as we struggled and began hugging me. *No, I do not want you to hug me! I hate to have anyone hug me, I told you!* I tried to push him away. He ignored me, pushing his body into mine.

"Stop that," I said a little too loud for him.

He slapped me hard beside the head. "You want more?" he said.

"I hate hugging," I say through gritted teeth, pushing him away still. "Do not touch me at all. I hate you," I said as we still struggled. "Please stop," I cried.

He hugged me tighter now, as if trying to irritate me, and there was that weird feeling again. I did not know what that was, and I did not want to know. I knew it scared me, and he kept trying to rub it against my body. I began to cry even louder. Finally, he let me go.

"Do not hug me, I told you."

"I will," he told me. "I will do whatever I like."

"Why are you doing this to me?"

"Because I like you."

"You do this disgusting thing to people you like!" I sobbed. Then he began to rub my back.

He started whispering in my ear again, "Don't say a word, or you will be in so much trouble, and everyone will hate you."

"What are you doing?" I asked.

"Do you want me to tell on you? Get you into trouble? You do know you would get into trouble now, don't you?"

You can do that? I thought to myself. I stopped struggling for a moment.

"Tell on me?" I said. "I have done something wrong here? You would get me into trouble?" I kept asking myself. I wish I knew what he was talking about. Could he be telling the truth? This could get me into trouble how? Could he tell on me?

"Yes, I will tell everyone you asked me to come to your bed. What do you think they would say about that!"

Everyone would hate me. What would I do then? I began to think as I cried a bit louder. *Oh no, this really would get me into trouble! What can I do now? He does not know what he is talking about, does he? That just can't be right!* He began rubbing my back again. We started to struggle yet again.

"You like me touching you. That is why you did not tell."

How could he say something so stupid? I shook my head no. I was still upset about him telling on me. He must be crazy or something.

"I hate you," I practically screamed at him.

"Be quiet," he loudly whispered back.

I began to gag again as he told me to stop.

This was all just so wrong! I knew everything about this was wrong. How would this possibly get me in trouble unless someone believed a lie he might tell about me? Now he was telling me to relax. What was that?

"Quit rubbing up to me!" I cried out as his other hand pushed up my shirt.

He began to rub my tummy. I cried out too loud. He slammed his hand on my mouth, hurting me.

I said, "Shut up!"

As soon as his hand left my mouth, I threw up all over it, all over me, the blankets, my pillow, I don't know what else. He took a corner of the sheet and angrily wiped his hand off then tried to help clean me up.

"Leave me alone. I can do it myself," I cried as I gagged. I did not want him touching me any more than he had to.

"You better learn to control that vomiting, or I will have to punish you when you do it. Do you understand?"

I said nothing, just kept sobbing.

"Understand?" he said louder.

I shook my head yes but wondered how a person controlled something like this. Did that mean he was going to come back to do this again? Oh no, it did. That was why he told me not to wear my clothes to bed again, letting me know he would be back! He pushed the covers all the way back, and the smell was gagging me again. He began to unbutton my shirt.

I grabbed onto my shirt, crying out and asking, "What do you think you are you doing?"

"Move your hand," he said.

"No. Why do you have to unbutton my shirt!"

"Move your damn hand now!"

As I moved my hand away, I cried out, "WHY?"

He got my shirt unbuttoned and pulled it away from me, rubbing my nipple as I cried louder. He began to moan. We began to struggle when he slapped me again.

"Lay still," he said. "I do not want to hurt you." Then he licked my nipple and bit it as I cried out and punched his head.

"What are you doing!"

"I told you, whatever I want," he told me.

"You said you do not want to hurt me. Well, that hurts," I told him through my sobs and shaking body.

His breathing was so strange. I was so scared, but I kept quiet, besides my sobbing. He stopped touching me, then the bed began to shake. *What is happening?* He grabbed my belly and reached for my nipple. He pinched my nipple. I cried out again.

"Give me your right hand."

"No!"

"Give me your goddamn right hand."

I was too scared to move. He grabbed me and jerked my whole body toward him hard, practically pulling my arm off. My hand touched something. He told me to touch it like this. It felt like a snake, and I pulled my hand away. Then he really jerked my body hard.

"Do not move again!"

I could not hear him talking. I was crying too hard.

"I am begging you to please stop this. I am too scared! I really think I need someone's help. It's my heart. It feels too funny."

"Shut up." He put my hand on the snake thing again. I tried to pull away. "You're really going to get into trouble now if someone catches us. You have touched me. If you do not want to be in trouble, then shut the hell up." The bed started to shake a little. "Do you hear me!" He held his hand over mine, squeezing tight. "Do as I say, or I will wake your sister up to help me."

"Please don't touch her," I cried.

"Do not make me!" He began pushing our hands up and down on the snake. His hand was tight over mine. My hand would not move. He was holding it so tightly. Then the bed started to shake again.

"Move your hand up and down like this, but do it faster. Do you understand?"

I thought of my sister. Yes, I shook my head. I sobbed, "Please do not make me do this. I am going to throw up."

"Don't you dare. I will punish you!"

I was so scared. He started moaning, telling me, "Faster, goddamn it! You better go faster and quit that crying." He sat up and said in a strange voice, "I am going to take my hand off yours. Leave yours on my penis. Keep doing what you are doing. Don't stop, or I will punish you."

"Your what?"

"Faster!" I tried to do as he said, but I could not stop crying and gagging. "That's right, just like that."

Then this warm liquid got on my hand, and I threw up again. He asked if I wanted to taste it!

"What are you talking about! No!" I told him, "How gross," as I gagged. "You are so disgusting!"

"That will come later." He laughed. This would get me in trouble? I began to gag out loud again.

"I already owe you two punishments for throwing up just now. You want another one?" I shook my head no. "You will be tasting my see-man," he called it.

"Your what?"

"My semen."

"Gross! No, I will not."

"We have to do this again!"

I started to cry louder. I said, "Shut up."

He pulled a handkerchief out of his back pocket and wiped off my hand as I got as far away from him as I could, shaking and sobbing like I'd never done before, waking up my sister! I looked at him as he put his finger to his lips and said, "Shh," and rolled off the bed.

"I'm okay, sis. Go back to sleep. I had a bad dream."

She rolled back over and went right back to sleep. He got back on the bed and said, "Good job!" He reached over, pulling me to him with one hand.

He kissed my cheek while we struggled and said, "Thank you."

What? I began punching and kicking him everywhere. I did not care where I hit. I got a couple good ones in before he stopped me. My hands were hurting. I hit so hard. He laughed at me, making me even angrier.

"Lay down," he said.

"No," I told him.

He pushed me down on the pillow. He held me there. I tried to start buttoning up my shirt.

"Stop!" he said. He laid beside me, putting his arm underneath me. "Do not forget! No telling about anything we are doing here, or

Entertaining Mommy?

I will tell on you. You will be the one in trouble after what you just did to me! I could tell you were enjoying that," he said.

"After what I just did to you? Are you serious? You made me! Just like you are making me lay here beside you, you pig!"

"Do you think anyone will ever believe an eight-year-old child over an adult? Don't you know by now, somehow, everyone adores me," he said out loud.

He was right. They did really like him. Mom did not like me and would never believe me over him. I would just have to put up with this monster until I figured out what to do about him! I thought I was smart. If only I could be smart enough to solve this problem, I could handle the rest of my horrible life! I knew there must be some adult out there that I should be able to trust. Who would it be that would not run right back and tell Mom and get me into trouble anyway? I should at least try. No, I couldn't!

There was nobody I could think of to trust with this kind of secret. Everyone I knew liked my mom and did not know all the bad things she did. I knew they would be shocked if I told them about this without my mother not knowing. I just couldn't take that chance I was too afraid of being in more trouble! Where was my courage when I needed it!

That coward is still holding it hostage, that is where it is!

Chapter 26

He Hurts Me

He pulled me, facing him, while I was on my side, bringing my thoughts back to the monster in my bed. He began to rub my bottom. I pushed back, kicking him with both feet. No one had ever touched my bottom.

"What are you doing?"

He laughed, whispering, "You will get used to everything."

"No, I will not, you pig!" I almost shouted through my sobs. *I truly have done something wrong to deserve all this. I need to know what it is I have done so I can please fix it.* I wanted to scream! I just knew for sure now I would be in big trouble. I have never been so afraid of anyone or anything in my whole life. Why me? What is it I have done that could have been this bad? I cried again even harder.

"Quit calling me that, ya hear me?"

"No!"

I tried pushing him away so many times but couldn't. He was just too strong. I thought, *I know Dad and Mom are going to be really mad when they find this out. Will they blame me? I am not sure. Mom probably will. What am I thinking? Of course, she is going to blame me. I think she really hates me.*

Just go to bed! Your own bed, I wanted to scream. *Go to your own house. Don't ever come back. I will always hate you. Just leave me alone!* I began to gag again. I could smell all these smells together. I swallowed it again. I stopped sobbing when he stopped rubbing my bottom. Immediately his hand went down the front of my pajamas and was in my private area. *What is happening? Will someone please help me!*

I let out a small scream. He clamped my mouth shut with his hand. "You are going to learn to be silent, girl, or I will spank your butt raw, ya hear me!"

I shook my head yes through my sobs. *Why is he doing that! Please let this stop.* He took his hand off my mouth. He started rubbing my private area. I made a crying sound.

"Stop," he whispered. "You know how much trouble you will be in if someone were to catch us?" He started rubbing harder, then faster.

"You're hurting me down there I tell him."

"There is no straightforward way to do this part," he said.

"You mean there will be more!" I cried. "When will this stop?"

"When I say so," he told me. "Now quiet, or I will be doing this to your sister. Do you really want that?"

I did not want him touching her! I tried to make no more sounds. Oh, how it hurt and burned. I cried being in pain, but only in silence, too worried to make another sound. It felt so bad he kept going faster and harder. It was hurting so badly, burning and stinging.

"It really hurts. You have to stop. I am going to be sick again."

His hand went back to my mouth, this time with so much pressure it took my breath away. I could not get air. I began to kick my feet. *Am I going to die? Is this what is feels like?* He was not letting go. I was ready to pass out. The pressure on my face was so strong. I think he forgot he had his hand on my mouth and nose. I began digging hard at his hand. Finally, he let go and stopped rubbing. I could just barely catch my breath. My heart was not beating right.

"Did you like that?" he said.

"You are such a jackass. I thought I was dying."

Then he began to hug me. "I would not have let you die!"

I still could hardly catch my breath. What was wrong with this monster? I was an eight-year-old child. He was a grown man! Why would he think I would like to be hurt like that?

"Stop hugging me, you monster," I said through gritted teeth. "Get off me, you ass!" I was struggling to still catch my breath. "I do not want you to hug me. I do not want you touching me in any way. My whole body is hurting so badly right now. I can't breathe, and you want to hug? What is wrong with you?"

"Remember," he whispered in my ear, "don't say a word."

Then all of a sudden, he was gone. I let out a deep breath, hoping he was really gone. I waited. I heard no sounds. I really did not care at the moment about all the pain I felt right now. I was so happy to have him gone. I turned my pillow over, still wet from vomit, and I began to cry into my pillow. Long, wailing sobs. I could not stop. I tried to understand how anyone could get this much pain from just rubbing. I really did hurt everywhere, but my private area was burning and throbbing. I could not turn or move without pain. He truly hurt me badly this time and told me there would be more? I couldn't take any more of this!

How was I ever going to cover this up and not be in trouble? I sobbed more into my pillow, not knowing what I was going to do. I couldn't believe he still had ways to hurt me, just like Mom. Did she know about this already? She couldn't let this happen to me and know it, could she? For what? Why? I did not sleep much at all that night, and when I did, I would wake up from such horrible dreams with so much pain I could hardly breath. So I stayed awake, mostly from the pain but also from being too afraid to close my eyes. *What is going to happen to me next?* I wondered. I just did not understand any of this, and I would not for a very long time. I just didn't know it yet. Because I never told!

Unfortunately, not once but twice the monster visited me that weekend, causing me more pain than I have ever felt in my life. Back then, I did not know it was pure terror in my dreams every night. I was not sure what to call the pain I was feeling inside me. I was so worried someone was going to find out. I could not stop thinking I was going to be in big trouble all the time. But then came the real pain. The very next night, I tried not to fall asleep. I just could not keep my eyes open. Not that it would have helped me anyway, but I thought somehow this would save me from the monster. The same thing happened as the night before.

Only this time, he tried to force my mouth on what he called the penis. He kept putting my head there, but I refused to open my mouth as he demanded. That was so gross. I cried out. I gagged. I fought the whole time. We struggled so much I think he actually got tired. I was glad, but he was furious. I would gag just thinking about it. I was not sure what I was supposed to do or what would happen, but I never wanted to find out. I was so very scared of him! I cried, and my body felt so sick the whole time we struggled. He finally stopped, and he told me I would pay for not listening and doing as I was told. We struggled again when he tried to rub my private area.

It burned to go pee or walk yesterday. I did not drink one thing so I would not have to pee so much. No one noticed the pain I was in or how funny I was walking. I did get to stay in bed after Mom saw that I had thrown up. So I did not have to get up very much. My mother actually could show some mercy. But what did she want in return? He held me down and began to rub even though I told him it hurt to move. After I had already been in so much pain before he started. If it already hurt to pee, what was this going to do to me after he was done? It was already burning more. Oh no, this was too much! I could not take this kind of pain. Could he hurt me any more?

This time, he rubbed a little bit inside my private area as I freaked out, where it was not so dry, he said!

"It won't hurt so much." He lied again; it hurt twice as bad. I cried worse and struggled harder. "This is what you get for not listening. Are you ready to listen now?"

I shook my head yes. I knew I had to be quiet, or my sister would wake up, and he would make her do these things as he had promised. I was trying to do as he asked so that would not happen. I just could not bear this pain much longer.

"Ouch! Please stop," I begged. I cried out, and my sister woke up. He laid flat and said, "Get her back to sleep, or she will join us."

That was my biggest fear, that he would make my poor, innocent sister do this. I could not forgive myself.

"I had another bad dream," I whispered to her. "Go back to sleep, sis."

She fell right back to sleep as I began to cry from the pain.

"Be quiet, I told you," he said in an angry voice. He began rubbing me again. Harder, faster, asking again if I liked it yet. What! I tried again to kick him.

"I hate you. I will always hate you. You're nothing but a monster."

He stopped then said, "You will learn to love me one day."

"Never," I said back.

Then he tried hugging me as I punched him in the head.

"I hate this too," I said in an angry voice. Struggling while he tried to hug me, I felt his gross penis against me.

Then he said, "Don't say a word. Remember the trouble you will be in." Then he was gone once again.

I cried myself to sleep for another night, beginning with trying to have a pleasant dream, playing with my siblings, then I watched as the monster and the witch came chasing my siblings as they began to run, screaming, and I couldn't help them because I was suddenly all tied up. I did not know what was happening to them. I heard their screams as I screamed their names one by one. Then nothing but silence. I heard the monster and the witch whispering my name, telling me I was next.

As I woke up, tears were running down my face. Then I swore, *I never told anyone! I promise! Just please make it stop. I cannot take another night of pain like that tonight.* Who would let this keep happening to me, and why? I was not a bad person, was I? Besides the pain and agony I was feeling, I was exhausted from trying to fight him off. *Please, someone help me! Do you not hear my cries? If I have done something bad enough to deserve this kind of pain, please show me what it is. I truly want to make it all better so this torture stops for me. In Jesus's name. Amen.*

Chapter 27

A New Game

I woke the next morning in so much pain. I thought I was going to be sick at that moment. It hurt to move. I knew all of a sudden that nothing could get worse in my life. Until it did. I could have become such a happy child if nothing else bad ever happened to me. I could have forgotten all about it. I know I would have. About the sexual abuse, mental abuse, physical abuse that has happened to me so far, I may have even forgiven it if it had stopped. What? My mother forgives and forgets very easily. Why shouldn't I? The monster stayed away a couple of weeks. It could have been three. It was such a long time for me. I had gotten some much needed relief. He had never stayed away this long, I thought. I had become less sore with the help of ice packs when I could sneak them.

But I still walked funny. It still burned, and it would still sting every time I would pee, making me cry out. I had become hopeful. I thought, possibly it could be over, except the nightmares obviously. Those became worse than I could have imagined. I had been punished by the monster for all the things I refused to do, and he had paid me back ten times over. I hoped we were done; I do not think I could have handled any more. I hid from everyone, not wanting to see or talk to anyone. I stayed in my room as much as possible, convincing everyone I had tons of homework and that I never needed any help with it. What second grade child had that much homework? Yeah, I did not know either. Tells you something, does it not?

I did not mind my siblings not asking a lot of questions. But my mom should have at least been a little curious about me being in my room for so many days! I knew it. She never cared about me! Funny, not even the teachers were suspicious of anything though. Back then, I would have thought, they would have at least asked me if everything was okay. Though they did not even do that. The hardest part for me was hiding it all from my mother, worrying about coming up with a story she would believe. Yet I also have been angry at her for not paying enough attention to notice. There really was something horribly wrong with me. Which one did I want?

I could not walk correctly for some time, but I knew I had to try. Questions I knew would be asked, especially by my family. Questions I would not know how to answer. Though I tried to be as normal as I possibly could. That was extremely hard when my face would scrunch up whenever I would take any kind of a step. Because I did not want to be in trouble, and I knew this was something big. The monster told me so, and he scared me into believing it. The teachers, my friends, what if they really did ask me? What would I say? Do you know how good I had to act being in so much pain? I deserved an award just for covering it up because the pain had gotten unbearable at times.

I stayed alone as much as possible. I lied a lot. Then Mom did not believe my stories after a while. So she began the beatings again. She would finally pay attention to me toward the end of my agony, naturally. As if I needed more pain right now. This was not helping my healing process at all. Mom said she did not like lying, but I thought I came by it honestly. I would find out later! I do not like lying either. Though I felt like if I did not, I might end up in the hospital or dead by the monster or my own mother. I thought if Mom found out I was in pain, she would tease and laugh at me like she usually did.

This time, of course, she whipped me good, and it made my situation ten times worse. She changed so much it was hard to keep up with her moods. I never knew who she was going to be from one day to the next. After some time, things started to go back to normal. I could walk, bathe, and pee without grinding my teeth or crying. I still wanted to be alone, not playing with siblings or friends. I felt so weird, like I had this awful secret that someone would find out if they got too close to me again.

Entertaining Mommy?

I still had not come up with a story that anyone would believe if they had started asking me questions about my pain. I didn't know what would have happened had they asked. Even when I started to feel better, I wanted to be alone. My sisters were so worried about me, making sure I was okay. The only two who worried about me, I sure love them for that. My answer was always the same. "I am fine. I did not feel very good." They did not believe me but did not pester me. They always thought I should tell Mom, but I said, "No!" I was no longer in huge physical pain; it was kind of tolerable. It was mostly inside that I had pain. I could not explain something I never understood, but I wish now I had tried, that I had gone with my instinct and trusted my sisters back then, as I do now. I was so sure it was finally over. Maybe my nightmares would not be so bad, that it would only be about one thing, not about both things.

This was the longest time it had been since I had seen the monster. I was so glad. Soon it would be summer. After that, I would be nine. Surely, something good would happen to me when I turned nine, possibly something to start my nine-year-old life off with a bang? Maybe a fun new game you tell me? Obviously, things like that did not happen for me. I was, however, introduced to this new game that I did not like. Without a doubt, I had no say in what went on in any part of my life, so let the games begin. How bad could it be!

This was just another childhood memory I had forgotten about yet, one that caused me almost as much pain. I have done a lot of suffering before, during, and after this lively part of my life! Both of my parents, unfortunately, I blame for this painful memory. This sad, unforgettable piece of my life was nothing but humiliation and emotional agony. I call this the "circle fights." When this part of my life started, I had just turned nine, and I was a wimp still, I will admit it. I did not like violence, fighting, or even arguments. I liked everyone getting along. I had already been dealing with a monster in my bed, my mom's beatings, the horrible nightmares I had every night. All the time I missed playing with my siblings, my friends.

All the lies I have had to tell, the pain of it altogether, and now I had to try to handle this too? I begged my parents to not let this game even get started, especially when they told me the rules for the game.

The torment I felt throughout these memories will haunt me forever now that they have surfaced. The suffering I had to deal with every time the circle fights ended was almost more than I could handle. This should never have been allowed to take place in my life. I had nightmare after nightmare. They just would not stop. My dad especially let this get out of hand, which surprises me today. I know Dad wanted his children to be tough, especially his daughters, for all of us to be able to handle ourselves in situations if they ever came up. Well, I did not plan on any coming up. He knew I was not tough at all and wanted to change that. I found out I will never be tough. I think they all did. I would never challenge anyone, probably never stick up for myself, and I was okay with that. My parents knew how completely shy I was, how different, how nervous. I was never a fighter. I believe they knew that was never going to change. I was afraid of everything. We all knew it and knew it would remain that way no matter what they tried to do to make me tough. They also knew I had never had a fight of any kind, and I probably never would.

My parents, my dad especially, said he was determined to toughen me up. I did not think I could handle any more, but I certainly was made to. I was a wimp, a sissy, I will admit it. I do not care what they thought I was. What they did to us next was criminal. I tried to understand how they could allow some of the things they witnessed happen to me, something they knew was going to cause me pain. How does a parent do this to their own child? My dad, who I knew loved me, hurt when I hurt, was sorry when he spanked us. I never understood his part in all of this. It hurt me terribly.

I felt so much rage toward them, when I would beg them to not let this happen again, and they would laugh, calling me a sissy while I cried, me telling them my body hurts, it could not handle any more. It did not matter what I said, how much I begged, or the tears they saw me cry. They turned their eyes from mine, looked past my tears, hearing none of my pleas or my begging for this to not happen. It fell on deaf ears. I was defeated in more ways than one. There was no help for me here. Why keep begging or trying? Nothing seemed to change them. I felt so hurt, betrayed, so unloved. Well, unloved by

Entertaining Mommy?

my dad right then. For Mom to love me or make me feel any of those things, I think would have been what some call a miracle.

Dad and Mom knew I was the child always upset if something or someone was hurt. How could they think I would fight? I do not like seeing anyone sad. They thought I would play this new game willingly? I was the one who could never watch something being tortured, something bloody in a movie. I still cannot. I do not know why I am this way, but my heart hurts when I see someone in pain. Why would they think this would be something I could do and be okay with it or take part in? I do not understand why they must make it so important for me to be a tough child when they knew this was *never* going to work! Why was it so important to let an audience watch? Why would this be entertaining for others?

To this day, I will never understand how a parent could be all right to see this kind of brutality as enjoyment for themselves or other people to sit and cheer about, especially when their own children are the center of it. To me, it is just sick! Even my siblings were allowed to watch and cheer if they wanted, never being allowed to participate in the games. At the time, why it was me chosen for this new game, we all knew. They told me for one reason, but it did not make sense. I never had to show this toughness in any other part of my life. Why now? Why for an audience? Why pick the weakest child? I would not fight, they knew it. What would they get out of it?

I began to think my parents just hated me when I found out what they expected me to do for this game of theirs. What were they thinking? I cried and begged at the start of each game, begging for my parents to stop this before it got started.

"Send everyone home please," I cried. It seemed the crowd liked that, but I did not care. I would scream, "Why are you doing this to me?" Never an answer. "I will not do it today!"

Dad would speak up and say, "You will do it until you join in. Fight! Toughen up! This is for your own good."

I cried out, but there was no one to hear my cries. No one wanted to help me. No one cared about anything but blood and fighting! If only we had cameras like we do now. Back then, if someone took pictures of what was going on, would my parents have been put in jail possibly? I do not know how the system worked back then. I know it would have been looked into at the least! Not that I would have wanted my parents in jail. Where would I have gone? Where would my siblings be? This kind of a life here would be better than not being able to grow up with my siblings. *I can handle this! Yes! I've got this! So let the games begin!*

Chapter 28

The Circle Fights

Dad would make me so mad with that same answer every time. I would yell at him, "I hate you! I hate all of you!" Unfortunately, it made me so angry I wanted to hit both of my parents, which surprised me. I never felt anger like that. Well, except with the monster, but he deserved it, and I never would have hit my parents, but let the violence begin…

The name I chose was very proper for this memory that I have retrieved. The circle fights are still a very painful memory for me. I did not get through this chapter without sobbing uncontrollably at times. It was like a knife opening a painful wound that had not yet healed from all those years ago. So it took a very long while to write this one. Just remembering how mistreated I felt is very painful, unloved and painfully hurt by my dad especially. Mom, I had already had thoughts on this from years ago, but it hurt no less. Such a waste of a childhood I had. That is what I thought. Therefore, I felt all alone again with no one to trust or that would help me. Let us get to these circle fights.

My younger sister, who was ten months younger than I am, was a lot smaller than me, a lot tougher, scrappier, and so fast on her feet. No one messed with her then or to this day. She was so dang tough! As a matter of fact, she was my protector when we were young and in school. If we rode on a bus together, whenever I would be bullied, if she were around or even heard about it, they did not dare come near me again. I am assuming my parents wanted me to be the same way. We already knew that was not going to happen. My sister never took any bull from anyone at her early age and, amazingly, does not to this day. My dad was proud of her for that. I was too. For all my sisters. They all turned out to be tough! Everyone but me. I am still that timid, shy person now.

Myself being older than her, my father thought I could take her (at least once). I did not think that was such a clever idea. I knew it was not going to happen no matter what stupid game they thought up. I guess I could have stopped it a lot sooner and tried violence just once! Had I been tougher and meaner, that could have happened. But I was not. I just could not bring myself to do it. I could not hit my little sister. After all I had been through, all I have suffered so far, this I did not need in my young, already messed-up, complicated life. I would not be forced into this stupid idea of theirs to toughen me up, or so I thought. But…here we go!

The entertainment was for our neighbors, family, and friends, anyone who wanted to watch and enjoy. They would all sit in a large circle, sometimes standing room only, usually in our dining room— it was the biggest for entertaining. Now that I think about it, I am truly surprised Mom did not sell popcorn and snacks, possibly cans of cold soda. Bet she will be upset she did not think of that when she reads this! There was only one rule for the circle fights: there were no rules. Whatever we wanted to do, we could do. Whatever happened, happened. Weapons were not allowed. They were never talked about, but I guess anything else was, so I guess that was a rule. We were told to put on a good show, or else!

My sister and I were to get inside the circle of idiots watching. My sister, being just as much a victim as I was, didn't forget. She would tell me before every fight, "Just give me one good hit. Knock me out. There will be no more fights. That is all they want to see—for you to fight."

I would always shake my head no. We would sometimes both cry and say we were sorry to each other then get in the circle. We were to fight until one of us (unfortunately, always me) went down. That, I guess, was the other rule. One of us had to be down and out. Nothing about the fight was out of the question: kicking, hitting, hair pulling, bruising, punching, drawing blood. No rules. No mercy, until I went down. Yes, it was scary for me! I know I should

Entertaining Mommy?

have listened to my sisters, about knocking her out! *Fight, dummy*, is what I told myself, but I could not. The names I was called from the crowd should have made me mad enough to fight, but again, it was not my sister's fault. I was just not going to fight her.

No matter what she was made to do to me, I could not hit her. She caused me pain, drew blood. But no matter how much she hurt me, she was doing what she had been told to do and knew she would get a beating if she did not show me how to fight. That is what she had to do for saving herself. She was forced as much as I was! I could not hurt her back. I ran around the circle, screaming at my parents, crying, pleading trying to get away from the hits, always holding up my hands, my arms, to shield her punches and blows. I could not hurt her back just because that was what they wanted me to do. I was not about to give in to what they wanted. I had my dad's stubborn streak in me, and I was happy about that!

This could go on forever. I did not care. I was not giving in to a bunch of vicious animals who could watch this and have no sympathy for me or my sister. I was not going to give them what they wanted. Sometimes I would end up in a fetal position while she pounded and kicked me as they instructed her to do, always cheering her on and booing me, calling me a coward and other foul names. I did not care. They were not getting me to fight no matter what they called me. My sister was being mistreated just as much as I was, and no one thought to get us help. They were all savages, wanting blood and tears. For an awfully long time, I got my butt kicked bad. I was always told, "This is for your own good." I never once learned one thing from all these fights! Certainly not how to be tough!

What good did it do either me or my sister? It sure never once felt like this was in any way for my own good. At least I could not tell it had worked for me so far! I only became more frightened of my dreams, scared, shy, and more cowardly as far as I could tell. You should have heard the crowd whenever I would try to make a run for it, and I tried a lot. I would see a break in the circle. Maybe someone got up to use the bathroom or get a drink. I would try to dash by them fast so I could run from this horror show, but I never got to run. They knew me well. I just kept trying time and again.

They would watch me like the savages they were. Some never took their eyes off me, just knowing! Someone would always push me back into the circle. I was again called names, laughed at when I cried or pleaded. They made fun of me, mocking me. Then they held their arms and hands up like I would do to defend myself then cry, trying to sound like me. My sister was always the champion. She sure earned it, and no one ever let me forget it! Did they ever cheer when she was able to punch me in the face! Especially if she drew blood! It took them a long time to settle down. If she got in a good kick, that would make them roar.

Humiliation was all I ever got. Bloody noses, bruises, cuts, and sores. Oh, and do not forget, I could hardly move for a few days. We did put on some impressive performances for them. They seemed to enjoy it a lot. It had to be some thrilling shows; they kept coming back for encores, many times bringing more friends every week. They liked it a lot when I just stood there and took the blows and take it. I did all those fights for an awfully long time. Many months, for what! Oh, yes, entertainment, my parents being the awesome neighbor and friend to be giving away such a great show for free. So many different people, and not one person ever thought to help me or my sister.

She was being forced as much as I was to play a game she wanted no part of. They were teaching my sister how to be cruel and to be a bully. I can still hear my mother's voice, "Oh, quit feeling sorry for yourself, you friggin' sissy! It is your own fault she whips you every time! No one will ever feel sorry for that!" How many times I have heard those words throughout my childhood? Sorry for myself! Really! How else should I have felt? No one else felt sorry for me, except my siblings, who tried to help me after the fights while my mother said, "Leave her alone. She will be fine!" No one helped me, except my sisters.

People sat there, waiting, no, wanting the bloodiest outcome, cheering the most damaging ending then booing me and calling me names again because I would cry from the pain. For the first time, I can call it its rightful name now, child abuse.

That is what it was! What they made my sister do also, child abuse. Having an audience watch, especially our younger siblings, child abuse again. Watching your child go through torture and pain and cheer about it yet do nothing but tell the crowd, "See you next week?" What would anyone who was normal have called it?

Do you even realize how cruel you were? Well, we are not done yet. Another week of the circle fight. This is never going to stop! When would they let it end? Would they let it end? I began to wonder if they would care if she, by accident, hit or kicked me exactly right and hurt me badly if my parents or the crowd would even care. Nope, I'd say, probably not!

On to the next child! I keep wondering what was going to happen to me. If it would be covered up if I were to be killed. How sad for a nine-year-old child to have to think that way! Then I began to think, what are they going to do, start their own neighborhood newsletter about the circle fights and that my mother was going to start selling tickets, maybe popcorn and snacks, like I thought before. During all these fights, my sister would not stop begging me to hit her. I felt bad, knowing it might end this craziness, give them what they wanted, give the crowd the best show they have ever seen. Her tears flowed, but I told her no.

"I won't hit you."

She says, "Fine, I will refuse to fight."

"Then an older or younger sibling will be made to get in the circle," I reminded her, "and you will get a beating or whipping."

"I do not care if I get whipped," she said.

"Please do not stop fighting," I asked her.

Sometimes we would cry together again. She cried for hurting me. I cried because she was made to. The circle was ready. The crowd was rather large tonight. Should be lots of booing and cheering. The cut above my eye was almost healed. She said she would try not to hit it. But if she did, she was already sorry. No one was going to help with this. How would this ever stop without me hurting my sister, which I refused to do? Would we get any help from anyone?

Not my parents, family, or neighbors. I could not get away. I had to think about this before I became really messed up, or they got an idea of putting a boxing ring in the barn and start charging admission—something else I feared. I had taken on the pain of the circle fights alone, the monster alone, my beatings alone, my nightmares alone. I could figure this out alone. I could not think. The crowd was so loud; everyone was talking at once. I was getting so angry. *How can I think like this? Everyone, just be quiet!* I began to feel lots of anger toward my parents as I looked at them, laughing and smiling; the crowd, waiting eagerly like vultures. I was feeling rage, surprising myself. *What is going on with me. I feel so strange!*

I started to feel like the underdog in a real dog fight. Everything stopped. I was in a cage. What was happening! I had sharp teeth. I was a dog! I heard growling. I looked and saw a vicious dog, his teeth hanging open with his wide mouth. He was ready to devour me. Where did I go! Why was I a dog? The crowd was waiting for the dogs to be released. I still wanted to cower in my cage. The crowd was cheering so loud. The door opened. The other dog ran toward me, drooling. I knew it was him or me. I ran toward him. The crowd went wild. Before he jumped on me, I grabbed him and threw him to the ground. Defeat was mine! The dog did not move.

The room was silent. I shook my head. Something was wrong. I blinked. I blinked again. I was not a dog anymore. What happened to me! I looked down. There on the floor laid my sister, facedown, not moving. I heard a loud scream, realizing it was me. I dropped to my knees, rolled her over. She looked so pale, so white. I cried out so loud because I thought she was dead. Then her eyes opened.

She winked at me then smiled. "You sure know how to knock someone out, and it's about time!"

I held her to me, which really surprised me. I hate to be touched, but this felt good to me.

She whispered in my ear, "Thank God. Good job. There will be no more circle fights! Stand tall and proud. Walk around the circle for your well-deserved victory lap."

I stood up so angrily, screaming at the crowd! "You got what you wanted. Do not ever come back! I hate all of you for not helping us!"

Of course, I got smacked across the face for that, but it sure was worth it! We will see what happens now.

Chapter 29

A Mother's Compassion

My sister was right. That was all they wanted. After that day, there were no more circle fights. I had looked at my parents after that fight and screamed, "I truly hate you!" I received another slap across the face after I hollered at the crowd again. How much they made me sick and the hatred I felt for them all. But the real hate I felt was for my parents. I did not want to feel hate. I did not want to be angry, but this was all their fault. I had no reason to feel anything else for them at that moment. They let all this happen without caring about their children one bit. For that, I will not forgive or forget! Should I feel this kind of hate? They should have known one day I would reach my breaking point.

They made me hurt my sister. I will never forgive them for that. I could have done a lot more damage than I did. That is what I hate them for. What could have happened to her or me. That was all I felt and still feeling, sorry for myself, of course, I was! I was still dealing with the rest of my horrible life. If only that could be solved now that the circle fights were over. I could handle the rest of the bad things happening to me. If only I could find my voice. Just one time, that was all I needed it for. To tell what was happening to me. If only the coward inside me would set me free, if I could have the courage to speak out, nothing else could hurt me. The coward had me trapped. I could not speak. I couldn't move.

It has made me so afraid. I did not even dare to play with my own siblings or friends. How was that for being a coward? I was so angry right now. I pushed through that crowd and dared anyone to stop me. How was a child going to get over this? My own parents had never helped me with any of my first sets of nightmares, yet they were the cause of the next ones. How does a parent find compassion for another child? Taking in a foster child who was, of all things, being abused, but have fist bloodied fighting among their own children? What was that? Compassion from my mom? How does a child possibly understand that? I remember my mom saying she cannot stand knowing what was happening to that poor child every day.

She said she just had to help him, and she did. She helped that poor child who was being abused. She felt sorry for him! Was it because he was male? How can they do one thing and feel another? Again, like the kissing on the cheek, the hugging, the smiling, saying "I love you," how fake is all this? *Is this real love? Has it ever been real? I am just a child. Can someone please explain this to me!* Fakeness, making others believe in the kind of love our family supposedly has to tie us all together. Why did I have to be a part of something I hated so much? Compassion my—! Why? I did not understand why. I thought part of love was helping someone with their pain, feel their suffering, see their tears, just care!

I was a child. I needed you. Where were you for me? Where was your compassion for me, Mom? I begged you over and over, please help me. Why did you not hear me? What do you do when your own mom will not help you? I have never felt your compassion or your love. When your children grow up, they learn from their parents, have traits their parents have. I had nothing from you. Subconsciously, I made sure I did everything just the opposite of how I was raised. I did it without knowing any of this, and I learned somehow…secretly… *never* to be like you! That is my miracle! You were not caring to any of the girls. You had no compassion for any of us. You made us fight each other. You tried making bullies out of your kids.

They could not be punished for that; they were taught horrible things. After all you have done to me, you expect to be cherished, respected, loved unconditionally from me? Then you are appalled at how we raised our own children, you tell us? I was always wrong because I did not spank my kids? They were going to turn out to be little monsters! You were wrong about that, were you not? My kids are GREAT! I do not ever think you have said that you are proud of any of your grandkids.

Now your great-grandchildren are not being raised the right way. You are telling me that I have no compassion as an adult, seriously? From my childhood to my children's, I have done it wrong. Seriously? It has totally changed for you? I heard you tell one of my sisters, "Do not punish your grandchild that way." Are you kidding me? They had to do chores; they do not get beaten like we did. You thought my sister had no kind of compassion! Where was your compassion for me? For my sisters, for our dad, and at times for our brothers? What happened to your poor child? Your poor family? Why were you not concerned back then? Why didn't you help us? We did not get any people. What is wrong with you?

I do not get any of this. How can someone go from an abusive, mean, uncaring mother to… "Oh my poor grandchildren. Do not holler at them like that. Those poor kids." That is what you say now, really? You found your compassion? Where was it when you were beating me? Torturing me? Ignoring me? Your other family members? Any of your children's kids when younger, you thought were hellions, they should have been punished. My children, always mine, you thought they should be spanked, or worse. I would be sorry when they grew up, you repeatedly told me. The ones you felt sorry for, the ones you loved the most, your favorites… "Oh, don't treat them like that. They didn't mean it. They are just being kids." You found your compassion for goodness' sakes, finally!

If someone swore in front of your favorite grandchildren, how could they swear like that, you say! Really? After the filthy, dirty names you called me, the awful swearing you did to all your children? When you watched me get beaten in the circle games, where was your compassion then, Mom? You do not know what compassion even is, so don't try to fake it now, like your hugs and kisses. When you did not believe any of your children had been molested, I think you should have found some kind of compassion then.

After all those years of pain, I finally found the courage to tell you what happened to me. When I thought, the coward had gotten scared off, had just left my body, I finally was ready and able to tell my story. You called me a liar. You slapped and beat me for almost thirteen years for sucking my thumb. Where was your compassion then? You paid no attention to your own children being abused! Even after they were abused, even after the fact, our abusers were still allowed into our house, by you. What was it you got from all your borders? Your so-called friends, you called them! You still talk to some of those abusers to this day!

Where is your compassion for us? Do you have any today? The odd men you rented rooms to? You let these men into our lives and didn't care what they were doing while they were there. How exactly do you want my respect now? Now all of a sudden, you know what compassion is, and you want me to find it for you?

My Mom's Compassion

The compassion you had for me
is the compassion I should have had for you.
I am so much better than that.
I can hold my head up high!
I was so innocent while you watched me suffer.
You will never have compassion "for me"
or what you've done "to me."
I grew up so different from you.
I am still a compassionate, loving mom,
despite your efforts.
I have bit my tongue for so long.
I never once disrespected you!
I still showed you love and compassion.
Although, it was not enough for you.
It is "never" enough for you!
Compassion you had none of,
but "GREED" you had plenty of that!
You even wanted more than I could give.
It has always been about you, and only you.
You pushed too far, wanting too much,
when you deserved nothing.
Do you have no shame?
I am okay now, not to worry.
My compassion for something better
made me the winner!

Chapter 30
My Mother's Nightmare

I was not always one to have nightmares, at least not when I was too incredibly young. Partially because I do not remember any. They did start for me; about the age of seven is when I can recall my first one. Maybe a few flashes or visions before I started school. Those I barely remembered, but the others were about bugs and the dark. Scary things like that. Probably not something a lot of people consider nightmares but they were for me. Again, everything scared me even at an early age, and I had nightmares of everything that terrified me. I do not know when it started or why. It always seemed to be on my mind, like something was going to climb on me or get me all the time. I was an incredibly nervous child.

The nightmare I am about to share has been a frequent one and I thought was one of my earliest horrors that still haunts me at times. This one followed me even when I was a young adult, always the same haunting nightmare. This was one of my first retrieved memories. While under medical evaluation, this finally surfaced. It was always the same horrible dream; nothing ever changed. Waking in a pool of sweat, always crying and scared. When I start this nightmare, it is like it is always for the first time. I was a small child. I was repeatedly the one hovering above the dream like a ghost. But I was in the dream, watching. I always just watched a young child walking down a path.

It appeared the path was leading to a beautiful park, but there were no other children to play with. It figures. There were never any children for me to play with either, it seemed. It looked like a nice, warm, sunny day though. Maybe kids were coming soon. The little girl was always alone. She had her arms wrapped around her like she was giving herself a hug, or she was cold. The sun would warm her if she was cold. I could only see the top of her head and her back, but I always thought I knew who she was. She looked so familiar. I tried to get around her, but I was only able to hover over the back side of her. I couldn't move unless she moved. This was so strange to me, yet always starting and ending the same exact way.

Her head was always down as she walked. I do not know how she could see where she was walking with her head so low. Then she lifted her head, looking side to side, always putting her head back down. I tried to get a quick look as she moved her head from side to side, but it was too fast. I still could not see who she was. We both knew it was coming. I do not know how I know, but I know. I saw what she was about to do next. *Please don't do it, little girl.* Then she did it. She glanced side to side again and finally started to glance over her shoulder.

I screamed, "No!"

She never heard me, obviously. She knew what was going to happen next. The clouds rolled in. Here came this big, dark cloud, hovering right beside me.

It couldn't see me, but I could see it. The young girl always tried to run; she never got extremely far before the black cloud formed a big arm, then a hand reaching out to grab her. She screamed. It was terrifying me, but I could not wake up. Something was going to happen! Something bad. It grabbed her by the hair, throwing her facedown to the ground. Her hair was pulled hard as she screamed louder and louder. The cloud showed no mercy. The sun blinded her as a foot stomped on her back, and her hair was pulled with more strength.

The little girl started chanting, "Please do not let the sun go down."

I started to chant with her. As her hair was being pulled, she was screaming from the pain. She couldn't breathe from the pressure.

The cloud let out an eerie, wicked laugh that echoed in her ears, frightening the little girl even more. The sky began to darken more.

The girl hollered, "Please, no!"

Suddenly something began beating the little girl's back as her hair was pulled tighter still. The young girl couldn't catch her breath. I could do nothing but hover and watch as I cried for her. The object beating her suddenly hit her hard in the back of the head. She knew she was about to die. She passes out for a minute or two. I wanted to help, but I was stuck because the little girl was not moving, so I couldn't move.

She woke in fear. She reached up to feel her head as it throbbed. The object came crashing down on her hand, crushing it. I could hear bones breaking as I sobbed for her. The young girl screamed out again as her hand fell limp to her side.

She begged to the black cloud, "Please stop. Why are you doing this to me?"

She felt like she was going to pass out again. The dark cloud let out another evil laugh. It began echoing through her ears again. The girl was kicked over, rolling onto her back. She screamed out in pain. Evil laughter rang the air. There was blood dripping all over her. She couldn't move. She could hardly breathe. The sun was almost down, now knowing death was near.

The sun covered the cloud completely just before it went down. A face appeared inside the dark cloud as it picked up the object, ready to strike the little girl again. The face was suddenly in plain view.

It was my own mother, chanting, "Never defy me. You will always be mine!"

I shivered from above. I screamed for the girl to move, but she couldn't hear me. "Open your eyes. She is going to kill you!" But it was no use. She laid there motionless. I kept screaming, and all of a sudden, the dark cloud looked up toward where I was hovering, like she heard me or that she could now see me. I was not sure which. She smiled this evil smile as it looked right at me. Suddenly we both looked at the little girl at the same time as she moaned. I was in tears, the black cloud with a smile.

The sun went across the ground so fast as it started to settle all the way down. I saw blood on the young girl's face; and there, lying on the ground, staring back at me was my very own face, as white as could be, while my mother stood over me, ready to strike, laughing hysterically. I quickly woke in a pool of sweat at that moment, every nightmare, every time!

This is the first time I have ever shared this horror with anyone. Back then, I was always afraid to close my eyes. Then a real nightmare begins. How could it have gotten so bad? All I could do was pray for it to stop.

Chapter 31

It Gets Even Worse

I truly hated the weekends when my cousin was around. I did think about running away more than once. If I got caught, what would be my reason for wanting to run away in the first place? I could think of half a dozen reasons right off quick, but none I would want to share with my parents or anyone else for that matter. I have been told now a hundred times, "Don't say a word" then how much trouble I would be in. I now believed my monster when he told me I would be in trouble as much as he would. He told me I should have told way before now, that everyone would think I liked it, and that I was a liar; that they would know all that we did and that I would be blamed more because I let him do it and never told!

You would think for as long as this had been going on that I would get used to the pain that had been forced on me throughout my childhood. But I had not and would not. I had to watch out the windows or in hiding spots at the gravel pit, just hiding everywhere, watching while my siblings, friends, and neighbors played and had fun. While I could not. I couldn't run, sit, or play games; climb or do any fun things kids should be doing. My private area and nipples hurt me so badly it was terrible the pain and torture I'd had to go through. But what could I do? I couldn't do anything that would make me happy. I tried; it hurt too bad. I did want to do what normal kids my age did. I just could not!

I still wish I could find the courage to speak out, for someone to hear my cries. If only my cowardness would not hold me back. Maybe one day I would learn to fight it. For now, it held me hostage,

Entertaining Mommy?

and I was too fearful to speak against it. So I would tell no one, keeping my secrets my own. I would not like anyone asking questions that I could not answer, especially my mom. If only I had not blown my chances in the beginning to tell. Now things had gone too far. I had done things I would really get into trouble for, probably things no one had ever heard of before. So many things I am ashamed of. I did not want anyone knowing what it was he had made me do. He truly is a horrible monster, and I hate him!

It is all so disgusting I cannot even think about it, and it makes me gag, sometimes vomit. I feel like I might die if someone found out now. Everyone would know. Everyone would look at me that way and hate me! If I honestly thought he would have been the only one in trouble, I would have told my secrets, but there was no way to be sure. I could not take that chance of only me being the one to blame. Then if he went after my sisters like he swore he would do if I told, I could never forgive myself. I could only hope this would get better for me; he would just leave me alone! *I want no more torture and pain in my life, please, Lord. Amen.* I wish everyone would have just known I was pressured. I was lied to, blackmailed.

How was I to know starting out at eight years old what was the right thing to do? He would tell me, "Look at all you have done with me. What will your parents say, your sisters, your friends, and teachers, when they all find out? You will have to tell them everything we are doing together, not leaving anything out. All this time together, all these things, you think you will not be in trouble?" That was what went through an eight-year-old's mind. Then he built on that for over four years. He forced me into believing I would always be in trouble. I was doing wrong too. I was young. I was innocent. I did not know yet! He was an extremely sick, devious man who knew how to manipulate an innocent child.

I was so afraid of him. He physically would abuse me for not listening to him too. Why couldn't he just leave me alone! Why did it have to be me? I have not been through enough in my life? I did not want any more trouble from my mom added to my misery. I did not want things to get any worse for me. I thought it was too late for me. I was a damaged child that no one loved, that no one could love after the awful things I had done and have had done to me. So I kept my secrets for me now, not him, thinking that was the best thing to do.

I still cried so many tears because I now know the truth about him. I never forgave him and never stopped hating him. I never felt he paid for his crime. Then again, I never realized until recently, I never forgave my mom either for her part in my journey to what I call coming back from hell. She never helped me with that either. She never wanted to help me. I know that now. If anything, she detoured me all the way! Now…back to my story. I would only wish my monster would move away. Far, far away. Anywhere out of my state.

That did not happen obviously. I saw him more, it seemed to me, still trying to bribe everyone, being the nice guy, fooling all my family. How could I compete with that? I would be doing something, and his smell or his image would come to me, all the sickening things he had done, and I would throw up right there. No one thought it strange how much I vomited? Just another reason for me to doubt how much my mother's compassion for me had become clear. I just knew she hated me. I did not know why she had to hit me at all. Why the cruel beatings? Why again not seeing her own child's pain that she herself was not the cause of for once? Then again, maybe she just did not care enough! (About me at least.)

Especially when no one was around, enjoying herself, it appeared to me. The way I saw her eyes gleam when she was beating me—how I hated those looks she gave when she was happy while mistreating me in any of her many ways. The witch in my nightmares looked at me the same way, letting me know how much she cared if I dreamt about her in only bad ways. Mothers did not really enjoy beating their kids, did they? I did not have enough of my own emotional stress in my life already? Why could she not keep the punishments I received something small like some of my other siblings received? Like extra chores, stuff like that? How much did she think one little body could take?

It has gone on too long. Does it get any better for me? I remained quiet and thought, *This is my life. Suck it up.* The coward was still building its sorry life inside of mine, its perfect little nest, and there was nothing I could do to stop it! I had no power over that coward. It seemed I have no power over any part of my life anymore. Sometimes I just felt like it would be easier to just give up the fight! But I couldn't! How could it possibly get any worse from here! No one could have predicted just how poor and sorry my life would become as a child. Because it did get so much worse. A new fear, a new pain. I should have known. Another nightmare to contend with. *What did I do that was so wrong?* I cried and screamed up at God!

I guess no one would ever find out. How would they ever know, especially me, when I myself could not find my own voice to ask! I never really got down on my knees to pray to God, to take all my misery out of my hands! We went to Sunday school a lot, but I don't think it was to learn about God. In my mother's eyes, she was only getting rid of us for a few hours. I was a child so confused with life I would never know which way to turn, abandoned like I have always been, left to deal alone. Then the following weekend, the monster stayed away. I was so happy I cried myself to sleep both nights. I never had many happy tears; I honestly enjoyed these kinds. My soreness got to heal some.

I was not kept awake half the nights, but I still had nightmares. I certainly was not so lucky the following weekend. The same stupid things continued, which meant I would still have to ruin any ideas he had as much as I possibly could, knowing that made him angry and hopefully want to give up on me. I could only wish and hope. I still fought him. I really thought he believed he could really train me someday. Not happening! I cried out too loud once, and he slapped me hard. Then he tried hugging me, saying he was sorry. I told him I was used to abuse, and I laughed at him for saying such an odd thing to me. How could he be sorry after all he had done to me? He became so angry.

He covered my mouth, began rubbing harder, then tried sticking his finger inside my private area so quickly and with such force I screamed out in pain against his hand covering my mouth as we struggled. My body began to shake from the pain. When my sister woke up again, I assured her I was okay.

She blinked, smiled, and then said, "Are you sure?"

I said, "Yes!"

Gemma

She went back to sleep as I cried in pain.

He whispered, "Do not ever laugh at me again."

I knew I would not! I did not want to go through that kind of pain ever again. I could not believe how badly that pain felt!

I told him, "You have to stop. I need to go to the hospital. There is something wrong."

He literally started rubbing again, like I had said nothing, then began rubbing himself! Oh, he was not making me do that tonight! I began to gag over and over.

"You just have to get used to it. Eventually, you will enjoy all these things."

"No, I will not. I hate all of this, you especially! This hurts too much. Stop! I need some emergency. Help!"

"No," he said. "No hospital. You are just making it up so I will stop, but that's okay, pretty girl. We will go slow so it will not hurt so much next time."

"It hurts so badly. Please stop. What about going to a hospital?"

"Go put ice on that. No hospital!"

"But I am not lying. I really need the hospital something is wrong. There is too much pain. This does not feel normal. It does not feel right. I am going to pass out." I began throwing up all over him.

"Shit!" He says, "You will pay for that later."

"I got to go clean up. What do I tell them if I do end up at the hospital?"

"They will interview you. Have you on cameras and then on TV, and the entire world will know what we have been doing here. Do you want that, missy?"

"They could do that?" I asked.

"Sure could. If I were you, I would keep my mouth shut! No hospital. Be a big girl now. Go on, get some ice. It will go away, I promise."

The pain had never gone away. It was always there! I knew that this was getting worse, much worse. It would be more than rubbing! Just pain and more pain and many more tears. I couldn't imagine how I was going to cover up this unbearable pain I was having right now. I felt down there, and there was blood. *Oh my god, what do I do now?* I decided to try and walk downstairs to make an ice pack and hope it would help.

I would not be able to sleep anyway. I prayed no one was up to see me walking this way and crying with each step. The coast was clear. No one saw me, but it sure took me a long time to get down and back. I must figure out a way to stay in bed a couple days. The ice just might help. It was already feeling better. I laid there, thinking about that monster telling me I would get used to this pain and that I would start to enjoy it. Never would that happen; this was all so crazy to me. How could anyone like being in this much pain? I cried all night until morning. I did nothing but cry. The pain was so horrible. What was I going to do now? I could not imagine the kind of nightmares I would have after that.

The following day was no fun. It hurt just to get out of bed. I drank nothing, knowing how badly it was going to hurt to pee. I found out it made me feel like I was on fire down there, especially when I peed. I made sure no one was in the house when I went. Sometimes I could not help the small screams that escaped my lips while I did go. I got a cold washcloth, hoping that would help some, and hogged the bathroom for as long as I dared. I did not dare make an ice pack, afraid Mom would not believe another lie, and I could not handle a beating right now. I cried more in silence and tried staying in bed as much as I could, telling Mom I thought I had the flu. She didn't want any of my siblings around me. That was a blessing.

I suffered so much pain. My sisters brought me soup and drinks, even ice cream. I have such good sisters. I do not know what I would do without them, especially on days like this. My shyness also helped a lot. I stayed away from Mom, and I got through it. I did it alone, without any kind of the medical treatment that I knew I should have received. But my understanding, kind sisters I will be forever grateful for.

They always helped me with my spirits and made me feel loved. I know now I could have trusted them with my secrets, that they would have helped me. The coward that got hold of me first would not allow that to happen. So I lost out again! I hated myself for the longest time because I did not trust them. I hated it when I looked at myself, hated who I was and what that monster made me do. I just hated almost everything about my life, other than my siblings. They were the only hope I felt I had. I believed the only adult who ever paid attention to me was my monster. He was the only one who gave me choices. Do it or be punished! With Mom, I had no choices. I felt so sorry I did not trust the ones who trusted me. That was why I hated myself.

That was why I was always sorry. I just could not stop myself from feeling that way. Now I say sorry out of habit, irritating some people. Sorry, sis. Then things still only got worse. I would never know what all the bribes were for. It was so disturbing to me, not knowing. Why the bribes? Who benefitted from it really? The kids liked it without knowing why. They received free treats. Mom got a free babysitter. There were so many other things that were so suspicious I could never figure it out. It still has me puzzled. The swimming trips. The ice cream cones. The bags of candy and treats. The groceries. Possibly the giving of money. You got what you wanted without the bribes from what I was seeing.

Unless someone was covering for him, who knew? I had no warnings from him. No kinds of signs whatsoever. But just before my thirteenth birthday, I never saw him in my bed again. He just stopped molesting me, taunting me, threatening me, and blackmailing me. No more hurting and pain. No more punishments. I was never so happy in my life. I still sort of held my breath then prayed that it was true every night before I slept for a long time, but I never saw him like that again. A very short time after that, I quit sucking my thumb… Just like that. No threats, no beatings, nothing! I finally just QUIT!

Is everyone getting the picture now? I did not care what the reason was he stopped, just so happy he did. I was not ever going to ask why or want a reason. I was just so happy it was over for me. Unfortunately, the monster stayed in my head with nightmares for a very long while. I still did not start sucking my thumb again because of the nightmares. That I was thankful for also. As I said, I did not think I was sucking my thumb as I got older for any kind of selfish reasons as my mother had thought. I still think I used it for some kind of security for myself. The monster may have left my bed, but the coward inside me lives on.

Chapter 32

How Could She?

It had become several months that I had no monsters in my bed. I was the happiest young girl. I missed a lot of my childhood, but I would be a teenager soon. We will see how my teens go. Nothing could get worse than my childhood. Could it? All of a sudden, I heard my sister crying. Then I heard my mom's voice not sounding so happy and being unquestionably loud. I wondered what she was angry about now. It was not me this time! Oh no, now my sister sounded angry. This could not be good! I wondered what Mom did now! It's no telling! I quietly listened for any more sounds. I only heard Mom talking, but not screaming at least. The door slammed hard. Mom screamed my sister's name.

Then I heard, "You get your ass back here right now, or you will be sorry you were ever born."

Then nothing but silence! That was one of my mom's many quotes. I knew my sister would not be scared, and she surely would not be coming back in either. I was in my room, reading a book, distracted by the thoughts of my monster. If I went down to see if my sister was okay, I hoped my mom would not see me. I put the book upside down so I would not lose my place. I quietly snuck downstairs. I saw Mom out of the corner of my eye, standing to the right of the door. Her back was to me, looking out the window; no one else was around. I went to the door, quietly going out. Phew, I made it.

She did not see me, then I went looking for my sister. I did not find her in any of our regular hiding spots, so I headed back to the house. Just as I got there, Dad was in his truck, peeling out of the driveway with Mom in the front seat, my sister in the back. It was no wonder I could not find her; she must have been in the barn with dad. Hmmm, I wondered what that was all about. My younger sister usually told me everything that was going on. I had to find out if someone was in trouble. I hoped it was not my sister. My older sister was standing in front of the barn, looking down the road in the same direction they just left in.

I walked over and asked, "Do you know what that was all about?"

"Yes," she said.

She looked like she had been crying when I walked up to her, then I became scared.

"What is wrong?"

"Dad is going to find our cousin (the one who molested me all those years)." Because he heard Mom and my sister talking about my cousin molesting her, my younger sister!

"What! Oh no!" I panicked. She also said that when Dad found him, he was going to kill the bastard. I was in shock, I started to cry. How could I not have known? Why didn't she tell me? My poor little sister. I guess she did not tell for the same reasons I did not tell her. Or maybe he threatened her too. Oh no!

At least she was brave enough to tell Mom, but we were both too afraid to tell one another. Please, no! Not for the mistakes I have made! My tears were for her. I was over my pain from that monster, or so I had thought. I still had nightmares for a very long time. I knew the pain she must be feeling, the nightmares, the loneliness. Thinking about that monster, touching her, and that it could be all my fault because I did not say anything. I would have noticed her not wanting to be around me though. I would have looked for signs. I thought I would know what to look for. I should have known! Maybe because there were none. Maybe he tried, and she told on him. I was hoping that was it.

She was so brave, just like my oldest sister. I wanted to be more like them, but the coward was still choking the life from me. I asked my sister if she knew anything else. She told me that my little sister had told my mother a few weeks ago about it and that my mother called her a liar. How could she! What was she thinking? Why would our mother stick up for a monster like that? How could she not believe the pleading voice of her own daughter? So who was going to be in trouble now, my cousin? My mom? Both? Now that my dad knew the truth, he would never touch anyone again, I can promise you that. How dare he touch his daughter? The story now goes like this… The three of them got to my cousin's house. My dad went to the garage first. I assume my cousin must have spent more time out there.

Mom ran into the house, hollering his name over and over, trying to warn him that Dad knew and he better get the hell out of there. I KNOW! How could she? He ran down the stairs. My sister witnessed it all and told this part of the story to me. My cousin got out a first-floor window just as my dad walked in the room.

He looked at my mom and said, "What the hell are you doing?"

My sister said, "Warning him! Mom told him you were after him so he got out the window."

Apparently, my sister told my dad on the way there what he had done to her and that Mom knew it weeks ago but called her a liar, told her she was making it all up, the whole time Mom telling my sister to shut up and quit lying. Mom kept trying to hit her while she was in the back seat. My dad grabbed Mom's throat and said, "Silence!"

The whole drive over there, Dad told Mom to leave her alone! My dad was so furious, my sister said. I know he wanted to hit Mom, she told me. When he got out of the house, he ran around the back to see if my cousin was anywhere around. He was not. When they got back in the truck, Dad started hollering at Mom. My sister said he sounded like he was almost crying when he said, "That is your daughter that man did that to! How could you stick up for him?" Dad never found him that day or that night. Later Mom told my sister to keep her mouth shut about the whole thing, that what she said was not true, to never repeat the story she had told about her cousin! That everything was a lie my sister had made it all up and that she had gotten slapped across the face for bringing it up again that day just for Dad to hear it and get all upset for nothing. How could my sister make up such a filthy lie! How could she do such a thing! Mom said. How could my mom do what she did! I could not imagine what she would have said or done to me if I had told her everything he had done to me. We had three cousins, all girls. Their mother told our mom that all three girls told their mom the same cousin molested them also. My mom said the girls were making it up and were trying to get attention! That they were lying! But all three of them? How the hell could she? Mom let him spend the night at our house again, even after hearing about what the girls said about him and what my sister told her weeks ago.

How could she! Well, my cousin sort of got his due. A few weeks after my dad went looking for him, my cousin went out joyriding with two of his friends, and some of our other cousins were in the back of a pickup truck. They were all drinking, raising hell and not paying attention to the road. They had an accident. Unfortunately, one cousin from the back of the truck was thrown and killed. The driver, passenger, and my cousin were all killed too. I felt extremely bad for everyone in the truck except my cousin who was the man molesting me and every other girl he ever touched. There were plenty more we found out later, one being his own sister! I never wanted to see anyone die, but as I see it, I think he deserved something for what he did. I do not deny I do believe he got off too easy. Yes, I said it!

If that makes me a bad person, so be it. For all he put me through and other little girls, I stand by those words and my bad thoughts of him. He had a family who thought a lot of him and, of course, my mother, who I am sure was devastated by his death. At least my sister was not a coward and had the courage to tell someone. She found her voice. She was brave just as my older sister was brave. They are both my heroes. Not everyone would be wrong like my mother and call you a liar, but you can see why I could not trust her with my secrets. She was part of the problem. I just do not know what part yet. But I am hoping before the end of this book that we all find out!

After the accident, my mother got right in my little sister's face and screamed, "This is all your fault he died. I hope you're happy!"

My sister said, "Yes, I am," and got a slap across the face once again! Let us read on, shall we?

Chapter 33
Getting Out with Regret

The rest of my childhood, I am not sure where the blame should fall. I never figured that part out. I only know I was still a child, with not one person who was adult enough to trust. Mom was just not there for me, and Dad, well, he did not have a clue what was going on in his own house. How could he really ever know what was really happening? We never had a chance to tell him. Mom still never wanted him to find out what went on when he was away at work. So he did not! Mom was not there for any one of her daughters, and at most times not for her sons either. She might have been for the boys if they had needed her. It was like she was not with us! If only I had someone to confess all my saddened secrets to!

My assaults, my shame, I think by now I maybe would have given it some thought. Then again, my mother never changed. If anything, she just got worse. She never learned from any mistakes she made. What am I saying! My mother doesn't make mistakes; she couldn't have helped me. First off, she never would have admitted she could have been wrong about anything. Second, she was not the type of mother who would have helped her daughters with any kind of problem, let alone a huge one like being molested or abused by someone other than herself. It just was never heard of in our household. No help for the daughters! She did not like us girls for some reason. We never did figure out why.

My oldest sister always had a theory that it was because we were not boys and we did not have a penis. I thought she was joking, but I am not so sure she was wrong. Mom liked her sons better than her daughters, very obvious, and there was no denying it. She also always said she would have ten boys rather than have one girl. I think we can all agree she is failing as a mother so far. Possibly, if Mom could have been the type of mom who I could have sat down with and poured my heart out to, I might have saved myself from other threats that came into my life later on, it seemed one after the other. If I had only had one person I could trust. You would have thought by now that should have been my own mom!

I am unsure of how my mom would have reacted. I don't think she would have believed anything bad that happened to me, no matter how I approached her or what way I explained it to her. I know my mom. She would have thrown it back in my face somehow, blamed me, called me her favorite names, and probably beat me for lying. What else could I have done? If I tried trusting someone else, they might have told only her, and the same results would have happened. I would lose! Do I blame the ones who should be put in jail, who assaulted me? My mother for not watching out for her child when I obviously cried out in pain, moved in pain?

It is over, yes, or is it? Should I forget what has happened to me, live with it, suck it up to misfortune? Or was it right for me to be in so much pain I blocked it all out, forgotten it all, let that coward build its wall all around me so I could not hear, see, or feel any of it? How could I ever forget such powerful pain without remembering some part of it? No one would have been shamed or blamed back then anyway. From the sounds of it, Mom would not have allowed it. Never discuss it—that is what she wanted us to do. So that is what I thought was the right thing to do. I suffered alone even after the fact, and I had my childhood taken from me.

I am resentful at times for the loss. Do you think you would have been, or am I being too harsh? Fighting what I have had to fight, fighting the demons, then your own mother not only cannot help; I have had to fight her off as well. Now she wants my love and respect after she helped sacrifice my childhood. She makes my fear stronger than my words… How do I not resent that? After all the years of abuse, do I forgive? Forget? I know I am better than that, so I try to move on without hate in my heart. When I finally did become a teenager, I felt so thankful. I am not a child anymore, maybe no more beatings? I can wish.

Hopefully, now that I am bigger, no more monsters. They will now leave me alone. No more nightmares! I knew I was wishing for a lot just by becoming thirteen, but I felt so happy. I felt like horrible things would not happen to me anymore. I really wish I could be able to forget the past and move on. For that part of my childhood, I did just that! That summer when I turned thirteen was an awesome summer for me, earning my own money, buying my own clothes from now on, Mom said. I was so excited, but I did not think I was really ready yet for a working world. I was only thirteen. I still felt like a child myself. My mind was still at the stage of. I wish I could have my mom to hug at times. I thought about sucking my thumb even, but I did not do it. I wanted to play with dolls! I still wanted to be a child because I did not get my chance. I thought I still wanted my childhood, but Mom rules, and I will not be getting that!!

There was this family about a few miles down the road from us, friends Mom knew from working at the store where she occasionally would work. Without asking me, Mom said that I would be able to watch their two boys after school and some weekends. I could not believe she thought I would be old enough at thirteen to be responsible to babysit for someone else's children. I was only told, "You have a job!" My first thought was, there had to be something wrong. What was the catch? Mom did not just do something to benefit someone else. There has to be something in it for her, but what? I could not think of anything. Then I thought, maybe she did feel bad for all she had done to me and wanted to make up for it.

Could it be possible she just did not like me as a child, and now we were going to get along like a mother and daughter should? Either way, she was letting me get OUT! Mom told me I could finally start buying my own clothes and whatever I needed. I could deal with that, I said. I would be free, and I would get my own money! I was scared of course, especially my first week babysitting. Mom had no advice for me, except, "Do not embarrass me."

Big surprise! The oldest boy was only a year and a half younger than I was. So he was truly angry he had to have a babysitter and then one so young. He gave me a super difficult time during my first week there, and I could understand.

I didn't like it when my siblings being one or two years older than me had to babysit me, but this was a piece of cake after all I have been through. I could feel the oldest warming up to me a little at a time. The youngest liked me the first day. This was my very first job. Even though it was babysitting, I would be the one responsible for someone else's kids. They were loved by their parents! I could not mess this up.

The older boy and I became friends even after I stopped babysitting there. I thought it was kind of odd that the parents and I never discussed the amount of money I would be making an hour or a week. I did study about cash in school. Apparently, Mom made the negotiating with them already, and I told her I did not think that was right. I also learned, always go with your first instinct. I was right about Mom getting something out of this. When I got my first amount of cash, which was a lot for a thirteen-year-old, I got home, and I was so excited. I could not wait for Mom to tell me how proud she was of me for the first time ever. Mom sat at the table, looking like she had been crying.

Me being the kindhearted person I was, no matter for whom, asked, "What's wrong?" She sniffled and said she did not have enough money to pay the light bill, and the lights were going to be shut off. She literally talked me into giving her, not borrowing, my first pay, but letting me keep a whole ten dollars. I thought, *Next week, I will have the same amount.* I did, ten dollars, again! She could not pay some other bill the next week. The third week, I was mad and started to cry, saying no! Mom just took the money and threw ten bucks at me.

"What would you do with that much money anyway, you little sissy!"

This went on for almost thirteen months. It was nice to finally get out, but it was with heavy regret, the way she stole my hard-earned money.

Just to be away from her for that long and not get beaten during the daytime just might have been worth the sacrifice I made. Although she did not care that I worked hard for that money. She did not feel one bit guilty taking it from me. Even though she had already known that was what would happen once I went to work! It was her devious plan all along. To keep on humiliating me once again! After that job was over, word got around what a good, responsible babysitter I am. So I got many job offers. Of course, Mom told me family comes first, but I told her, "No, thanks. I do not want to babysit anymore."

She got extremely angry, grabbing me by the hair, and said, "Why the hell not?"

I said, "I tried it. I thought it was okay. I will try something different. I will get my own jobs from now on!"

"No one's going to hire you at your age, dummy!"

"That is right. I am too young to work."

She let go of my hair, went, and sat at the table before I said, "Besides, it's exhausting to work hard all week for ten dollars."

She screamed at me, "You ungrateful little bitch! I have fed you, clothed you, made sure you were warm, took care of you. You used my electricity, my hot water, and I washed your clothes. I bought you extra things when I could afford it for how many years now, and you want to cry over a couple hundred dollars? Do I get compensated for any of that?"

I said, "It was a lot more than that."

If I did not have a coward still living inside of me, I would have said, "And aren't parents supposed to supply those things?" Then I would have said, "Do I get compensated for unnecessary broken bones, cuts, bruises, black and blues, the physical and verbal abuse? The neglect, like withholding food from me? What do I get for that?"

I still found no courage, saying nothing, once more letting dear old Mom control my life and what I said because of how she still terrified me. At that moment, she made the decision that I would be going to work, babysitting for my aunt and uncle who did not live very far away, and I knew there would be no arguing; after all, she was the breadwinner (literally). She was making out well, my money for nothing, and she got her borders money for rent, groceries, and the praise she needed from my cousin, who still had been welcomed in our house after my younger sister had talked about him molesting her! She also told me, she did not want any of my goddamn money, even though we both knew better than that. I had been so happy for about a year, with my new job, meeting people, making a new friend, feeling good about myself again, coming out of my shell a little bit—not a lot but a bit. I might have only made ten dollars a week, but there was no sexual abuse. I was so very happy about that. I was getting used to the physical abuse. Mom was now being a lot more careful. She knew I was out in public with people, now out in the world, just like at my last job, so she was incredibly careful not to leave any visible bruising or cuts. She could be a smart woman when she needed to be.

I started my new job three days later. I was even more nervous this time around. My aunt and uncle had a young boy and a newborn baby. Talk about nerves. I had never taken care of someone so tiny or young before. My aunt could tell, and she was so good about making sure I knew everything I would need to know before she was confident enough she could leave me alone with her little ones. The first day, of course, I was extremely on edge, trying to remember where everything was, making sure I read all the notes my aunt left me before I finished anything.

The next couple of days, it got better. I was still a bit nervous because I had never taken care of such a tiny baby. Every day I seemed to relax more and more. By the middle of the following week, I had a good routine going. I was even doing light housework because I got bored. They had a TV, but that was boring too. I would have to remember to get a couple of books to bring over for when I get time to read. They had a telephone, but not a lot of my friends were allowed on the phone for long periods of time like they are today. The housework began to be fun, and I was a pro at it as much as I did at home. But it was a lot better doing it somewhere other than your own house, for someone who appreciated it. I thought about my life more. It was getting on fairly well. Things were going better than I thought they ever could. I was happy, except for the fact I was still being physically and verbally abused by my mother. I could handle that though. I was so used to it by now. She hardly hurt me anymore.

That is, until she got even smarter with her choice of weapons. She was also still taking most of my hard-earned money, then trying to make me feel guilty for being born just because she has to dole out things a real parent is supposed to give out freely (kindly, even) like just common necessities, food for one. I felt so guilty if I had to ask for anything in the past, like things for my menstrual cycle, so I never asked for anything once I began making my own money. I guess being a teenager was all I had needed just to forget all about my childhood. I could do that. I hated it anyway, what childhood I did have. Who needed to remember a painful childhood like I have had when I could become a teenager, forgetting my past, moving on with my life? Possibly being happy for the first time in my life! I could hope, but the way my life had gone so far, I would not hold my breath. Things might have been going a little too well. See, I just knew it! Nothing in my life would ever go smoothly, no matter what my age would become. I couldn't even wish for a little bit of happiness.

> I wish someone could explain to me
> why a man thinks he has the right
> to molest a child without consequences!
> You should know,
> you will always pay your dues!

Chapter 34

Not Going So Well

By the end of the next week, everything was running so well. I even had a great routine for the housework, which my aunt said was not needed but that she sure did appreciate. I genuinely enjoyed taking care of children. The kids were taking a nap. I had just put a load of laundry in the washer. I picked up both the kids' rooms of toys and laundry, got out what they would be doing when they woke up, then went out to start the breakfast dishes. My uncle walked in as I was about halfway through. I looked up, and I knew my face was beet red. I never got rid of that bad part of me. I hated that my face would always get red. I wished I could stop it somehow.

I've known my uncle a good amount of time now, but I was still shy around so many people, especially men, except kids; I was great with them. My uncle said he decided to take a well-needed break and come home for lunch just to see how things were going. Then he had made a joke.

"Checking up on you, making sure you are not doing anything illegal."

We both laughed, but I did not turn around. I knew my face had gotten even redder. I kept doing the dishes while he ate, and we chatted about the kids and family occasionally, which made me calm down a bit.

"I love kids," I said with confidence as I began to relax a little.

Suddenly my uncle was standing right behind me. Oh no!

He began pushing his body into mine. I closed my eyes, looked up, and said, *Please not again. Please do not let this happen to me. Why does anyone think I deserve this punishment when I don't know what I have done wrong?* I closed my eyes again and made a silent prayer. *Please make this be a dream. I will open my eyes, and he will not be behind me, that this is not real! That I have fallen asleep, and it is just a bad dream.* Then I felt his breath on my neck and ear as he talked. It did not stop. He only pushed me harder, trying to get his arms around my body while we struggled, then I screamed out as loud as I dared, without scaring the kids, of course, and tried to get away from yet another monster! He was too strong. Oh no, his penis was pushing on me. His breath on my neck as he began to whisper. It made my neck feel very damp. All the things I hate most. Not this again.

I began to cry and said very loud, "Please do not do this."

He whispered for me to settle down; he was not going to hurt me. *Right*, I thought. *Where have I heard that before?*

"What do you think you are doing? Get your hands off me! Get away from me!" I yelled. I tried to sound grown up.

"Quit yelling, or I will have to spank you," he whispered, making a small laughing sound. He straightened both of my arms to my sides while I struggled to get away. "I want to play house," he whispered.

I stomped on his foot as hard as I could, even though I did not have any shoes on, but neither did he. I wanted to make him feel some pain, and I knew he did.

I gritted my teeth and said, "Let go of me, you ass! Do not whisper in my ear. I cannot stand that when someone whispers to me. Now get your filthy hands off me!"

I was terrified but tried to sound mean and like I was not scared at all, thinking it might scare him off. It did not. Flashbacks of the past made my voice shaky, and I began to cry out. He turned me quickly, knocking me off balance but catching me before I fell. He pushed my body against the sink with his own. I instantly felt sick to my stomach.

I gagged as he told me to stop. Suddenly his hand is in the front of my shirt, inside my bra, grabbing my nipple, squeezing it. I tried kicking him while I sobbed louder and louder.

"You're hurting me. Stop! Get your hands off me, you pig!" He pulled my breast out and tried sucking on my nipple. I did everything I could to make him let go of me. I started to scream.

"Shut up," he said through his gritted teeth as the baby began to cry.

I was never so happy to hear a baby cry before. We stood there while the baby cried, staring each other down. I was trying to look mean, and he was trying to play a game I found out later that he laughed about as he told me a few weeks later.

"Let go of me!" I said firmly.

He reluctantly let go of me and said, "We will be talking about this at another time."

I ran into the baby's room, fixing my bra and shirt before entering the nursery. I wiped my eyes with my sleeve then went to pick up the baby. *Why is this happening to me?* I begin to cry again. *I just have* Stupid *written on my forehead, or I do not know what the joke is yet.* I turned while rocking the baby in my arms. There he was, standing in the doorway.

"You are not stupid. You're beautiful," he said.

I jumped, not realizing I had spoken out loud. "Oh, shut up and get out of here!"

"But this is my house." He smiled.

"Go away. Don't you have somewhere to be?" I said sarcastically.

I continued rocking the baby so he would not cry again.

He said, "Remember, little one. Do not tell anyone about this. I will tell them it was all your fault, and you will be in all kinds of trouble with your auntie. Now what would she think of you, letting me suck on your nipple?"

When I turned to tell him, "Oh no, you will not. None of this was my fault," he was gone. I was so relieved. I put the baby back down as soon as he went back to sleep. I quietly went back to the kitchen.

There was no one here. I let out a deep breath I did not know I had been holding. I was so thankful I was alone. I had to think. Telling me this was my fault. My god I hated men. *Who do they think they are!* My tears began to fall once again. *Now what do I do. This kind of stuff all over again?* I went to the sink. The water was ice-cold. I drained the sink, and as it went down, I began to cry uncontrollably. *What should I do now? I cannot let anything like this happen to me again. I just can't handle any more.* I filled the sink with hot, soapy water and finished the dishes. After wiping my tears, I decided that I would just quit babysitting. Problem solved.

I kept my mind off things by keeping busy. I really deep cleaned today, until the kids woke up from their naps. We began our regular routine: change, have a snack, throw a blanket on the rug, get some toys out. We read stories, played a game. We were still playing when my aunt came home.

My aunt looked over at us, and she smiled and said, "We have the best babysitter around. You are so good with them. Hold on," she said as she left the room then came back in with a camera. She said, "I want a picture of the three of you. Everyone has to smile and say baby." When she was finished, she asked, "How were the kids?"

My face gets beet red for some reason, like I did something wrong.

I wanted to tell her, then I looked at the kids. I couldn't do it. "Perfect as always," I replied.

I was quiet once again. What a coward. I couldn't do that to the kids. This was not going so well. "Everything went fine," I lied. After all, I was going to quit babysitting anyway. No sense in possibly upsetting a family over one incident. She asked if I wanted to stay for dinner.

"No," I answer a bit too sharply.

She gave me a funny look. "Are you okay?"

"Yes. I'm sorry. It's just that I have so much to do. I have to get home. I have a lot of things to get done. I have a ride coming." More lies.

"Your uncle will not mind bringing you home." I just knew she would say that.

"No, thanks, I already have a plan. I am walking up to my friend's house, then her mom is going to bring me home." A third lie.

"You did a wonderful job cleaning. Thank you! But it's not a requirement, I keep telling you."

"I know, but I do not mind."

"I told your mom what a major help you have been."

"Thanks, but I do not think she cares whether I do an excellent job or not. Only if I make money."

My aunt laughed and I said, "I am not joking." It was her turn to get a red face. "I help Mom pay bills with the money I make."

My aunt said, "You are kidding me!"

"No, I am not! She says she needs my money to help with the household."

Oh no, I said something I shouldn't have. This was not going so well!

"That is horrible," my aunt said.

"Yes, well, please do not say anything to Mom."

"I will not," she told me.

"About the housework. I told you, I get bored easily. Besides, doing housework takes my mind off things."

"What kinds of things?" my aunt asked, looking concerned.

"Oh, just things I gotta do."

I asked Mom to pick me up at my friend's house. I told her I wanted to quit babysitting.

Mom said, "Only if you are dying! They are counting on you. Why do you want to quit your job already? You have not worked there awfully long."

She already sounded angry. I had already thought of an answer for this, knowing she would ask, knowing she wouldn't like any answer I happen to come up with. I moved as far away from her as the car would allow me to go before speaking, knowing her arm would reach me anyway. I told her I had never taken care of such a tiny person before and it was truly making me nervous.

"What if I do something wrong or if I hurt him!"

"Oh, you won't," she said.

"What if I get sick?" I asked. "I will not want to give it to the boys."

Mom said, "Well, if there were ever an emergency like that, I guess I could fill in for you. But I get to keep the money for that time!"

"Of course," I said. *You do anyway*, I thought to myself.

Entertaining Mommy?

I wished I had thought before I spoke! I could have been sick tomorrow. Maybe Mom would have taken over for me. I would have to think faster next time.

Looked like I needed to go back for now. I would just have to take my plan into action faster next time. I was so happy my uncle's vehicle was gone when I got there the next morning. My aunt put her coat on as soon as I walked in. Wow, Mom really was right! She truly was counting on me if she was leaving when I got here.

"I am sorry. Am I late?" I asked her.

"No, no. I just want to get to work as soon as I can. Lots of paperwork today." She was trying to put her coat on, eat a breakfast sandwich, talk to me, and remember everything for work. She was trying to explain about the instructions on the list she left on the counter, that I had her number, and there was a breakfast sandwich waiting for me in the oven. Then she was gone.

This time I hurried and finished the dishes first thing. Second, I made sure the baby would be falling asleep in my arms around the time my uncle came home for lunch. I was watching TV, praying he would stay at work. Then he ended up walking in.

He smiled when I glanced up, turning my face red, then telling me, "You do not really think that could stop me, now, do you?"

I read his mind like he just now read mine. How did he know?

I said nothing, angry he had known my plan to hold the baby, trying to keep him away from me. He walked to the table and ate his lunch, staring at me every time I glanced his way. After he finished, he walked to the living room, walked over to the couch, taking the baby, kissed his cheek, then brought him to the nursery. I got up, thinking, if I kept myself busy, he would leave me alone. I started picking up his mess on the table.

He came out, saying, "Do that later," as he sat on the couch. After he sat, he then patted the spot on the couch beside him. I thought, *Who does he think he is, and what am I, a dog? He is not my father. He can't tell me what to do! I am not doing this again!* I told myself.

"No," I said firmly. "You are not my dad, and I will not sit down!" *This is not going so well for me*, I thought. My life had taken a turn for the worst, and I did not know what to do about it again.

I knew I was too cowardly still to fight anything or anyone, so I stayed silent and scared. I just stood my ground and was not planning to move an inch. I was trying to act like an adult so he might be swayed to leave me alone if he thought I was serious enough! He just laughed at me. I told him this was not funny.

He said, "It is when you look like that. Telling me you're not going to do something when I know you will do everything I say!"

"No! I will not be doing anything you tell me to do. Who do you think you are anyway!"

Chapter 35

Starting All Over

I felt like I was clear enough, telling him no. I was not doing as he told me. Then I warned him that I was going to tell someone about this.

He laughed way too loud and said, "If that were true, you would have already told someone. I bet you liked it, didn't you? I can tell you did."

He began laughing as my face got redder by the second. I did not sleep well last night because of more nightmares creeping in, of him being childish and laughing at me while he chased me, trying to rip my clothes off, chanting my name as he, too, sounded like an evil witch. He was flying above me as he reached down, tugging at my clothes. No matter how fast I ran from him, I could never get away; he would always catch me again, yelling, "Let's play. Come on, let's play," Almost as if he had turned into someone my age.

It was so strange because he had no eyes. I was scared the whole time. For some reason, this one felt more disturbing to me. Again, I was just not being brave enough to use my voice to talk to someone, and I let that coward win once more. No, something felt very wrong. I worried all night he would come home for lunch, and he thought I liked it? I hated almost every man I have ever met! I knew nothing about a woman or a man or sex, except what I was taught by a molester. I surely did not want to know anything else. What I knew at fourteen was too much.

"You are an ass," I told him, "and I will not be doing anything you tell me unless it has to do with babysitting!"

"I told you to sit," he hollered a bit angrily this time.

"And I told you no," I repeated.

He got up so fast. It scared me so much I wanted to run and hide. He headed straight for me, grabbing me in a tight hold.

"Get your filthy hands off me! Who do—"

Slap across the face! He smacked me hard, reeling my body backward, while holding onto my arm tightly with his other hand. I grabbed my cheek, and I started to cry, making me angrier. I began punching him and kicking anywhere I could. I was no match for his strength and size compared to my own. He turned me around and planted the hardest slap on my butt. It stung like it was on fire.

Then turning me back towards him, he shook me and said, "Let's get one thing straight! I make the rules! You follow the rules. You got it!"

"Says who?" I shot back at him as I began to rub the sting out of my butt.

"You want another?" he asked.

"You're nothing but a big bully! You do not scare me if that is what you're trying to do! Hit me all you want to. It phases me in no way, so do it if it makes you feel big! I am used to bullies!"

"Well, I was thinking," he said, looking at me funny, "I may just have to fire you and hire one of your younger sisters to watch my boys. Maybe they would be a little more cooperative. What do you think?"

"No," I cried out. *Not this again*, I thought to myself. *This is starting all over!*

"I am not playing this game with you," he said.

"You can't do this!" I told him.

"Oh, but I can and I will," he answered back.

He reached for me, and I stepped back where he could not reach me.

"Already, you are not following the rules." He angrily grabbed both my arms, pulling me to him, trying to put his arms around me.

"You have not made any damn rules yet, you jerk, so how am I supposed to be following them?" I began to cry.

"Don't cry. I am not hurting you now."

"Yes, you are! I hate hugging. It makes me so uncomfortable," I cried. "Please, no hugging," I screamed at him through my sobs.

"Okay, okay, no hugging." He laughed.

"Stay away from me, you ass, or I will tell my aunt."

"I'm sure you will" was his response back as he said it and sneered at me. "Don't forget, I already have a younger sister in mind. Don't you think they would enjoy me?"

"You stay the hell away from my little sisters, you sick creep!" I just could not let that happen. I knew what it was like to have unwanted touching, hugging, unwanted demands, and the pain that came with it. I could never let that happen to any of my sisters. They could not know the fear that I was feeling at this very moment.

He put his hands on my shoulders and said, "See, that's what I thought. I knew you could become cooperative. I just had to word it correctly."

I tried shaking his hands off my shoulders to get away.

"You're a real comedian, you are," I said. "What is it you want from me?" I struggled to get away.

He tried using his strength to pull me up to his mouth for what I thought was a kiss on the lips! How disgusting! Oh no, he was trying to kiss me as we struggled! I started to gag at the thought. I practically spat on him.

He only grinned and says, "I like it when they fight."

They? Maybe this was why they couldn't keep a babysitter. I just had to ask.

"Did you just say *they*?" I asked through my struggling breath.

"A figure of speech," he said.

"A what?" I shot back.

"I keep forgetting how young you really are."

"Yes, a sign you should leave me alone!" I acted like I had no clue what he meant.

"Never mind," he said.

I knew he looked at me like I was an idiot. But I was trying to distract him any way I could think of for this crap not to happen to me again. I did not want to kiss my old adult uncle. *How gross*, I thought. Right now, all that we were doing was nothing but struggling. He seemed to be enjoying himself doing it. I would love to have wiped that stupid grin off his damn face! I screamed a little loud, hoping to wake the baby or possibly his older child this time.

"Enough!" he said a bit firmer, just a little louder than my voice had been, which frightened me.

"Okay!" he shouted. "Now listen very carefully to what I am saying and understand! These will be the rules for now, until I think of new ones. I promise we won't have sex if you will let me have some foreplay."

"Some what?" I looked at him like he had three heads because this time I really did not have a clue what that meant. But I was scared to death from the look on his face to find out. I had never heard that word before, and I already knew I had not yet had sex. I was not starting with my old uncle. How disgusting. I did not even know very many details about sex, yet I still did not want to have it with him. Or anyone else for that matter. I guess I could act like I was listening. Maybe he wouldn't try and kiss me again. Yuck!

I was thankful that was one thing my cousin who was molesting me did not force me to do—to have sex or kiss. Well, he asked a lot, but I always said no and was terrified we would. But at first, I thought we were having sex, even after two years had passed. At least after two years, I had said no to sex. I had heard kids talk at school, and I had never done anything like what they were talking about. I never wanted to, so I was pretty sure I had not yet had sex. What happened to me was all I could stand and was painful enough.

I asked my uncle through clenched teeth, "Don't you think I am a little young at fourteen for all this?"

"Oh, I like 'em young," he responded.

"How gross you are," I said. I could feel my face getting redder and redder as I was becoming angrier.

He finally gave up on trying to kiss me, and we stopped struggling, both out of breath. When he began to breathe a bit more normally, he started naming off his rules again.

"Sit," he said as he pointed to a kitchen chair while he sat down.

I did not do as he asked right away, making him angry, which was what I was trying to do. I was not doing anything willingly, and I wanted him to know it. I said sit! He looked up at me as I stood there, and suddenly he jumped up, grabbing my arms and plopped me into the chair he was pointing to.

I was so angry I stood right back up, making his face red, until I said in a sarcastic voice, "I have to use the bathroom."

"I want to watch," he said.

"No! Are you crazy! I am not letting you watch me go pee."

"No," he said. "I just want to make sure that is what you are getting up for. I want to make sure you are going to follow the rules before we even get started because if you do not really have to pee, I am going to put you over my knee and give you a spanking like you have never had before!"

I was glad I did have to pee, but I laughed at him, telling him, "My mother already beat you to it. She does it on a regular basis."

He said, "You mean when you were little?"

I said, "When I was little all the way till now!"

He got this sympathetic look on his face and said, "I want to hear more about this."

I told him, "I do not need your sympathy, and I do not tell my life history to anyone."

"Tell me this," he said. "Does she beat on you?"

I looked up at him and lied, "Of course not."

He said, "I know you just lied to me. I am sorry for what you have been through. I will never spank you again."

My spirits lifted. I thought he was going to have a heart and change his mind about the foreplay thing. If that was true, I would tell him anything he wanted to know just so I did not have to go through this again, so I told him so. No such luck.

"Well, I can't promise you that," he said, "but no more violence. That I promise."

"Gee, thanks. You're still an ass!"

He still followed me to the bathroom, standing outside the door. I hollered through the door as I peed and said, "I thought you would not punish me anymore?"

"Oh no. I said no more violence. I will not strike you, but I will still punish you if you do not follow the rules."

"If I refuse?"

"I will hire one of your sisters," he said as I flushed.

I was taking my sweet old time because I knew he had to go back to work soon.

Just as I thought that, as I washed my hands, he said, "I am the boss you know. I can go back to work anytime I please. You may as well come out now."

Damn, how does he do that! I thought. I kept washing my hands until they felt like I was washing the skin off. He tried to unlock the door again.

As I stood there, looking in the mirror, I asked myself, "Why can't I help myself? Why does this coward inside me live and feed on my fear and just keep growing? Why can't I do that with my confidence?"

"Who are you talking to in there?" he asked.

When I finally came out, he said, "That lock will be broken tomorrow. I promise you that."

We walked back to the kitchen. He said, "Will you please sit down at the table with me so we can talk?"

Now I was afraid he was being too nice. I sat down, and he said, "These will be the rules, and I will punish you if you do not follow them."

I could feel my face getting red again. How embarrassing for a young girl to be talking to an adult man out in the open like this about something so inappropriate yet so disturbing to me. He knew by the way I was looking at him and the ten shades of red I was turning, I had never talked so openly about this.

He began to smile, jumping up and down in his chair, chanting, "I got myself a virgin."

"What are you doing, and why are you talking like that?" I looked at him strangely.

"Have I got a lot to teach you!" he said, smiling.

It was definitely starting all over.

"You are not teaching me anything!" I practically shouted at him as I began to cry because he did not understand I did not want this! I couldn't do this. "Don't you understand how upsetting this is for me?"

"Okay," he said as if I was not even there and he heard nothing I said. "Foreplay is when you willingly let me touch you wherever I want to and whenever I want to, without you saying no or complaining about any of the things I want to do as long as it is not having sex with you. That is what foreplay is."

My face turned even redder if that was possible. I gulped then I shouted, "No way!"

"I guess it will become a choice of one of your younger sisters then."

I then really began to cry harder than I ever had in front of him. I knew he must be telling me the truth, that he really could do it and probably would do it without anyone stopping him. Mom would again never believe one of her daughters, especially me, if I told her what was about to go on at this place.

"What have you done now" or "How could you?" she would say first. It would be the same old thing. "You are a liar and a whore," whatever name she can think of. I would have to be the one who saves my sisters from this new monster. I had been through it after all. How much worse could it get to start it all over again? As I thought about it through, my stomach began to turn.

Could I start this mess all over again? Would my mind mentally handle it? Could my body physically handle it? Would I be able to look my aunt in the eyes ever again? I ran to the trash can and threw up my breakfast. He came over and started rubbing my back, trying to hold my hair up, as I tried to push him away. He went to the bathroom and got a warm washcloth, which I gladly took and not because I wanted him to be nice to me! I wiped my mouth off and wobbled back to my seat. He tried to get around me and help. I looked up and give him the most evil look I could.

"Keep your hands off me."

"Already not following the rules," he said and shook his head from side to side.

"There have been no rules discussed yet, you idiot," I told him.

"You will become my girlfriend. We will not have sex. Unless you say it is all right to do so. See, you have a say in this!"

"I do not think you're funny at all," I told him.

"You are not allowed to have any other boyfriends."

I started to protest even though I didn't want one, and my parents would not let me if I did. He did not need to know that.

"You are married," I reminded him.

"I am making the rules," he reminded me. "Like I said. No sex as long as you do what you are told."

"Hey! You never said that before."

"Well, I just thought of it, and I am the one making the rules, you know!"

"What if I do not go along with any of your stupid rules?" I asked.

"You know what happens," he said. "You change the rules, then so do I. You will keep watching the kids for as long as I tell you to. This one is especially important. You will tell no one! You are already in trouble for what we have done so far, so there is no point in getting us both into trouble when you would be the only one in trouble right now."

"Wait, why would I be in trouble? I am not the one chasing you around."

"I will make sure they think you are though. That you open your shirt up to me, things like that."

"This is so not fair!"

"You know they will believe me over you," he told me.

"How dare you!"

"Do you understand the rules so far?"

"There is more?" I cried. I begin to cry even harder.

"Is there anything we need to discuss? I want you to be completely clear before we make this agreement, and if you mess up, you cannot say you did not understand. Now is your only chance."

"This is so dumb," I told him. "Tell me you understand the rules before we go on."

I nodded my head yes, as if I was going to go along with this stupid idea of his. I was fourteen. What could he do but threaten me? Then I thought of my sisters and began to shake.

"Did you hear me?" he asked. "Are you even paying attention?"

"Yes, go on," I said, still thinking he had lost his mind if he thought he was going to get away with this.

"You will see me when I tell you to."

I started to protest because I knew that would get me into trouble with Mom. He held up his hand as if to stop me from asking questions.

"You will get away any way you have to without getting caught. Have a friend cover for you or something. If you do not get away and I have to wait for nothing, I will become angered, and you had better have a damn good excuse as to why I sat alone. Do you understand? Don't forget, I will get one of your sisters if you try anything funny You are getting the rules so far?"

I shook my head yes, in fear for my sister who could be in this seat. He stood, taking my hand and pulling me out of my chair. He tried to pull me toward him. I resisted and pulled away.

"Already, you are not following the rules," he said, incredibly angry. "Are you going to even try?" he asked.

I shook my head yes as if I would go along with this childish idea.

"I am not done," he said.

"There is more!" I cried even louder.

"I want you to call me at work every day at least once a day. Even after you go to school. If it costs money at the pay phone, I will give you an allowance."

Now I felt sick again. I was going to throw up again.

"No, you are not," he said and tried to rub my back.

I tried pulling away. He pulled harder just to rub my back. I did not throw up, but my skin crawled where he touched me. I stepped back again.

"I want to know what you are doing during your day. I want to hear your voice, and I want you to tell me if there are any boys bothering you."

"Oh my god, you must be kidding me."

"Do I look like I am kidding?"

I began to protest. "I cannot use our phone at home. Everyone will hear me."

"You find a way," he told me, "or you will be punished."

He turned me around so fast I almost lost my balance again. He caught me and tried to hug me again. I pushed away.

"Do we need a punishment for the first day of you being my girlfriend?"

"I have this thing about hugging. It really bothers me and makes me uncomfortable."

"Why?" he asked.

"I don't know why," I told him.

"Two more rules. No lying and no name-calling, unless it is cute names for each other."

That made me sick again.

"Do I get to have any rules?" I asked him as we remained struggling just a little more than I wanted to.

"That depends on what it is!"

"No hugging, please!"

"Name another. I want to hug you."

"Why do I have to follow all of your stupid rules?"

"Name another!"

The next one I would really think about.

"No kissing."

"Deal," he said. "Now let me hug you. I promise I will not ever hurt you."

I did let him, not hugging him back, turning away and struggling a little.

"Hug me back," he said.

"No, that was not a rule. No more rules!"

He lifted my chin up to look at me. "Try harder please?" he said.

"Give me space," I said.

"All right. Please tell me why you do not like to hug."

"No, I do not have to talk about personal things. Not a rule. Okay, you had a hug. Can you please let me go!"

"Such trembling," he said. "I will take it slow." He tried putting his hand down the front of my pants.

"That is not taking it slow," I cried out, jumping back again.

"I just want to touch you, then I will go to work."

Entertaining Mommy?

I sobbed and shook. "You're hurting me," I cried out again.

I was feeling so humiliated once again, knowing this was starting all over! I hated him, but did not dare to tell him just yet, but oh, I would! I had to promise to call him in an hour as he handed me his business card, telling me not to lose it.

"One day I want you to tell me who hurt you besides your mother. I will take care of them."

"It is fine. Mind your business."

"So it was someone," he said.

"No," I lied.

"You're breaking a rule already. No lying, I told you!"

Then I said, "Go to work," as the baby started crying, right on cue. Loved that sound.

"Call me in an hour!"

"Yes, master," I said sarcastically.

I had to go along with this stupid plan of his, at least for a while. I even asked my little sister to lie for me sometimes so I could go sneak off and meet this idiot to save my sisters, I thought. How stupid I was! I sometimes wonder if I deserved any of my abuse. Shouldn't I have known better? Mom always told us, "You asked for it."

It really was starting all over for me. The most horrible nightmares of my life started again. I had to start calling him every day also. How would I ever explain any of this unbelievable story to anyone now? I even started walking down to the farm a few houses down where we get our fresh milk from on the days that I could without getting caught. How was I to know it was a toll call, eventually being found out when the farmer got his bill?

I was glad. I thought this would be done and over with. No one would get into trouble. I knew I did not want to babysit for my uncle another day, let alone another week. Let's see whose fault this would be! I wanted my life to start all over, but in a good way, not this horrible insane way it was going now. I thought becoming a teenager was going to save my sanity and not hurt me any longer!

It sure was starting all over again.

Chapter 36

It's My Fault?

My aunt came to our house one night. It had been about five months since I had been babysitting for them. I was just walking down to the gravel pit to meet my second monster. When he got there, he told me to get back to my house as fast as I could—he would explain later—that my aunt might be there and for me to not say a word, that I was to lie, or I would be in so much trouble. He did not have to tell me twice. I hated meeting him. My sister and I got to the driveway; my aunt had slammed her car in park. As she got out, she apparently saw me, hollering like a crazy woman, slamming her door, and screaming my name. This did not look good, I thought. We were both out of breath from running. My sister had been at the brook on the lookout for me in case anyone was looking for me.

My aunt screamed at me, "Are you having an affair with my husband!"

Of course, it had to be just as my mom came out the door.

Mom looked at my aunt, "What is going on?"

My aunt said, "I think your slutty daughter is sleeping with my husband."

"Is that true?" Mom screamed at me.

"No, I am not," I answered.

"You are fired," my aunt yelled.

"That does not make any sense," I told her. "I am not having sex with my uncle!" I was not only saying it because I wanted it to look good in front of my mother and I did not want to be beaten. I really did not want to go back there to babysit if I had to keep seeing him! It also was NOT TRUE!

This could be a win-win for me. If she only knew how happy that made me deep down. I wanted to run over and hug her before she got in her car and drove off, but she probably would have slugged me, and I would not have blamed her. Her car laid rubber going down the road. We could all see the black smoke. My mother walked over, and I instantly put my hands in front of my face.

"What are you doing that for if you're innocent?" she asked.

"Because I have told you the truth before, and I still get beat or a slap across the face anyway."

She punched me in the head. "See, I told you so. I am going to ask you one time. You better tell the truth, or you will get the worst whipping and beating you have ever gotten in your pathetic life. Are you sleeping with him?"

"Take me to a doctor. See if I have ever had sex before. Maybe then you will believe me."

"Right," she said.

"I told you no, and I am not. I will swear on a stack of Bibles if you want me to."

"I believe you," she said.

I almost fell over. Then she belted me across the face anyway. I held on to my face and said, "What did you do that for! You just said you believed me."

"I do. That was for getting fired!"

"Oh right. No more income for you to take from me!"

I am sure I heard her call me a whore anyway as she walked away. Thanks a lot, Mom. The very next day, the farmer came to our house. He said he was investigating his phone bill, and he thought that one of mom's children might be the culprit.

He would like Mom and Dad to pay the bill as soon as they found out which child did it. I thought, *This just became my fault!* The farmer stood there while the kids that were around were called in. I happened to be one of them and my little sister who walked down to the farm with me. She knew that I did it; she was there too. She listened in on the calls and made faces at me while I tried not to laugh the whole time. It was a good thing they were not long phone calls; they were not that expensive. I would somehow get down to the farmer and pay the bill. This was all my fault, and I had no way to explain that anyone would believe. I had no idea the phone calls I was forced to make were toll calls, or I never would have done it. Now what do I do?

This did not look good for me if anyone found out. As the farmer laid the bill down in front of Mom, she saw that it was all for the same number. She asked each one of us kids. I said no, as we all did.

Then my oldest brother, who I looked up to and thought the world of, walked in, asking, "What is going on?" He was already mad at me about my aunt accusing me of sleeping with my uncle but said he was giving me the benefit of the doubt.

I promised him I was not sleeping with him. He said, "I know you would not lie to me."

I did not care if I had to pay this phone bill or not. I would go down tomorrow and pay the farmer. I just couldn't let them find out whose number it was or that I was the one that made the calls. It was bad enough I just lied to Mom. I knew how my brother would feel if he thought I lied to him also. My younger sister and I looked at each other, like, *Oh no!*

My brother said, "Let's find out whose number it is, then we might know who did it."

I knew my face turned red, as it always gives me away. Of course, I was found out as soon as they saw whose number it was, and I knew I was in huge trouble this time.

It made me looked so guilty just from lying to them. Mom asked me again. I really wanted to explain, but what was the use? No one was going to believe such a stupid story now anyway. I was caught in a lie! I was doomed! Mom told the farmer I would be down tomorrow to pay the bill in full She thanked him, and he left. My brother stood beside me. When I answered my mother, it was my brother who slapped me across the face, almost knocking me down. I grabbed my face and screamed because it was my brother who did it. It hurt worse than any beating I had ever received from Mom. The look of disgust he gave me made me want to die on the spot. How would anyone believe my real story now?

I would not believe someone if they told it to me either! So I took the punishment, was labeled a whore, hurt my brother, and no one knew the difference. It was my fault. Nothing I could do.

"I thought you were not having sex with him," Mom screamed at me. "You whore!" Then Mom began beating me in front of everyone there.

I guess I looked guilty enough to deserve it. For at least not trying to explain, but then, what was the use! It was a hard story to believe, and I knew nothing I said or did would change their thoughts about me now. I did not care at this point. They believed what they wanted because the coward had always been beyond my capability to begin to stop whatever I needed to say without any help, and how would I get help now when no one believed in me? The coward always took over. It seemed to overpower this force, taking over my life, yet I could do nothing to stop it while it grew stronger and more powerful than my truths!

It's okay. I took it and tried not to complain. The worst of it was, it was not over yet. In the same immediate family, I was babysitting late one night. I had to sleep overnight because it got to be so late. I woke up to my other uncle with his hands on my private area. *Are you serious? This can't be happening to me! Why? Do I have a sticker on my forehead saying,* whore? It had only been a couple of months after the incident with the first uncle. I jumped and began to cry. He instantly stopped doing it and began to whisper how sorry he was and that it would never happen again.

He was right about that; my babysitting skills were over. He apologized again the next morning, but I was done being put in positions where men could take advantage of me. No matter what it was all my fault and why not, I always looked guilty. Men knew how to make me look guilty. No stopping that label now! Even after that incident a good family friend (so I thought) was asked to build new kitchen cabinets for my parents. He came over, did an estimation, giving my parents a terrific deal, and went to work right after that.

He was more than halfway done when I came downstairs one morning and knew it was laundry duty for me that day.

It was quiet. I asked him, "Where is everyone?"

He said, "They all went to get groceries, but they did not tell me you were home."

I said, "Not for long. Laundry duty, then I am out of here!"

It was unfortunate I had to go past him to get to the summer kitchen, which was where the washing machine was. When I went to walk by, he grabbed my laundry basket and quickly took it from me, setting it down.

"What do you think you are doing?" I asked him.

He said, "We are all alone."

I said, "Yes, you told me. I do not care. I have to get this done." I began backing up as panic started rising.

I knew someone had to be in the barn; there was always someone there. I would scream if he started anything. I tried picking up the basket again, and he stuck his hand down my bra and began fondling my breast.

I pushed him backward with the basket I had brought up between us and said, "Keep your filthy hands off me."

"Pretty fast on your feet there, young lady," he said as he stumbled back.

"Yeah, I have had some practice with pigs like you around! I have had lots of ignorant men who do not know how to keep their hands to themselves." I sneered. "Now get away from me before I scream."

He said, "I told you we are all alone. Scream all you want."

"There is someone always in the barn. That is how much you know."

He grabbed the basket out of my hand again, throwing it, then tried putting his filthy hand down the front of my pants. I began to scream as we struggle. He was behind me, so I stomped hard on his foot. That did nothing. I screamed again. *No one is coming. Perfectly great*, I thought. I struggled away from his grasp, turned around, and I brought my knee up to his restricted area—a trick a friend told me I should do if I was ever being attacked. He moaned and bent over, but before he could get to me, I ran into the summer kitchen, locking the door. *How about that?* I thought. I outsmarted a man.

I decided I might as well get the laundry started while I was in there, so I threw a load that was already piled up into the washer, then I heard voices. Someone must have been in the barn after-all and came in to see who was screaming. I smiled and unlocked the door just as I saw someone entering the barn.

"Who was that?" I asked.

"One of your brother's friends."

"Oh, good to know they are out there. They must have heard my screams."

"Yes," he said as he lunged for me, catching me by surprise.

"I will just scream again, and they will come back."

"No, they won't. Everyone knows how afraid of mice you are. I told him you saw a mouse and was screaming about seeing one."

If they heard any more screaming, that was what it would be.

"You are an ass," I told him as we began to struggle again.

He was having the hardest time getting his big hand inside my tight jeans, which I was so thankful for. I started screaming again, but he put his hand over my mouth, and it smelled like gasoline. I gagged, almost throwing up. He pushed me against the door where he could see the driveway if anyone pulled in and the barn if anyone came out. I kept right on struggling, giving him a real fight. He got one hand between my body and the door, holding my body tight with his knee, and began unbuckling my belt buckle. I began to cry out.

He said, "If you scream anymore, I will tell your mother you came down the stairs without any clothes on."

I thought, *You are crazy if you think my mom would believe that!*

"Yes, she will believe me." He smiled.

I thought of my mother's non love for me and knew he was probably right; she would believe him. I also knew I was not giving up that easy as I scratched and kicked to fight him off me. This would be right up her alley to think of me as a whore again. She would believe anything bad about me after what she thought with my uncle. I did not care. I knew the truth. I knew I was not a whore as my family has thought of me.

He put his arms around me, like he was trying to hug me.

"Do not do that to me, you jackass."

Why did men have to hug? He got my pants unbuckled no matter how much we struggled. Suddenly I saw my mother drive in. I was never so happy to see my mom before. He quickly went back to work.

I fixed my pants while he said, "Remember, you came down naked. You started this."

"Go to hell," I shot back, grabbing the basket of clothes he had flung, then I ran upstairs to collect more dirty clothes. Just another man that thinks he can do whatever he wants. I made sure I was never alone with him again. Of course, I lacked courage, still never telling anyone. I knew the coward was winning still!

Chapter 37

My Rage

Naturally, I do not think back too much about how old I was when I got my first spankings. I do not really know. How would I? I probably would not want to know. I am still unsure if I was against getting them back in those days or not. It sounded to me like a lot of people got them, but a spank on the butt, not hit with objects, switches, other places other than the butt. Normal spankings. Not full-blown rage from your own mother! I was never an angel when I was a child. I am sure I did things like kids do: being a brat, being selfish, crying a lot, throwing fits, tantrums.

The older I got, the more I thought about somehow paying Mom back for some of that abuse I received by getting into mischief, unimportant things: skipping school, dating a boy she did not like, hanging out with kids she called the wrong crowd, things she forbids me to do—the so many things I should not do, or I would get into trouble by her. Like I was not always in trouble anyway. Besides a beating, I would have to do a sibling's chores for a while, things like that. I would do normal teenage things, nothing bad. I already got into trouble without doing anything wrong anyway. How much worse could it get? What could she possibly do worse than what I had received so far! It always seemed that I would be sorry for even wondering or that I tried to get her back.

She could still whip my butt good. It seemed the older she got, the stronger she got; the difference was, the weapons she would use. I deserved a good spanking as a child, I am sure, and I probably deserved more than my fair share of them. I believe I would have been okay with that, if they had been spankings. When I was young, I remember even then getting angry about what she would be doing it for, about hitting me and with what. Then she would always have to go overboard with it. I remember I would feel rage. Overboard anger. It started out that I was seeking her attention. I wanted and needed it, I thought. I also looked for her approval in almost anything I did, especially as I grew.

No matter how hard I tried, I never received it! Yes, I got mad, and hell yes, I felt rage. If I worked hard, I deserved something for it! I got nothing, and I felt more rage every time I tried. Your spankings that turned into beatings turned me into a child of rage! You did that to me, Mother! I stayed by myself so much, missing so much, while you humiliated me, breaking my heart and my spirit (almost). You caused my nightmares! You made me want to be violent. You turned my love into anger. I went from wanting and needing you to uncontrollable rage and hate for you! That is what you did to a child. I felt your hate toward me, and so many times I wanted you to feel mine. Yet I had no feelings after a while.

Time passed, and so did my feelings for you. I do not feel love. I do not feel hate. That is what I felt as a child. The rage came out of me as I grew. I was not even aware that I had it in me. Until I discovered that you could have a feeling other than love for a person. I know you wanted me to become afraid of you and to stay afraid of you for a long time. I was and I did. Hell, I still am at times. Now that my head is clear of all the toxic bull, I have been fed throughout the years of my life. I am enraged once again at what you did to me. I do not understand this at all. From three years old, really? How dare you treat another human being the way you have treated me, the way you have treated all your children?

You may have thought you were doing the best you could with what you had, kept us all together, as you remind us so often. But who is to say that was the best choice? I would never have wanted to have been separated from my siblings, and I am so happy and blessed to have grown up with them. The rage I am feeling for you at this very moment just to have to think I would have been better off away from them, just to get away from you, makes me feel that kind of

Entertaining Mommy?

rage you may have had as you were beating a poor, genuine little one that you must have felt hate for! What other reason does a mother mistreat their children that much in that way?

Your rage was real? Well, so was mine once I realized who you really were and what you have done! Now others will also know when they have truly found out who you really are and all that you have done to your own children. But mostly due to all the pain you caused that poor little heart, that lost, lonely toddler. The trap you set from the first day of rage you felt for that poor young soul, an attack you set up on one confused, pleading, innocent child. Yes, I felt rage. Maybe even still at times. The nightmares I now remember and the ones I am sure I had when I was too young to remember of how a child of that age must have felt to fall asleep, dreaming about their own mommy being a monster, a witch!

Help me understand how you beat me for years. Watching me cry, laughing at my pain, attacking me time after time. Why? I am sure there were times when you were looking into my eyes, watching my fear, that you felt something other than contempt for a child that came out of your own body, wasn't there? When I began remembering you reaching with one hand to find a weapon and holding on to my skin or my hair, I wanted to do the very same because you made me feel bitterness while you had power over me as a child. That is what you wanted; it is what you were happiest feeling. I remember that I could see that! I now remember the very first time I saw your eyes, the way you looked at me.

You were not having any kind of insane emotion. You were enjoying yourself! You think you were feeling rage back then? What do you call what I felt? There are so many things I have no answers for that make me angered still. Like what was the feeling, the enjoyment possibly, of you having me cut my own whipping switches off a tree, knowing you could have picked a better one to beat me with? I always thought if the switch broke and you made me get another one, a better one, if I'd bring back the best one I have ever found instead of handing it to you as I have always done, start taking out some of my own rage on you just to see how it felt, feel that satisfaction you were getting, then maybe I would not complain or cry so much about it.

Gemma

While you were beating and whipping me, sound fair to everyone? Well, thankfully, I did not have a heart like your heart, Mom. My heart grew kinder, even as I should have felt my rage. While you beat me, my heart was getting kinder, softer, feeling sorry for all that you were missing out on as yours became more bitter. I felt nothing but pity for you, knowing someday, you would get yours somehow, in some way. My kindness would overpower your bitterness, as it now has.

I would never take out my rage on you or anyone. Even to this day, if I had any for Mom from the past, I could never have become Mom. The hardest thing is, it is not just one thing I could get enraged about. It's such a combination of things you did to your children. I do remember trying so hard once to do the best work I could, getting gold stars on everything, getting an award from the teacher. I just knew I would have to become one of your favorites then. I was so proud for working so hard to win your love. I waited until after dinner that night. The excitement was unbearable.

I waited until you sat in your favorite chair in the living room, waited while you relaxed. I happily passed them to you, one by one. As I thought, you looked at them, you watched the baby crawling, talking to her. I would point out what each paper was and what each gold star was for. You did not even go to the next one. I had to do that for you too, and you could not say one word to me after you saw each paper, after I told you what all of them were for. I was not sure if you understood what they even were. So I tried to explain again what they were for. I kept holding your face in my hands, trying to get your attention toward my papers, but you kept slapping my hands away.

I should have known then I was going to be hurt once again. I tried not to show it. So I would ask, "Aren't you proud? Didn't I do a great job, Mommy? I worked really hard, especially on this paper."

You looked at me, and I can't be sure, but I think I remember you rolling your eyes. I do, however, remember for certain you saying, "I do not have time for such nonsense."

I remember walking up to my room after grabbing all my papers in your hands. You still were not paying any attention as I started ripping every one of those papers up into little pieces. I cried because I thought for sure it would be something you would be proud of. I had worked so hard all week while leaving a trail, and you did not know, but there was my rage left on that trail as I dropped each little piece of paper all the way up the stairs while no one noticed.

Even back at that memory, I feel my rage slither out of my heart for you, just a tiny bit, and even now it hurts. But still, it felt so wrong what you did and how you made me feel at that moment! There are things I will remember after I am finished writing this. When I think about all that you put me through, like these kinds of moments, I can feel the rage peak, and then I have to remind myself, *I am not that person at all,* that I will never be you or never be like you; that your opinion then and now should never have mattered to me, except that I was a little girl and once again trying to win your love! I could never become you, to turn it off and on like a faucet. How does someone do that?

My rage did not boil long enough to get hot or to stay within me. It is okay though. I am over it. But once again, you want something from me. Be your friend, love you, forget the past, respect you. For over fifty years, you have had something you did not earn or deserve. I think I will give it a rest. I have broken my very small rage cycle.

I am through now!

Controlling My Rage

If ever there was a time
to learn how to control my rage,
it was when you needed to feel my heart…
I did that, no thanks to you!
I put up with having to force my rage down deep
for so very long,
keeping it restricted, and at bay
while your rage broke out freely,
making me its best and favorite victim.
Now your heart has found
something it has never felt before, truly?
I am now to somehow control
the way my heart feels?
Sorry, it does not work that way.
But I have no hate in me at all.
I never really have.
I did not get that trait from you!
I have peace and love in my life
and in my heart,
something I begged you for
so many times,
and for so very long!
You can't have it both ways now.
That doesn't work for me either.
Shame on you for even asking!
Live with what you have done.
Own up to your rage,
and all that should keep you awake
at night!
Funny, I still feel sorry for you!
It is the way my heart has always worked,
loving and caring, no matter the hardship.
Seek help!
It is the only way to live with it now.

Chapter 38
The Voice Inside Me

I had close siblings I could have confided in. I know now I should have done so. I should have shared my many horrors, my pain, my secrets. I wanted to. How I wanted to! It was not that I could not trust them. All those damn voices inside my head would outweigh my logic, always telling me, *Don't say a word. You will be in trouble.* It almost became a chime in my head over and over. Trouble—I have had enough of that in my life. No! Telling might just have caused me all kinds of problems. I did not know how to deal with anything more at my youthful age. I also felt so ashamed. I could not bear the thought of my siblings, especially the bond my sisters and I had, to change in any way.

I couldn't have handled that. It would have possibly destroyed what little bit of hope I clung to, for my peace. I knew them, yes. We were close, and I trusted them. I did not know if anything that had happened to me would change the way they thought of me. What if I told them, and they thought I was disgusting for what I had been made to do? Even worse, if any of them blamed me? I could not have lived with myself. For them to look at me so differently or feel differently about me, it would have crushed me at such an early age. Besides, how could I think another child could help me if none of the adults in my life were willing to help me with anything bad in my life?

Possibly telling someone would have made it worse for me too. I had not one person to ask beside the voices and the coward who always lurked. According to the voice inside me, it would have caused me too much trouble. I knew my mom would have thought the worst of me, blaming me, as she had done in the past, and not only me; she could not believe in any of her daughters. There was no way I could take any chances. So I stayed as quiet as a mouse. No one had seen me; no one heard me. I have stood alone, waiting patiently still for help and to find out if someone, anyone, could explain to me what it is I have done wrong still. For me to deserve all that I have been through in my life so far, why me?

I wanted an answer from anyone who knew. Even the voices in my head would only tell me that I was an evil child, that I was an ugly child. I did not know how either of those would keep me in so much trouble, but at that age, I believed! If only I would have conquered my fears and not given in to the voices in my head. My sisters and I possibly could have played one of our many tricks on my monsters, scaring them into leaving me alone. I think about these things now. How many what-ifs make a whole lot of oh-wells. No dwelling on the past. We are moving forward to the future, one I hope turns out to be healthy and happy. I want that so much.

I do not know how others deal with abuse. I was not sure at the time that was what it was or if it was healthy to do as I had done, block it all out as I had and kept hoping to do and never think about it ever again. Truly, I did not know that was what my plan was going to be, to block it out forever. I think it must have been bad enough to do just that! Forget about it, like I have done all these many years. I can tell you, that is one of the worst decisions I have ever made. I really was not aware I had done that, and not sure when I began blocking it out. Deep down, I could always feel something troubling me. I could never remember much about my childhood. Good things I always talked about and remembered.

When I tried to get details of the rest in my head, the voices would slowly start to whisper. It frightened me, so I would stop and wait for time, for things to calm. I could never ask a sibling. How stupid would I sound to say I do not remember my childhood? Maybe there was a reason, and I should just leave it alone. The laughter starts, and I know it is the coward inside, letting me know, *I am here and not going anywhere*, always reminding me. Then the stories as I got older, getting together with my siblings more and more, I would be so confused.

Sometimes a memory I would see flash before my eyes, but most times, I would think they were brought up in an altogether different house than I had been. *Where and what were they talking about?* I would call myself names, put myself down, think myself crazy. But the voices, they knew! They started to talk, whisper in my head. Unfortunately, I could not share this with anyone. I would look like a fool. I already felt stupid enough with how I thought of things now. If I were to contribute something like this to their stories, how would I explain something I did not have any answers for? I always went home so disappointed in myself, always wishing I would not have to go through this again.

Sometimes I was only confused, other times so sad. I would cry myself to sleep that night. I was feeling like I was losing my mind every time those voices whispered. I knew no one could help me. So I remained hidden behind my fears. I tried not to get involved in conversations, stayed away as much as I could for lengthy periods of time. My mother always thought it was my partners keeping me from my family. So, of course, she did not like any of her children's choices for partners, but that is another whole story. If only I could get help and knew which direction to go and look for it, if someone would notice me, really see me; if they could feel my pain and they could ease it; if they saw my tears falling and dried them, heard my cries and soothed them.

There was no one there for me to have hope for. I made no sound while the voices remained unclear and unwanted. The voices in my head, always stronger than the secrets of my heart, are clearly telling me again, *Keep it all inside. Tell no one, and just remain quiet.* I would think past the voices and pray that someday my voice would be heard. I knew I would have to fight, knowing I would have to be strong and remain alone. Yes, always alone. *Just be patient. It will happen one day*, I always told myself. I had to have some kind of beliefs, to keep faith, make wishes, to try to expose my deepest memories, make them come to me all that hide from me, and take away my pain, just for myself. That is all I wished for, all that I could hope for.

I do not want to be alone anymore with just the voices to talk to and listen to me. My coward battling in my head time and time again was always destroying my good thoughts. No more battles. No more looking through the window to see only emptiness! Blue sky is what I wish to see. Sunshine and feeling happiness are all I want to touch and to feel coming through my window of hope. Suddenly the only thing rising up for me to hear and feel is the coward inside me, rising above my common sense, laughing through my window, making it become dark and dreary all over.

I become a child of fear once more. I have no voice. I see only nightmares waiting for me in the dark clouds hovering. I hear a voice, *Don't say a word… No one is coming to help, and you will never be able to help yourself. Ever!*

The voice inside me makes me, once again, cower in fear.

To Have a Wish

Sitting near the ocean
or standing by the sea.
The waters where I dream about,
it's where I'd like to be.

If I could have a wish of mine,
I'd want to be near there
instead of hiding from my mom,
who's looking everywhere.

I know she'll find me soon enough.
She always feeds her rage.
I'm the child she likes to beat
when she gets to that stage.

I hate it when my mother screams.
She makes me fear my name.
I wish sometimes I was not here.
She'd have no one to blame.

If I could have my wish today,
it would be to disappear,
to get away from Mom right now
just to stop my fear.

Chapter 39

Mom's Rage

Talk about child abuse! Everyone turned their heads the other way on this day. When I got in high school, I talked about how I did not care. Well, I should have. I could have saved myself a few scars. I got brave one day and skipped school with a neighborhood friend. I should have known my mom was right; she did have eyes in the back of her head. She really did when I was younger, I swear, and it just got kind of creepy when I got older. My friend and I thought we would be safe if we were a couple towns over. No one would go there during the day. It was small, and all they had was a very tiny movie theater. We could hang out in during the day and take breaks during intermission.

Well, after a movie was over, we went outside and was walking up and down the sidewalk in front of the building. We were smoking a cigarette while we waited for the next movie to start. There were a couple of adults there with a couple of small children. No one we knew, so we were safe. We had about fifteen to twenty minutes between movies but decided to just hang out there, where we would be safe. Just before the next movie started, I heard a screeching of tires, but we could not see very well. The sun was in our eyes. We started to walk toward the noise, almost at a trot, when all of a sudden, I heard my name being called. It was not in a particularly good way either.

Suddenly I grabbed my friend's arm to keep her from hurrying. I knew that witchy voice could only be one person. How on earth did she find me! We were unaware that a relative of mine happened to come to town to run an errand and, living in that town, would have to go through the main street to get to his destination. How fortunate for me! He saw me walking, thought about what day it was, looked at his watch, and decided to be on the safe side and call Mom. She must have flown to get almost three towns from our house to get there. I do not even care to know the dangerous speed she had to be driving. I could see her now, parked in the middle of the small street, cars stopped in both lanes, horns just a-honking.

Her car was blocking both ways so everyone could enjoy the show, and that was exactly how she had planned it. That was all I could see. *Uh-oh*, I thought. Right up her alley for entertaining, and she could be the center of attention too! I had just made her day. It had been a couple days since she could find anything to beat me about. She was leaning against the car, calling me a whore and pointing to my belly. I looked down, and the shirt I had on, having an elastic waist, had risen above my pants a little bit and showed some skin. You could not even see my belly button.

I yanked on it and pulled it down as she screamed, "Oh no, you like showing off what you got apparently. My daughter the whore!" I got almost to her, and she screamed, "Get in the car."

I was very hesitant. I knew she could not do much with her hand if I got in the car quickly. I devised a plan to just make a run for it. My plan failed miserably. The rage I saw on her face was like nothing I had seen before, but I knew what it was all about. She had not yet controlled me for this week. Mom stopped me by grabbing my hair and then produced a belt she had been hiding in her other hand. She took her hand with the belt and lifted my shirt up past my bra.

"See, everyone, this is what my slutty daughter wanted everyone to see." I began to struggle to pull my shirt down. She said, "Oh no, let's show your breasts too. You like to show things off. How about we show off your breasts?"

"Stop it," I screamed at her while she controlled me by pulling my hair tightly.

She did not lift my bra and let me pull my shirt down. While I did that, she began beating me all over with the belt. I tried getting in the car. She pulled me out by my hair, making me lift my arms to hold onto my hair because it was so painful; that way, she could get some good hits in with the belt. I cried and screamed during this whole ordeal and kept pleading with people watching to help me, but they looked just as terrified of my mother as I was.

I finally was able to move around to get a glimpse of my friend, and she stood there, looking white, with her mouth hanging open, wanting to help me, and I mouthed the word *no* to her. Then she got this look of hate on her face, and I gave her the thumbs-up as my mother beat and humiliate me in front of my friend and a bunch of strangers who did nothing but watch a teenage girl get beaten up by an adult. It was impossible to tell just how close Mom came to passing out with all the energy she was using, beating me and screaming names at me while trying to hold my hair. Plus, the sun beating down on us was so extremely hot.

Mom did not care what kind of foul language came out of her mouth either. There were young children there listening, people hanging from out of the windows above us throughout all the stories of buildings, just watching, not saying one single word. Like they were watching a movie, waiting for it to end. Well, people, so was I, waiting and wanting it to end. Thanks for all your help, everyone who watched and did nothing! I never stopped begging and pleading for her to stop. I twisted around and got a glance at my mom's face. The rage I saw in her eyes, she was not even there anymore.

I finally got in her face and screamed as loud as I could, "Mom, stop!"

She quickly pushed me into the back seat, with the belt raised halfway in the air, trying desperately to catch her breath.

She turned, looked at my friend, told her to get in the (swearing) car. My friend started toward the car pointed at my mother and said, "I will get in, but you touch me with that belt, bitch, and it will be the last thing you do!"

She got in the car with no problems. Even though I was crying and in severe pain, I wanted to high-five my friend for having the courage to stand up to my mother. Instead, I kept my head down, cowering in the back seat and whimpering all the way home, like a coward. Mom finally got in, still trying to catch her breath after swearing at honking cars. Mom moved the car, and the cars started moving around us then began to stop honking finally.

I could see through the window as I would look up, several people hollering at Mom and giving her the finger. My friend's mom and my mom happened to be best friends. She only lived a couple houses away from us. The whole way home, no one said not one word.

When we finally got to my friend's house to drop her off, Mom got out, turned around, and with the deadliest voice, said, "Do not move a muscle."

She did not have to worry about that, I was scared stiff because I knew, from the sounds of her voice and the rage in her eyes when she just looked at me, she was not finished with me, and it was far from over. Mom came out of my friend's house in a couple minutes, probably trying to get her in trouble for being disrespectful. Mom's face was as red as mine. I couldn't wait to find out what happened in there. Little did Mom know, her best friend was appalled after hearing about the way she beats on her kids.

We were home in less than a minute. Mom came around the back of the car, opened my door, and screamed, "Get the (swearing) out. Go cut yourself a good switch, not one of those petty things either, a good one."

I knew it, I thought. She still had lots of rage to get rid of. I went in the house. I was glad no one was there; I did not want anyone to see this as they usually did. It was humiliating. I got a good dull knife so it could at least take me a while to get a switch and get my body ready for the next beating. I was still sore from a few minutes ago.

I just got one cut when Mom hollered out the door, "What the hell is taking you so long?"

I began to slowly take off the leaves and little nubs because those hurt when she switched me. I finally got it done, brought it in, and as soon as I got through the door, she ripped it out of my hand, swearing filthy names. Then she began to use it on me with such force I almost fell over. I dropped the knife because I knew that could be an accident waiting to happen.

It was like she had gotten a second wind, and the rage started all over again. Wow, I got an extra good switch. This one hurt and was leaving whip marks on my hands and probably the top of my head, legs, and back, which was where she was hitting the most. I was really crying and pleading while she was calling me names when suddenly the door opened. I was so thankful. She stopped; it was my siblings coming home from school.

My younger sister hollered at my mother, "What the hell do you think you are doing?"

Mom said, "Mind your own business or you will be next, you mouthy little bitch!" Mom started whipping me again, reaching up, pulling on my shirt, like she wanted me to get on the floor.

But no, she was ripping my shirt off me. She ripped part of the front and most of the back off, calling me a slut and that I wouldn't be wearing this slutty shirt again! Which by the way, my mother had made for me! She began whipping my bare back with the switch. I really screamed out then. The whole time, my sister was calling Mom names, telling her to stop, trying to get Mom to turn the switch on her, but Mom would not. My sister became angry, ran in between my mother and I, grabbing the switch from my mother's hand, and began breaking it into pieces over her knee. All while Mom screamed at her, slapping my sister across the face. Then she started beating my sister with her hands.

Mom told my sister to go cut another switch. My sister swore at her and said, "No!" My sister instead turned to me and said, "Go get a shirt on. We are going to go hide until Dad gets home."

Mom screamed at me, "You stay your ass right there."

My oldest sister walked in, "What is going on?"

My younger sister tried to explain while Mom began to scream at me to go get another (swearing) switch. Both of my sisters said no at the same time, scaring me because they both screamed it. I started to pick up the knife to go get another switch, but my sister kicked it across the room before I could grab it. The rage in my mother's face! I could tell she wanted to kill all three of us. My oldest sister called my mom a bully, telling her to stop, that I was bleeding. I had had enough!

Mom said, "I do the disciplining around here, not the two of you. Now go get me another switch!" Mom looked at me and yelled.

I, the coward that I am, did as I was ordered to do. I walked across the room, picked up the knife, while my sisters both screamed, "No! Don't let her bully you!" My youngest sister was trying to stop me at the door while my mom began to hit her again, distracting her from stopping me, but I just knew my sisters would help me. I went out and cut the switch that would not hurt and the easiest for my sister to break. I walked through the door and thought she was going to use it on me again, but no, she started using it on my little sister.

I began screaming louder than before. If I had known she wanted it for her, I never would have cut it. Then my oldest sister went over and started screaming for our mother to stop! Mom got her a couple of times before my little sister could get that one away from her, also breaking that one. Then my two sisters began to laugh together while running out the door, hollering for me to follow. I was between the door and Mom. She grabbed me by the hair, grabbed the knife out of my hand, screaming at me that she had not been done with me by a long shot! I knew I was in for it. I was going to get the rage she had for my two sisters also. My sisters had not seen me getting caught again, or they would have helped me. Mom pulled me by the hair outside, cut a switch while holding onto my hair, pushed me up against the back of the house, ripped the rest of the shirt off me that I had been wearing, and she began whipping me again.

I tried to keep my back to the side of the house because that was hurting badly, and I could feel that it must be bleeding. That made her even angrier, so she got me in the face a couple times. I still screamed and pleaded with her, but she didn't stop. She still got my back some, and I could feel it when she would hit the blood, I knew she would be hitting raw flesh. Oh, how that stung. I was surprised all the neighbors did not come see what all the screaming was about. She still had hold of my hair, but I finally twisted enough so she painfully let go of it. I fought my way up to the door, keeping my back to the house; and just before I got in, she brought that switch down my back so hard I thought I was going to pass out. But I managed to get away.

I ran to my room, put on a loose-fitting shirt, then waited until I heard no sound downstairs. I ran to the pit and found my siblings.

We were all laughing together. They were glad I got away too. I never told them about the second beating. I had not wanted them to know I was a bigger coward than they ever knew. They had assumed I had taken longer checking out my back and finding a bigger shirt to wear. So I just never said a word and covered my pain as well. Later Mom told Dad about me skipping school and that I needed to be punished, also that the three of us girls have begun to be disrespectful to her. Dad did not have a lot to do with our discipline, so Mom was pretty angry when Dad only grounded my two sisters one week, and me for two. Then I had to promise him I would never skip school again.

"Okay, Dad, I will not skip school again."

I did not keep that promise. I am sorry, Dad. There were a few times more that I skipped school again. I thanked my sister so many times for being so heroic and standing up to our mother, the monster, the evil witch! That I wished I could be more like her and my older sister. She told me I could be. Everyone told me I could, but I knew I never would be. I was too afraid, and no one knew the coward inside me had control over what I could and could not do.

No one would ever believe a coward could have that much control over my fear! My sister laughed and said, "You do not have to keep thanking me. I can handle our mother."

Then we both laughed because she could handle her fairly well. Whenever my sisters would try to tell Dad about the whippings or beatings that especially I was receiving, Mom would do or say something to get them out of the room, making sure none of us were ever alone with Dad. That must have been one exhausting job for her! Trying to keep us all away from our dad at all times. I cannot imagine how much time and energy that took. Can you imagine what could possibly have happened if only she had put that much time and effort into watching us when we were younger, worrying about where we were, what we were doing, all that she might have saved us from? If only she had kept constant track of where we were at all times. Maybe she already knew where we were at all times. Who knows?

The next morning, my friend who skipped school with me told me that everyone in her family thinks my mom has anger issues.

Entertaining Mommy?

I said, "Do you think?"

As we all waited for the bus, they asked how things went after I went home. Before I could say everything was okay now, my sister said, "Not too well. Look at her back!"

She began lifting my shirt to show them, and I tried pushing it back down, knowing if Mom found out, I would get it again. I was such a coward. It also did not do me any good for anyone to see my back or know about it, so I asked everyone there to not repeat it, please.

After school, I was in my room, doing schoolwork, when Mom came up behind me. I turned around real quick when I saw a shadow, never trusting her. She had a long switch, ready to come down across my already stinging back. I could see the rage in her eyes already and asked what I had done this time as she brought the switch down over me. Mom knew that I had seen the switch, so she did not surprise me as she had planned, which angered her more.

"You like showing your marks to your friends at school, do you? I will give you something to show them. Did you show any of your marks to your teachers too?"

"No, I swear I did not!"

I wanted to tell her I did not show anyone, but I did not want my sister getting into trouble. So I kept my mouth shut. She was in the perfect position to beat me with this switch. I had nowhere to go, but I picked up a thick book to soften the blows. I could not handle the sting if they were ripped open on my back. My younger sister said, "Grab an object to soften the blows, and do not put it down. She will get tired of you easily."

Mom screamed at me, "Put it down."

Instead of saying no, I said, "Can you put down the switch?"

She said, "You are not going to act stupid like your sisters."

"I don't think they are stupid," I said.

She still swung that switch down and switched my fingers and wrists, almost making me drop the book. So I just kept moving the book around like my sister would do, and my mother got tired and said, "Do your (swearing) homework." Wow, it really does work. As she walked out the door, she said, "And no supper tonight!" slamming the door.

I could have told you that, but that was the least of my problems. I was hurting bad and had no way of getting something for it without running into my mother, so I looked out the window, hoping to see one of my siblings. No such luck. I knew they all had to be at the pit.

I told them I would be down after I did my homework then added, if I got it done, so they would not come looking for me until around dinnertime, with Mom stopping them, I am sure. My two sisters came to the rescue, sneaking me food and something to drink later. They turned on the light, and both said at the same time, "That bitch," when they saw the welts on my face.

I told them what happened, and my little sister was so angry, saying, "I am telling Mom the truth. That I told them about your back, not you!"

"No, sis, it's done and over with. I am fine."

Then she said, "For what she did to your face, I am going to beat Mom up."

We all laughed. They got some ice for the welts on my face while I ate the food they brought.

After I finished eating, we sat around talking, then we all decided that we hated Mom, then we laughed together, told some jokes, then snuck down to the gravel pit. Hey, she did not say I could not leave my room. I did start to become an angry, rebellious teenager after a while. It was only directed toward my mother though. The whippings and beatings were getting out of hand, and I was finding myself at times wanting to turn on my own mother. I never did. I just had enough some days. I began writing letters to my friends, not portraying Mom in an exceptionally good light, we will say. I said horrible things about her. Nothing that was a lie, just some names you probably should not be calling your mother.

I said in one letter just how I felt about good old Mom. I skipped school a couple more times. Smoked pot a few times. Started dating a guy I knew she would hate. We only saw each other in school. I did nothing that was really criminal. One day, I came in from the bus. Mom was sitting down at the end of the table. She had been crying. I swallowed hard because when she looked up at me, I could see the rage, and I believed it was directed toward me again. I looked in front of her. She had a piece of paper that had been folded all up. She pointed to the chair beside her then told me to sit down. I swallowed again, thinking, *I really do not want to sit that close to you*, and I had hardly ever seen my mother cry unless she was getting sympathy from someone.

I thought to myself, she really had to tear my room apart to find that letter. I wondered how long she had been snooping in my room. I bet she could not wait to find something bad just to have a reason to beat me. I would not leave anything else lying around, maybe a joke kind of note to her, saying, "Nothing here, Mom. Sorry you did not find it today. Maybe tomorrow," things like that. Mom brought me back to the present time by hollering my name.

"Sit down," she repeated, pointing once again to the chair closest to her.

As I sat down, I tried to see if it was the letter I had written yesterday, but I could not tell.

"Why!" Mom said in a long, drawn-out whine. I looked at the floor, not knowing what to say. "Why would you say these things about me to a stranger who does not know me?"

I wish I had the courage to laugh at this moment or to at least smile, but I couldn't do it. The coward still draped me with senseless fear, still holding me hostage with no way to control it. So I had no nerve to do such a simple thing. I thought about all the things she had said to everyone we knew about me, things that were not true to people who did not know me. But that was her way, not mine. So instead, I told her I was sorry, a lie she wanted to hear. Suddenly a hard slap across the face.

Please, someone give me the courage to slap her back before the moment passes! It slipped away. She won again. I looked at the rage in her eyes, on her face, the way she was looking at me. I wondered again if that was hate. It sure felt like it, certainly looked like it. I checked for bleeding. She asked why again, still the whiny voice. I knew I couldn't tell the truth. She would beat me again. I was not healed from the last time. She moved. I held up my hands to protect my face. She stood up. I kept my hands protecting my face. As she walked by me, she punched the side of my head so hard my ear began to ring.

I will have to see if that is bleeding later, I thought to myself. She told me to get up and go to my room. No supper, again. Great surprise! She thought she would use the letter against me. She kept it and secretly showed it to family and friends. Like that would bother me. She even secretly showed it to any guys I dated, even my husband. I think she thought she could scare them away. Why else? She showed it to my favorite cousins, anyone who liked me. I think she was trying to get people to dislike me. I wrote many other letters, and I was not sorry for any of them. It got my anger off my chest some, and I told the truth about a mean mother who could not control her rage! I never wrote down one lie about her!

Mom's rage had gotten out of hand for so many years now I think it has become a part of her emotional baggage. She gets lost and out of control, and I used to think she did not know what she was doing. I now know, she enjoyed her moods because it was nothing but entertainment for her. She enjoyed losing herself in the pain she caused others. It was such fun for her. The more she found to entertain herself with, the happier she became. I call that evil! Mom was not the only problem I had in my life. People who were supposed to care about me and love me, I could never count on them! I have had people tell me how much they cared, and then, *boom*, I am hurt by them in some way. I couldn't seem to trust some of my family or my friends at all. If you can't trust them, who can you trust?

Chapter 40

The Hits Keep Coming

We all knew him. Kind if he liked you, but if you were his enemy, you may want to hide. Luckily for us, a family friend that we trusted. You may as well say he was a family member. He was around that much. I was very close to him, a brother/sister relationship. That is the way he was with the whole family. He had been around for many years. Since he was a young boy. As he kind of grew up with us, he became a really bad influence when it came to some things. If Mom and Dad only knew what a rebel he really was, they would not have trusted him so much. We would go to the store sometimes, and he would scare us to death with how fast he drove. I am so surprised the cops did not pull him over more.

I hardly ever went with him after a few times. I did not trust his driving. I never wanted my younger siblings to go with him, but didn't want to rat out a friend, so I remained quiet. Once in a great while, he would promise, no speeding, no tricks, and he would be good, but I would rather just stay safe at home. He would sneak a beer to us girls occasionally. I never drank any yet; I did not like the smell of beer. We stole his cigarettes all the time. I thought he suspected and did not care. We even smoked pot with him a couple of times, but I did not like it, so I passed on it after the second time. Some thought he was a cool guy, and they thought he was tough. I knew him as just any other boy growing up, trying to find his way.

Not too many people dared to mess with his tough act he put on. We were close enough that we told our secrets to each other. He knew about some of the problems I had in my life. I knew about his. He would tell me about a girl he liked. I did not really like boys yet. From my experiences, they were all pigs so far. He knew Mom got out of hand when she spanked us. He thought that was when we were children and that she was done with all that. I never told him it was still happening. He never asked. He did know how I felt about males, at least most that I had ever met, and he did not blame me for the way I felt.

Still, I never told him the truth about anything that had ever happened to me either. He only thought older men had made passes at me and that I thought men were all the same. That is what I had told him anyway. Lots of times I would stay home by myself when Mom and Dad would visit relatives, family friends, or go shopping and take my siblings, just so I could be away from everyone. I did love my siblings, but I wanted some quiet time once in a while. It was so nice to have some time alone that I could think about my life. I liked being home alone. Never did I have so much peace and quiet. It did not happen often. I was really surprised it happened at all because of Mom not trusting any of her daughters.

I don't know what we could have been doing wrong back then, but I am sure she thought it was something bad. I was not, however, supposed to have any of my friends over while I was home alone, and I never did. So this family friend was there, but he was there all the time no one cared. He was not only my family friend, he was everyone's, so he did not count. We spent a lot of our time together, alone with the older siblings a lot, and we spent time together with the whole family for a lot of years. He was there now and had a beer, the small bottles. So I said one little beer wouldn't hurt. Well, I did not like it still.

He said, "You have to keep drinking it to get the taste, then you will like it."

I did not believe I would ever like the taste of that stuff. It reminded me too much of the smell of my cousin's breath.

Every time I smelled it, I would think about my dad always telling us, whoever drank beer was drinking skunk piss, so I tried to smile every time I smelled it and thought of my dad now. I kept it in my hand and took three very tiny sips of it. I did not like it.

Entertaining Mommy?

Obviously, I knew I would not drink it. He wanted to hear some music, so we both went to the stereo. We argued over music sometimes, like a brother and sister would do—like we did about a lot of things, actually. We found a station we both agreed on, and before I made it back to my seat, he grabbed my arm and started dancing.

As well as I knew him, my face still got beet red because I did not like to dance. My face got red if I had to do anything out of the ordinary. I kept protesting, trying to break free. He finally let go, and he stayed in the middle of the floor, laughing and dancing by himself. He never got embarrassed like I did, and he never made fun of me when I did. Another reason I liked him—we were comfortable. Since no one was home, I lit a cigarette. I did not drink any more of the gross beer. I told him I was sorry, but I just could not do it. He finally stopped being silly and sat down in his seat and lit a cigarette.

"Don't you ever tell your mother I give you cigarettes."

"Don't worry. You can trust me. I have never told her about your crazy driving, have I? Or any of the other things you have taught me to do, like lie better!"

We both laughed so hard. Mom would not think that so funny, but she was the one who taught us to lie the best!

He said, "Why don't we watch a horror movie."

"No, you know I hate those things."

"We will pick one we both like."

We decided on a comedy that we had already seen, but it was worth watching again. I got on the couch and wished I had made popcorn, but it was too late. I did not want to miss any of it. We were not extremely far into the comedy when he moved over to the couch.

"What is wrong?" I asked him. I was afraid something bad had happened, and he needed to talk.

He did not speak, so I gave him a moment, thinking he had to have a couple of minutes to get started. He had done it before in the past, so I sat quietly, waiting. Very quickly, he threw me back on the couch, and I hit his back, laughing. He had been playful like this before.

"Okay, get off me. I can't breathe," I told him. "This is not making me laugh anymore. Please quit. You are not being very funny. I really cannot breathe. Get off me! You're too heavy."

I was not afraid, of course. I could never be afraid of one of my best friends. We wrestled all the time. He started pushing me into the couch.

"Hey," I said, "enough! I really can't breathe. Knock it off."

I saw his eyes for a couple of seconds. It did not look at all like him.

Oh no, what was happening? I did not know why I suddenly felt so frightened of him. *What is going on with him!*

"Hey, it's me," I hollered a bit louder.

Then he tried laying over me to kiss me. Then we really started to struggle. I got one of my arms loose, bringing it up and hitting him beside the head as hard as I could, thinking he might snap out of it. He acted like it did not affect him at all. He never even blinked. He grabbed that arm, found my other one, putting both of my hands together over my head, holding both my wrists tight with one of his hands over the arm of the couch. I could not move. This was getting real. I began to scream as loud as I could.

He slapped me across the face with his free hand. I cried louder, sobbing his name, trying to get through to him. I could not believe this was him, that he was assaulting me this way. He needed to stop before it got out of hand. I thought, if only I could just get my hands loose.

I continued screaming, "Why are you doing this to me? Hey, it's me. We are still okay. Talk to me." He was trying to get my pants unzipped. "Oh no, please. This cannot be happening."

He got my button and zipper down then began pulling my pants down. I begged and pleaded with him. It was like he could not hear me or see me. He was getting my pants down while he laid on top of me and held my hands. I did not know how he was doing it.

He knew he had to finally let go of my hands. I began my attack. He could not see that it was me, then I would not see that it was him. I started to slap him anywhere my hands would hit or punch him. Then I began slapping him as hard and as fast as my hands would go, screaming the whole time. I tried to buck him off me; he was too heavy. He stood up and, in one swift move, slid my pants right off. I screamed as loud as I could.

"What is happening to you? Why are you doing this to me? We are best friends!"

I tried scrambling off the couch as fast as I could over the arm, but he caught me, dragging me back. I stood up hitting, kicking, anything I could do. I even tried putting him down with that knee to the crotch move, but he was too fast. He had me back on the couch, and on top of me, he somehow got my panties off without me even knowing.

"No," I screamed again and again. "Please don't!"

He put his knees across my legs with his full weight, hurting me again. I tried hitting him with my fists as I screamed and remained screaming his name, never letting up! He just slapped my hands away. I never once stopped screaming or crying, hoping a neighbor or someone walking by would hear me. He undid the belt buckle on his pants then the button and zipper, taking off his pants and underpants. His penis went straight out, and I was scared to death just seeing it.

"Please do not let this happen. You know I have never had sex before. You do not want to do this to me! Please, I am begging you. Stop before this goes too far and you cannot take it back."

He climbed on top of me. I was kicking and hitting him. He tried to spread my legs, as I tried bucking him off. I was slapping him as he grabbed my wrists again, telling me to quit or he would slap me again.

"I don't care, you bastard. Get off me."

He got my legs spread with his knee, causing me pain, but I tried kicking. I still did not know a lot about sex, but if that thing was supposed to go inside me like I read that it did, I knew it was going to kill me.

"Please don't let this happen. You can stop this. I know you don't want this!" I screamed at the top of my lungs.

I recalled the last time I had an experience with a penis, and it was in the dark. I did not really get to see it; this was all new and scary to me. I did not know what was going to happen, but he was being so rough.

"You are hurting me, you ass."

I really thought he was going to rub me. That was all I had known about sex so far. Then someone told me about a penis going into a woman's vagina. I went to the local library and looked it up. I was so embarrassed! I wanted to ask my friend how the hell is that possible, but I did not want to sound any dumber than I already did. I could not move an inch. I tilted my head back and prayed for this to stop. Then the worst pain I have ever felt went through my whole body, starting in my private area. It burned. The pain shot through me so fast I could not stop from screaming. It hurt so bad. I cried and cried for him to take it out of me.

"You're going to kill me, you jackass."

Then he pushed himself up and his penis slammed back into me. I screamed so loudly I thought I was going to pass out. The severe pain. How could anyone enjoy this? I felt the pain way up in my belly. I cried. I screamed. I begged for him to stop.

I screamed, "Please, you have to stop." The pain in my vagina was burning with piercing pain like someone had taken a knife and cut me, and I knew I needed help! "Please, I need someone to help me. I need some kind of emergency. Help! It hurts. You're killing me!"

He laid still for a few seconds then whispered in my ear with his voice cracking, "I am so sorry. I do not know what got over me. I do not know what happened. I truly don't. Please forgive me."

I could not believe what I was hearing. I reached up and slapped him hard right across the face as he let go of my wrists.

"Get off me now, you filthy pig."

He rolled his head back, made some weird noise, pulling his penis out of me, then his semen sprayed all over my belly. "Oh god," he kept saying. "I am so sorry. I did not think you were serious about being a virgin. I am truly, deeply sorry. Do not get that semen near your vagina," he told me! All I was doing was trying to cover up while I was sobbing.

He tries to help clean me up.

"Get your hands off me. Get the hell out of here. I never want to see you again!"

"Don't say a word to anyone. You know how much trouble we would both be in," he tried to tell me. As if I have never heard that before. "If you tell anyone, I will have to tell everyone that you tried to seduce me, and I could not resist you."

I did what? I had no clue again what that meant, another word I would have to look up. I was crying too much now to think about anything but my pain.

He grabbed his jacket and, before leaving, said, "Don't say a word."

"Get the hell out!" I screamed at him. "I hope I never see you again. You are no better than any other man!"

As soon as he was gone, I grabbed my clothes, ran upstairs to get my pajamas, then ran downstairs, locked the door, and took an extremely hot shower—as hot as my body could take it—scrubbing my skin until it hurt!

Even though the water was almost burning my skin, it felt better than what I had just experienced. I felt like I would never be clean again. How could this have happened? With my best friend! Why? What did I do? Why was that so painful? I wish I could just die! I stood there and cried until I thought I had no more tears left to cry. I hated him! I hate all men! Why was this happening to me? What in God's name have I ever done to deserve what I was getting in my life? Why did the hits keep coming? I still was not able to tell one single person.

Naturally, the coward wins again.

Chapter 41

Having Enough

If only you had listened for once in your life. Then again, that would have been one of those miracles I kept hearing about. You never believed anything I said before. Why start now? I had been working out in the public for a few months now, one of the hardest things for me to do, considering how shy I still was. Customers would approach me, and I thought my face could not feel so hot or get any redder. I also began to get tongue-tied while talking to people. It was the hardest few weeks I have ever been put through as far as embarrassment goes. I thought changing schools was tough, high school being the worst. I found out, it was not.

It does not compare to feeling like this, being thrown out into the world without somewhere to run and hide when you make mistake after mistake in front of everyone—like your boss other staff or the customers—as they watch your hands and voice shake and your face turn redder as they talk while you do nothing but fumble. I was so fortunate to get so many understanding people to work with, and I made some really nice friends. I still was very shy and nervous, but I was working on it, and my new friends helped. A lot of the customers seemed very understanding, which also got me through. On the weekends, I would try to do fun things with a few of my friends from school to give myself a break, or my younger sister, and I liked hanging with our friends from school mostly together.

Although one summer night, we talked our parents into letting me drive a couple of cousins, my younger sister, and one of her friends to the fair one night. I was a good responsible driver, so far, so they agreed. We had been at the water that day as a family, swimming, having a picnic, and spending time together. One of my sister's friends produced a bottle of alcohol for the fair tonight, not knowing where they got it from and I not wanting to know. After they showed it to me, I told them to put it under the seat in my car before someone saw it and they got into trouble before they even got started! We went to the fair that night, and while we were there, my little brother had been telling our mom a secret.

He had seen someone put a bottle of alcohol in my car. Mom, being furious, sent my dad and uncle (father of the cousins we had in the car with us) to find all of us and bring us home. What parent would not be upset! Of course, I understood and was not really upset with my little brother; after all, I was not getting into trouble, I thought. It wasn't my idea or my alcohol. My dad found me first, asked me if I had brought a bottle of alcohol to the fair with me. I was shocked. How could he know that?

"Did you?" he asked again.

I said yes, but before I could get out another word, he slapped me hard across the face, which hurt worse than any of my mom's beatings. Dad had never slapped me in the face before.

He told me to get in my car; my uncle was driving my car home. I got in the passenger's seat, and my uncle patted my shoulder as I cried. I told him I did let them put it under my seat, but I would never be stupid enough to drink and drive.

My uncle said, "Did you tell your dad that?"

I said, "I did not get the chance."

He patted my shoulder and said, "Everything will be okay."

I still cried all the way home, still very upset that Dad had slapped me. Dad had found the rest of the gang, put most of them in his vehicle, and we followed them home. It was a quiet ride back, besides the sound of my sobs, with both of my cousins wanting to ride with their dad, who was in my car.

One of my cousins asked his dad something every once in a while. My cousins would not have gotten into trouble, whether they had a drink of the alcohol or not. We all thought their dad was so cool at the time.

When we pulled into the driveway, my uncle looked at me and smiled, saying, "Any last requests?"

It made me smile, and I felt better. I would just go in and explain that I let them bring the alcohol, but I would never drink and drive, that it would be okay.

"Come on, kid, it will be all right," my uncle said as we got out of the car.

"Yeah, I will just explain it. It will be fine. Just give me a minute."

I wanted to wipe my face off and look more grown-up when I explained it all to Mom. I was the last one in the door and still feeling the sting from Dad's slap. As soon as I got through the door, there was Mom with her hands slapping me in the face, not willing to hear me at all.

"Shut up," she kept telling me.

Everyone else quickly made a beeline for the living room. It was Mom and me, with my aunt staying at the table to enjoy the show, I guess. I already knew she would not say anything to help me, the way she was smiling. Mom did like to entertain people! The sting from Dad's slap and the ones Mom just laid across my face were hurting pretty bad. I was up for it though, since Dad was there to protect me this time. I just knew that I was really angry now!

She wouldn't even listen. I knew this was not going to end well, but I have already had enough! I tried covering my face.

She kept screaming, "Put your hands down."

I did not as she chased me all over that kitchen, hitting me with anything she could grab before it flew out of her hands. She kept screaming like a crazy woman, not wanting to hear me talk at all, telling me to stand still, put my arms down, put my hands down, that we could and would do this all night if we had to! I was angry because she just would not hear me! Was everyone scared of her? Where had my dad and uncle gone? She kept pulling my hair, trying to swing me around like a rag doll. That was one of her favorite things for control.

I screamed in toward the living room for my dad, but he did not come out, which made me even angrier. This was not happening again. She was not going to win this battle. I finally got in behind the woodstove where there was not a lot of room for her to swing her hands or pull my hair. I was screaming for her to stop it when she put herself between me and the huge woodstove. I took my body, and I shoved her back as hard as I could, knocking the wind out of her. I think the weight of us both even moved the heavy woodstove an inch or two. Mom began to fall, and I did not turn around to help catch her fall. She caught herself then jumped back up in just a couple of seconds.

She tried to grab my hair again, but I got out from behind there. Mom started screaming for Dad, saying, "She tried to kill me. She tried to kill me."

Drama queen she can be when she thinks she is hurt! I smiled at her like she was nuts and just tried to keep her from hitting me anymore.

Dad came out and screamed, "Enough!" Mom tried attacking me again and again while Dad hollered at her to stop. My dad had to shake Mom to get her to stop. "I said enough!" he told her.

Then I screamed, "I never took a drink of that alcohol, you crazy bitch!" I felt pretty brave with my dad there to protect me.

My dad said, "That is enough out of you, young lady, and no more swearing!"

She lunged at me again, but I was too fast. I dodged the other way, and Mom, almost falling over, blamed me again for trying to hurt her!

Mom screamed, "See how she talks to me."

"That is the very first time I have ever called her a name," I said, "and I have had enough of her crap!"

My dad said, "Well, look what you have done to her face! What is wrong with you? Is this how you treat the kids when they do something wrong?"

"Dad, if you only knew! She loses her mind when she starts one of her rants!" I said.

My sister and her friend came out, the friend who had brought the bottle of alcohol, saying, "Yes, Dad, she does. We have tried to tell you, but if you have ever noticed, we are never left alone with you. Mom always seems to beat her more than any of us. Take a look at her back. You will see what I am talking about. Now do you believe us?"

"Don't you stick up for that little whore!" Mom said.

Dad slapped Mom across the face. "Don't you ever call one of my daughters that again!"

I smiled at her, and I said, "That is mild, Dad. She does it daily, and that is a nice name she just called me compared to other days," as I sneered at Mom.

Dad said, "I do not want to hear anything about this again. Keep those names to yourself." He pointed a finger at Mom. "If I ever hear of you beating one of my girls again, I will take you out to the woodshed, and I will show you how a real beating is done. Do not lay another finger on her ever again!"

Tears of joy were stinging my eyes! I wanted to stick my tongue out at my mother so bad, but I had won finally! I knew I would never have to deal with dear old Mom again! I knew after tonight, I had truly had, had enough! I wanted to rub it in, but putting my plan into action a couple of nights early would not hurt anyone but my mother! I ran to the bathroom, locking the door. I had a bloody lip and a bloody nose. Dad was right, my face was a mess.

I ran out of the bathroom and said, "I hate you. I have so had enough of you!"

I ran out of the house and out to my car. I knew I would never have to live under that roof again with that witch! I felt hate and rage and just wanted to forget she existed! I was moving in with my sister, just a few nights early! I had lived with a crazy woman of horrors long enough! How could it possibly have gotten any worse, I dare ask!

Now, about some other unbelievable stories I had totally forgotten about, a memory of my oldest sister that saddens me to think about, so late after all my sad stories. She recently reminded me of this story, and I wanted to share this before I go on. It is beneficial to my story, and I have more depressing observations of my childhood, but it is always more about my mother. This story seems to be becoming about her, and I did not want that even though she is the root of most of the evil that has happened to me. You do not even know the half of it, and you certainly do not want to miss the rest of this! Now back to my sister...

She found it exceedingly difficult to go to my mother with the heartache she did not understand and did not know how to explain to anyone, especially our mom, because she was such a hard person to approach. To find the courage to say something she knew nothing about as a child of only six at the time it happened, naturally, she could not do it at that age, but it stayed with her for over five years. A burning pain in her memories, knowing that it had happened, that she did not dare to do the right thing by telling our mom like she was supposed to because someone lied and convinced her not to somehow, only to be told, "You are a liar," years later when she finally did tell our mom. But when something else took place, something that caused her panic and fear, she had no other choice than to tell a secret she had been keeping.

She took Mom aside and begged her, "Please, you cannot let my younger siblings go with him." My sister was now eleven, telling Mom of a time of being six years old. She repeated, "Please do not let them go with him."

Mom did not believe what my sister had just told her. "How dare you make up such a story!"

My sister could not believe her ears. To finally get the courage then be told it's a story she made up! To be told that she is never to repeat such a thing. My sister was made to go with this man and do the same job at six years old—that she had done the day before, mind you—cleaning the church pews. Then day after day, because my sister of six did not know that a pastor who would molest her would be doing anything wrong, she was told a lie to keep from telling her mommy. The pastor would never lie, and Mommy would never make a mistake or let bad things happen. It had been the pastor who she accused of molesting her for all those days and all those years ago. He had somehow found his way to where we had moved to, wanting my sister and all her younger siblings to start coming to Sunday school that day. Mom, being the person she had become, let us go with the pastor. Yes, after just finding out he could have molested her six-year-old daughter! She told us nothing!

Free babysitter? Who knows! But my oldest sister refused to go. I happened to be old enough that the pastor knew I would probably say something, so he did not bother me. I, of course, knew none of this had happened at the time. Just a couple of weeks after that, for some reason, we started going to Sunday school at a different church. No idea why, no explanation. Mom still thought my sister had made up such a story. What kind of mother does this! Really? Oh, it does not stop there.

On another occasion, one of my mom's friends had let this same sister stay overnight to play with her friend's daughter. Her husband told my sister that when she put her nightie on, there was only one rule. No one was allowed to wear panties under their nighties. My sister was incredibly young still, so she thought that was the rule, and she had to do what everyone else did. The husband had her sit on his lap while he molested her, watching TV. This time, my sister thought, *She has to believe me. She cannot think I could make up two stories.*

The next day, when she returned home, she found the courage to tell our mother again. Mom again told her to stop making up stories. How dare she tell another lie about such a good family friend? "Why are you saying these things? Where are you getting these stories from? Who is telling you to say all these lies?"

A couple of weeks later, that man, that good family friend, was kicked out of his house by his wife. She wanted a divorce, and our mom, being so kindhearted, let him move into our house—with five young girls living there! To hear this now, what was she thinking! This same man was the man who left stacks of dirty magazines outside his bedroom door.

I am sure he was hoping for someone to pick them up and look at them. He had plenty of places in his room to keep them. He tried calling us in his room. None of us would go, but he forced me by grabbing me, covering my mouth. Sometimes he would catch me upstairs or catch me over beside his door, sometimes going into another bedroom, grabbing onto me then pointing to pictures of nasty things in the magazines he had, telling me, "We can do this" or "I want you to do that." He was such a disgusting man. He started

Entertaining Mommy?

getting braver when he thought Mom would leave or she was taking a nap or knowing she was too busy to notice, pulling me into his room, covering my mouth with his hand, always promising he would not hurt me if I did not scream.

He would try to show me dirty pictures, and I would try to make a run for the door. He never molested me, that I recall. While in that bedroom, the dirty things he tried to show me were enough for me. I had to get help with getting all my memories to surface. I could not remember most of them. I had blocked out all the bad ones. The rape I will never forget nor will I forgive. I still see that same person we called our family friend occasionally. I treat him like he is not even there when I see him because, to me, he is not. That was a nightmare I carried with me from the night it happened. It is still a painful one to think about. You never know someone like you think you do… You only know them like you want to. I knew I had to get help after not receiving any as a child.

I could not even attempt to approach my mother back then about any of the things that had happened throughout my childhood. Then after I discovered what really happened to me and I remembered how she treated my sisters when they approached her, what a painful way to be slapped in the face without being touched. I knew she would never be able to help me with any of my problems that I was having. Besides, I saw firsthand her problem-solving skills. I also knew she was the center of all my wounds. Why would I ever want to find my voice to tell a mother that would call me a liar. Another thing I have had enough of—all my mom's nonsense!

She has never believed a word of any of her own daughters for what they have told her. Called molestations nothing but stories, all made up? The rest has not peaked quite yet. There is more. My question is, how could she trust all these men and not her own daughters? Even more, why would she? What did she ever get by not investigating at least one thing?

She found out she was wrong later and could not bring herself to admit she was wrong, or she did not want to have to say she was sorry to her daughters! Never would she have! What kind of mother has evidence put right in front of them then turns around and says it is a lie? Calling her child a liar! She never could have admitted it if she had found out she was wrong anyway. It would have meant she was mistaken, and we could not have that! Trust is not something I could ever say my mother and I have ever had between us. I knew I would never be able to feel comfortable with her, talking to her, trusting her even at an early age, and not just because she scared me.

Even her two youngest daughters, who she knew she should have been keeping a watchful eye over, and did she? No. She did not! They also were molested right under her watchful eye. You would not watch because all or any of what your daughters have told you were lies, right, Mom? Isn't that what you told my sisters? Even your younger daughters were molested because you were wrong. The same kind of men you trusted hurt your other daughters too! From the sounds of it, you should have kept an eye on all your children. You could have saved some of your children some shame, humiliation, the confusion, embarrassment, and maybe all that pain? You were too busy looking for things to use against your own children, things you could punish them for, looking for things to entertain yourself!

You sure had time to snoop for things like that, but no time for me! When I was eight years old, why could you not be there for me! Years nine through thirteen, where were you! I wanted and needed to tell you! I needed to be able to trust my own mother, and at eight, I knew I could not. What were you doing to be a mother? I should not have known what some of my own body parts were called, nothing about sex, and I should not have known that it was even called sex. Why should I have known that? I found out about a penis at eight. You think that is a story I could have made up, along with all the other things that I should not have known at my age?

You still would have called them stories that I somehow thought up, slapped my face and called me some bad name, then tell me to never repeat that again. I was supposed to trust you then or now? Which is it? I am supposed to trust a mom who helps men that you have no business helping, when you cannot help your own children? You sounded like you had enough of your daughters as soon as they started walking. Let me tell you, I had had enough of you as a mother way before your time. You had a great chance to be a mother, and you blew it, failing miserably. You never gave any of your daughters their chance. I am not sure you even let me get a start, never understanding why. Not even sure I want to know why anymore.

It really upsets me that you always think you do no wrong, never saying, or should I say meaning, the words "I am sorry" for anything. If there is something you do not want to talk about, *we* do not talk about it, and that is final! I guess some people could say I was a lucky child. My mom would say, "Oh, quit your whining." I guess she is right. There were some who had it worse than I did! I did not get as abused as some children I have read about. I made it out alive. You must have thought I had just had a change of heart, swept it all under the rug, forgive and forget? Because I never gave it a thought what you did to me?

When I grew up and got married, started my own life, my own family, you thought that I was that kindhearted and I forgave you for all you had done to me? Well, it was only because I had not remembered! It was too painful to believe that a mother could do that to her child. I did not want to believe it, so I had to block it out, I am assuming. What other explanation could you possibly come up with, Mom? You had a part of me that you would not have had otherwise had I remembered all that you had done to me throughout those years, entertaining yourself the way you have.

All that you did not do for me many of those years and all that you took from me all my years, you are one lucky woman to do all that you had done. Never held accountable as a mom, as an adult, as a citizen breaking the law. Yet still was able to carry on a great relationship with me. Yes, lucky is what we will call you. That is why you never wanted to discuss the past. It made you look as bad as a rotten tooth. You changed some and became a slightly different version of yourself. Now you deserve, what was it again? Remind me because I have forgotten what it is you think you deserve. Now that I realize who you are and what you have done, I think I have had enough—enough of you, enough of your abuse!

There is nothing forgiven here. Nothing forgotten ever again! One day I wanted you to discuss my childhood with me, but never mind. I desperately wanted to know back then. Now I know all I need to know. Do not talk to me about a past you would probably lie your way through anyway. I wanted that talk. I wanted your answers. I do not even want that from you anymore. Now that I know all this and am not missing anything now, I have had all I can take on this chapter in my life. You thought I would forgive you again? Forget all that you have taken from me, done to me? I should have respect because you are my mother!

Just recently, as a matter of fact, you said a child should praise, love, and worship their mothers. I thought that was meant for someone else altogether. I do believe you have gotten enough of me, all that I am willing to give. You have gotten more of me only because you guilted me into spending all my time with you instead of my own family. I was stupid enough to do it because you still intimidated me in more ways than one. That is all I have ever gotten from you. You made me feel guilty of anything in my life, including the time I spent with my own children. I do not think I owe you anything else. But you sure made me feel like I did. You would be doing it at this moment if I was still allowing it to happen.

I could never talk to you about anything bad or sad in my life. You always used it against me—some form of torture, I guess—because it sat me on pins and needles. I never dared to tell you anything good in my life. Because in some way, somehow, you were going to make me feel guilty about it. Well, I have certainly had enough! I think it is because it is something you had never had, or never received, or never wanted. I am really not sure. You sure made your kids feel guilty if they had anything that made them happy. Still, I cannot get over those memories of you overlooking me, not seeing any part of me when I was in pain for all those years, when I needed my mom to hear me even when you could not love me.

That still hurts to know I was in front of you, and instead of giving me any type of help, you beat me instead. Every chance you got, you added to the pain I was already feeling, but you did always say, "I will beat you into somebody." Thank you. I believe you accomplished that. You beat me into just the opposite of you! A good mother, good person, someone kind and loving. I got through the heartbreak, tears, and loneliness by having enough and making sure

Entertaining Mommy?

I would never be like you. Even after forgetting, I kept that promise to myself. But the coward kept me from being any braver. I lived through my neglected childhood. I was indeed one of the lucky ones.

I am almost thankful that I had forgotten most of that childhood. I might have become a whole other kind of person had I not. I could have become my mother or someone like her. I am happy with the good person I have turned out to be. I was so thankful for all the happy memories that came into my mind freely. I love all those memories. There really were not enough of them, not enough for what I have endured. But I am not bitter. I am happy. My life makes me happy. Can you say that about any part of your life, Mom?

My children make me happy, no doubt about that. I have had and still have many joys and good times with my children. I think mine enjoy having me around still. Do yours? They do not need to visit me every other day or do things for me every time I see them. I do not need to talk about family to them. I am happy just the way I made my own life, fulfilling and knowing I have love! You took those many things from me, but I still learned to cope and survived with the help, love, and bond from my sisters. They got me through it all. Because we had all had enough, back then and to this day! You haven't changed, and we all know you're never going to. Now, find something else to entertain yourself with!

Chapter 42

My Last Assault

I wanted to work as many hours as I could to pay back my parents for a big old boat of a car they bought for me to, as my mother said, pay back every red cent when I was a young teenager with my very first job while I worked out in the public. That was a convertible that ran well. Always got me where I wanted to go, but had no back window. The plastic I would replace all the time, which was what I could afford at the time, worked for as long as I owned the car. It was hard to get the car paid off though. Mom still had her way of talking me down and getting money out of me the only way she knew how—guilt. Go figure. Only now she was using my younger siblings to do it.

Every Friday, when I would try to make a double car payment, I would hear, "Your sister has no winter coat. She outgrew the one you all have worn out. She really needs one" or "Your baby brother has no outfit to wear for this occasion, and I do not get paid before he needs it. I ordered something through the school and have no money. I do not want to look like a fool. Could you pay it?" Just something every single week. When it was about a sibling, she knew I would not say no. My mother kept the papers to the car. She said that she and Dad had to take out a loan to get it for me, so there was interest. I never believed that for a moment, but I did not have the money to pay outright for a car. Unfortunately, I had to believe whatever she told me.

I promised myself I would never owe my mother anything again. It seemed like that $1,000.00 car ended up costing me almost double, even though I made many double payments. I would get backhanded in the face if I tried accusing my mother of cheating her own daughter. The thing I remember about the most. The day I finally made the last payment was when I handed her those bills, smiling my biggest smile, knowing the time had finally ended for a lot of good things in my life. She had to spoil that moment too. After all the money she had suckered out of me and lied that she needed for this and that, she had the audacity to hold out her hand and say to me, "And nineteen cents!"

I just looked at her and said, "Are you serious?"

She held up the paper she had been keeping track on and showed me a balance due of nineteen cents.

I said, "Come on. You must be joking."

She said, "I am not! The car is not fully yours until you pay the full price," and held out her hand again.

I ran out to my car to retrieve nineteen cents so I could cry my tears. But do not worry. They were happy tears. Tears of utter joy! I had, what we call, had enough. I was making plans with my oldest sister to move in with her and get a job closer to her and get out of that ridiculous house! I was glad she did not make up that I owed her .92 or .96 because I barely scraped up the nineteen cents.

It would have just meant another time for her to humiliate me had I waited to give her some change I owed her. That is how greedy my mom was, right to the very last penny.

Anything to be away from the insane woman we call our mother as soon as possible. As excited as I was, my only regret was the same regret every single one of us had as we made our plans and when we finally moved out. We were leaving our younger siblings with the crazy lady. There were still four more kids at home she could torture and abuse, whose lives she could make miserable or a living hell if she wanted. Who was going to save them! One by one, we all worried. But we tried to watch out for them as much as possible, never moving extremely far away, talking to them on a regular basis, making sure they were okay, letting them know what not to let her do to them, what she had done to us, how to stay safe and for them to call anytime day or night.

We at least gave them someone who watched out for them. We know, we were horrible siblings. We should have done more, but she did mellow out some with the abuse as the years went on. I had a plan to move out on a certain day. Then Mom and I had a fight, and I left a few days early. I slowly forgot almost everything that had to do with my childhood, being on my own, away from my mother. I was living with my oldest sister. Freedom! Yes!

Finally, I was out of that house. I started a new job, and it paid a lot better than my earlier one. I would miss the other one though. I was still this shy young girl who just turned seventeen, a greenhorn trying to make it in the world on her own. My sister said I could stay with her and save money to get a rent of my own when I could. My life seemed to be on the right path. I was happy, and my past was my past. I did not even think about my mother, one way or the other. It was still hard for me to make friends right off, but my cousin worked there, and he made it a lot easier for me. As a matter of fact, he introduced me to my children's father there.

I met a couple of girls I spent time together with. We went out on Fridays for dinner. I had the time of my life for a while, doing what older teenage girls do, spending my own money on whatever I wanted, not feeling guilty about it. My new friends shared an apartment together. We had dinners there mostly. Sometimes we would watch movies. We never got into trouble. There was a police officer living in the next house who happened to be one of the girl's dads, so we behaved. I was always an incredibly nervous driver and refused to drive anywhere if there was snow coming. So if my friends and I made plans and there was a storm, I always canceled, unless one of them came and picked me up and I would spend the night at their apartment.

One day, going to work, the sky was clear, no sign of a storm. It was spring. Things were blooming. While we were working, we had gotten this freak snowstorm out of nowhere. No one had predicted anything like the storm we had that day. We all watched it come down out the windows, thinking it would stop soon. Well, it did not. People started going home early that lived far away. I was not too worried yet. My sister only lived about a mile down the road. I would just keep track of the snowfall. There were still lots of brave people staying, so I thought, *I live a lot closer. I can stay. They do need me.* It was really coming down, and many people had gone home by now. I was starting to panic.

Not that I was not before, but I tried not to look out as much as everyone else or think about it as much. Everyone decided to call it a day only a half hour earlier than we normally left. I looked at my car and was so scared I was almost willing to stay in my car, until my sister and her husband came looking for me. I watched the plow go by then the road fill right back in while I tried to brush off my car. By the time I got it done, got back in, buckled up, it was covered again. I turned my wipers on, and said, "You can do this." I just prayed my plastic window covering held through this, or I was going to have a mess. I would just keep watch of it when I got home and keep coming out to it brush it off.

I backed out of my parking space without getting stuck. So far, so good. I pulled down to where I turned to get on the road. There was so much snow. I was breaking my own rule: never drive in a storm, unless someone is dying or unless absolutely necessary. As soon as they plowed, it was almost impassable again. I slowly got out on the road. You could not see ten feet in front of you. I was staying in what I thought was the middle of the road. I could not see any lights coming my way. I just hoped it stayed that.

My car was fairly good in the snow, but as good as it was, it was still pulling me everywhere. I was doing what I thought was a decent job. Then I looked and had only passed the first house closest to the shop. This could take all night. I was white knuckling the steering wheel for sure and straining my eyes when a bump from behind me pushed me right into the ditch, surrounding my car with nothing but snow. Only hitting the snowbank, I was so thankful. Of course, straight into panic mode I went.

I laid my head against the steering wheel and told myself, "You are not going to cry over and over."

I remembered Dad always made me keep a shovel in the trunk of my car. He said it was for my protection, but he knew I was always nervous. Thanks so much, Dad! I opened my door to get out, put one foot out, and there was nothing to stand on. I looked down, and I swear, that snow was going to go up to my neck if I jumped out. I think it was going to take an awful lot of shoveling to get out of this one! Well, I had to get out somehow. Here goes. Down I went into soft snow that went over my waist. I turned to head to the back of the car to get my shovel when I thought I could hear my name. I stopped walking, and there it was again. I looked toward where I thought the road was, and I could barely see what looked like someone waving their arms. It must be someone I knew if they were calling me by my name. I waved back and began the hike toward them. I turned back around to retrieve my purse. I almost got stuck. That was how much snow there was.

I slowly trudged along, looking to see who was there to rescue me, and I still couldn't see. There, standing in the road, was a friend of the families I recognized. I was so happy to see a familiar face I told him. Somehow my car slid off the road, but I was happy I did not hit anyone or that no one was hurt!

"Why are you so happy?" he said. "I am the one who bumped your car and ran you off the road I am so sorry. I did not see you in time."

"I thought I felt something touch my car, but it's okay. My sister's husband will get it out," I told him. "It's not far. I can walk. I was thinking, maybe this was why Dad always made me carry a shovel in my trunk, but after I got out of the car, I knew that was not going to help me any."

"Your dad is a smart man."

"Well, it is because he really knows how nervous I get when I am out in a snowstorm of any kind."

"Then here I have to run you off the road."

"Don't worry about it. I told you. We just live down the road. I am sure my brother-in-law can get me out."

"Don't be silly. You can't walk home in this storm. I got you in this mess. I will get you out. Get in. I have my secretary, who I am taking home to this house here. Then I will tell you the rest in the truck."

We got in the truck, dropped her home, then he started backing out the wrong way.

"No, I live that way."

"That is what I am trying to tell you. I have a neighbor who lives right beside me. He owns his own wrecker service. I will pay for your car to be pulled out. It's the least I can do," he said as he turned up the heat, seeing that I was soaked.

"Are you sure it's not a bother to anyone?"

"No bother at all. Again, I am terribly sorry I hit you."

"Don't worry about it, and it's good about your neighbor. I appreciate it."

"Let's see how the roads are this way."

The roads did not even look like they had been plowed. We slowly crawled to his house even with a four-wheel drive. We got inside, and I did not realize how wet I had really gotten.

He went over to the phone to call his neighbor and told me, "He must be out on a call. I will try again in a couple minutes." He left the room as he said, "You look soaked. I will be right back."

He came back carrying a heavy bathrobe and slippers and handed them to me.

"Oh no, I am fine. I do not need those. I will dry off as we wait."

"I insist," he told me. "Go to that bathroom down the hall. Take off all of your wet clothes, including your jacket and gloves, put the robe on, and throw your wet stuff in the dryer right across from the bathroom."

"Like I said, I am fine. I will not be here that long."

"I told you, I insist." He was pushing the robe into my hands. "It will not take long for your clothes to dry. I do not want to be the one who is blamed for you catching a cold or worse! Now go and put the slippers on too."

"Okay, fine!" I went in the bathroom and locked the door.

He sure had an awfully clean bathroom for a man who was engaged. He must have a housekeeper. No man was this tidy. I took off my pants and socks, and my outer shirt was damp, put on the bathrobe and slippers, picked everything up, threw it in the dryer, with my jacket and gloves, putting my boots upside down on top of the dryer so they could dry a little. I felt very embarrassed to walk into the kitchen with someone else's bathrobe on. I could feel my face getting red!

I hated that part of me. He was standing at the stove, cooking something.

"What are you doing?" I asked.

"Making us dinner," he said and smiled when I looked up at him.

"Oh no, I am not staying that long."

"I just called my friend, and he said it is going to be a couple hours before he can get to your car."

"I need to call my sister. Maybe she can come and get me. Can I use your phone?"

"Go right ahead."

No answer. I left a voice mail and told her what had happened. Then he handed me a glass of wine.

"No, I do not drink, sorry. I have had a couple of sips of beer before, and I did not like it."

"Wine is much different, more sophisticated. Try a sip. It will relax you. Keep your mind off your car being in the ditch."

"I will have to drive in a while."

"Wine has hardly any alcohol whatsoever. You eat, and you're fine. Just try a sip. If you do not like it, I will drink it."

I tried it. I liked the taste, and it did not taste like alcohol at all. I took another sip and wanted to go sit in a chair in the living room.

"I thought you said it has hardly any alcohol," I said as I took the last sip. "I sure feel funny."

He was right behind me, grabbing my glass out of my hand, then all of a sudden, my legs were not working as I fell back and he caught me, laying me on the carpet gently. I could not feel my arms either. *What is happening?* I could talk, but my head could barely move. *Oh no, am I paralyzed? What the hell is going on?*

"You're going to be just fine," he said.

"Wait, you did this to me? What did you do?" I began to scream at the top of my lungs!

"No one is going to hear your screams. My house is soundproof. If you think I am going to listen to that, though, you are wrong. Keep screaming all you want, and I will keep slapping your face, then you will look like you have been in a bar fight. Now, I would shut up if I were you!"

I began to cry as he untied the bathrobe. "Please do not do this. I am begging you."

He smiled at me and opened one side of the robe, laying it out flat like a blanket.

I kept begging through my sobs, "Please, I will not tell anyone. Just let me go. No one will know I was here. I can go back to my car and walk to my sister's. Please!"

He reached down and opened the other side, laying it the same way.

"Just as I suspected. You are someone I have wanted ever since I saw you grow up."

"You are a pig!"

"And you are beautiful."

"Keep your stupid opinions to yourself."

"I guess this freak storm worked out in my favor. You...not so much. Now, you will be able to feel everything sexual," he told me as he lifted up my bottom and began to pull off my panties.

I couldn't even feel him doing it. What was it he gave me? I cried out as much as I dared to. I did not need him slapping me too.

"Your legs and arm movements will start to be coming back in just a few moments."

"Good. I can kick you in the crotch when it happens."

"Oh, I do not think you will be doing that after we have a little chat."

"About what!"

"Not now. I do not want to spoil the moment."

He got down and started rubbing my legs, then he pulled up the undershirt and bra I had left on.

"Don't do this please. I promise I won't tell."

"Oh, you're not going to tell anyway. Now stop talking."

"What did you put in my drink, you bastard!"

He reached down and slapped me across the face. "I said shut up!" He stood up and began to undress.

I turned my head as much as I could. I sure as heck did not want to see him naked! All that I heard was my clothes spinning in the dryer, around and around. That was what I would concentrate on while he did his thing—rapes me, I was thinking!

He got down on his knees. I looked down, and he put his hands under my butt. I couldn't stop crying. He lifted me up, so I was the same height as his penis. I wanted to scream, but I took him at his word that no one would hear me. He drove his penis into me hard, and it hurt. He held onto me tight and kept pushing harder.

"You're hurting me. I can feel that, and it hurts. Please stop it."

He did not stop. He kept pushing as hard as he could. It looked like doing nothing but causing me pain. Then he let his sperm go inside me after just a couple hard pushes.

I screamed, "What are you doing!"

He was not wearing protection, and I had no protection. I was not planning to have sex for a long time when I found out about protection.

"Do not worry. I cannot get you pregnant. I am sterile." I looked at him funny through my tears. I had no idea what that was. "My sperm can't get anyone pregnant."

I finally felt my arms and legs coming back to life. I couldn't wait to kick him where it counts, as my sister calls it. He looked at me and smiled.

"I know the feeling is coming back. Don't even think about injuring me. I have the power for you to keep your new job or to lose it."

"You can't do that!"

"I can and I will."

I called him every foul name I could think of as the feeling in one of my arms came back, and I lifted it straight up.

"I told you," he said, "no job if I get injured."

I couldn't believe all this crap I had gone through, and now this assault. I promised myself, *This will not ever happen again. I will never be tricked or talked into anything by a man ever again.* My arms and legs were almost feeling normal.

He stood up and told me, "Do not tell our secret, and you will keep your job. Go shower. Get your clothes out of the dryer, and we will go have your car pulled out."

"Oh, that was not a lie too? That is a miracle."

"If anyone finds out about this, I will say you seduced me, begging me to bring you to my house."

"You are a sick man!"

When I go to sit up, I saw blood that should not have been there.

"Oh no, I have to go to the hospital. What did you do? I am bleeding!"

"You will be fine. I was just a little rough. You got me excited."

"You're such a pig!"

I wrapped the robe around my almost naked body and tried standing up. Still very wobbly. My private area hurt so bad; I wondered if I really did need to see a doctor or the emergency room.

"I'm bleeding," I cried, scared to death!

"No doctors, no hospital," he said. "That is part of my deal."

"You can't make a deal with me."

"Put that robe in the hamper please. Everything you need for your shower is already in there. Take your shower, then we will eat dinner."

"Have you lost your damn mind? I am not eating with you! As soon as I am done my shower, I am going to my car if I have to walk there! I will never speak to you again if I do not have to. Tell me the truth, your friend could have pulled my car out at any time, couldn't he have?"

"Of course, he could have."

"I hate you. I hate all men!"

I quickly got my clothes out of the dryer, slamming the door so hard it could have broken off the hinges. I would not have cared if he had a dryer or not! Then I grabbed my boots. I went to the bathroom, slamming that door and locking it. I took a shower without closing the curtain, water going everywhere. I even took the sprayer and sprayed out as far as I could, soaking everything in its path. Took the covers off the bottles in the shower, tipping them over so they could empty out. Any cleaning products, perfumes, anything I could get the covers off, I dumped each and every one of them all over what looked to be brand-new towels, some shelves, the toilet and sink, and the cupboards. I topped it all off with baby powder everywhere. *There. Clean that up, you jerk!* At least some payback, and he could not be half as angry as I was. I got dressed, put my coat on, went to the living room, grabbed my purse, and went to open the door.

He grabbed my arm and said, "Remember, tell no one. I will tell them you seduced me anyway."

I looked at him in disgust and said, "In your dreams, asshole," as I slapped him in the face! "This will never happen again. Don't ever speak to me again! I know you raped me, and you will go to jail if you ever come near me again. Now drive me back to my car and get your friend there to pull my car out NOW!"

When we got there, just before I could get out of the truck, he put his hand on my leg. I punched it as hard as I could.

"Don't ever touch me again!"

"Remember," he said, "keep your mouth shut, keep your job."

I slammed the door as hard as I could, making the window rattle. He got out, came around to where I was, saying, "My friend will be here in a couple minutes. We could be friends, you know. I could help you out a lot."

He then tried to hug me. I punched him in the stomach as hard as possible, and he bent over just as the wrecker pulled up. After I finally got in my car, I let it warm up as I sat there and cried and cried, knowing I would go through this alone too, with nothing but my silent tears, knowing the coward still lives on.

Chapter 43
Accountability

I wondered, who would be the one for me to blame for most of my childhood suffering that I have been through so far? The pain, loneliness, the nightmares, always being afraid of something that was not there? But I didn't know that. Should I make accusations at all? Or do I just keep it pushed aside? Forget it and keep it hidden? For fifty years, that's exactly what I did, but that did not help me. What is the answer? Should I just blame myself? I was the one, after all, who could have saved myself by using my voice, even though I had been scared and blackmailed starting out as an eight-year-old. Still, I have wondered that often. Should I be the one accountable?

After all, I thought I had been the coward throughout my childhood who could never find her voice. If only I would have screamed, things could have been different. That is all I knew to tell myself. So the blame fell on my shoulders for as long as I can remember, and that is what the coward wanted. The monsters, rapists, perverts, or possibly my protectors—do I blame any of them, all of them? I was eight when it started. I believed what the monster told me, the coward, the voices in my head. I truly thought there was no one who could help me. I never trusted myself, never trusting my own voice and too frightened to use it. There was no one else for me to ask, I thought.

My only real guidance was inside me, controlling most of my emotions, what I did, how I felt. They were my adults, my authority, making me as scared of them as much as I was of my own mother. She would have liked that had she known. It would have made her taunt me even more. I am glad I had some secrets she did not know about that I kept to myself. More secrets, how to keep them all straight in my head, where did I put them all? I was too intimidated to communicate my pain or fears, my secrets. Not brave or courageous enough. Certainly not able to fight conflict, stop my nightmares, or get the circle fights out of my already bullied life.

I became so vulnerable, easily frightened, yet not smart enough to know I was being manipulated; that without help, I would keep becoming my predators, targets. I was at fault, yes, but to what extent? An eight-year-old who was very weak, frightened, and just beyond the shame I had felt for myself endured all my misery alone. This does not admit blame, but some accountability should become mine, even as a young child. I will take some fault. Again, my mother would like that. Though she has not taught herself how to accept her own accountability quite yet even after all these years. I like the thought of putting the accusations onto someone else though.

Like blaming my mom for having no love for me, that is on her. She should own that! That had she known, it would have put a smile on her face just to sense that it killed me to feel that from her, not one ounce of love; that I know she would not have cared at all, at any time had she known how much I suffered alone. I kept those kinds of things from her because I thought they could possibly make her happy and my tormented life had already pleased her enough. She never helped me when I needed her most. Where were you exactly? A mom should be the person holding the family together, I was told, being a positive role model for everyone to witness, yet you were not. I am not sure she wanted to be.

Negativity though, that could have been her middle name, trying to get under her children's skin, keeping them agitated, laughing at the turmoil she causes. Those are part of her hobbies. Who does anyone know that enjoys animosity among their own children, even more with her children's spouses? It is an adventure to her. She wants to push enough buttons to get exactly what she wants from each family member without pushing too hard or all at once. So she could have just her children all to herself. If she can push the spouses out, make them mad a little bit at a time, they will not want to visit anymore. But her children will always visit, so all to herself she gets us.

She makes dysfunction in our family a game she likes to play, and she does like her entertainment! Do moms really do that? Do not kid yourself. It happens. At least it has in our family. I wonder if she would take accountability for any of her actions like that, or would she just say that, too, was wrong? Or something like, "I would never do such a thing." Sorry, Mom. We are on to you. We all love her many phrases. She would not even care that we sit around and mock her when she does my not-so-favorite one, "I'm seventy-nine years old, and I don't give a shit!" Of course, the number changes with the year, but that one is like a broken record. How many times she has said these many quotes over the years.

Now it sounds as bad as nails going down a chalkboard. I like the one, "What did I do?" or "What did I say?" When she knows exactly what it was she purposely said or did! Later in life, while our parents have been of sound mind and retired together, Mom likes to upset our dad as well. She gets as close in his face as she can and says, "Ya wanna hit me, don't ya!" No, she is not drunk when she does this. They do not even drink. She is just being a bitter woman. Because she wants to pay my dad back for their past when the children were young and Dad was not a good husband our mother always tells us. But then she says, "I'm only foolin'."

Let's see, so far, who shall we hold accountable for that, her or him? When years ago, she swore everything was forgiven, but we now know it was not. That she only said that to torture him for life! This one would drive anyone a bit off their rocker. The whole few weeks before a holiday, their anniversary, Mother's Day, her favorite one, her birthday. She tries every day to remind us what day is coming up, always wanting someone to remind the other of her children what day it will be. Like she would ever let any of us forget. Then the day of especially her birthday, she is worse than a six-year-old. "It's my birthday today!" Telling strangers! As many people as possible before the day is over. Depending on how she is feeling that day, we sometimes have to make a holiday extra special.

Do not upset Mom by forgetting her holiday. It does no good. If you care, you will have to make it up to her. If you have forgotten and even if you do say you're sorry, she will tell everyone if you did not do something for her holiday, calling friends, relatives on the phone, as she does with any kind of gossip or something she just wants to spread because she doesn't like a person that week. She will tell what a horrible child you are to forget her holiday. After all, we only get one mother! Oh yes, she is the gossip spreader, the pot stirrer, the storyteller.

Mom will tell a lie about you or spread gossip about you before it is out of someone else's mouth, especially if you ask her, "Please do not repeat it." Those are her favorite ones to tell. Remember, this is the woman who does nothing wrong, will never admit to anything she has done, even if you have pictures of the crime. You will never hear "I am sorry" come out of her mouth. If two of her daughters are visiting and one has to leave, you know you're not going to be the favorite that day. She will talk bad about you, your husband, your children, their children, whomever she can gossip about within that particular family. Or if she has nothing to gossip about, she will make something up. That is another favorite thing to do.

She also would say, "You know what she said about you yesterday?" Animosity much? Who is accountable for that? We never listen to it. We all know how she is. But sometimes she will hit a nerve and someone gets mad, and she is laughing inside, bathing in her glory! She does like her entertainment! A vicious cycle is what she likes to start if she possibly can. She used to have her grandchildren and great-grandchildren visiting her, but she talks about the child's mother or grandmother so much they refuse to visit her anymore. Then she literally cries when no one visits. Accountability? We should just forget she said that or let that go. There goes some of that disguised feeling again.

Or how about this question, how did the people who were always in need that she felt persuaded to help always happen to be male? They ended up at our house. What would have happened if there were no men allowed to sleep in our home? Who is accountable? Or maybe I should have just gone to someone else's house in my time of need when I needed help. I always wondered why there were never any females who came to live with us, even stay overnight. Why did that never happen? There were never any female family

Entertaining Mommy?

or friends in need? If there were, would they have been allowed to stay at our house or move in with us? I am looking for someone to blame for that, someone who would like to take accountability for this one. Anyone? Mom always seemed to know when men needed somewhere to go, somewhere to sleep, or that they needed her.

Where could I have found you if I needed that, if I had needed you? They knew they could find my mother when I could not find her. Then once they got behind closed doors and they did not need you anymore, you just let them do whatever they wanted? Did you know anything about them after you were done helping them out? Did you really know any of them at all? Especially knowing now that you allowed us to be driven off with them? What could he have wanted with a small girl for two or three hours? You never asked. You never wondered about why they would drag around a girl of four, five, or six? A joyride, they would tell you. Accountability I am asking!

A man accused of molesting my sister, and a couple of weeks later, no questions asked, we have a new roommate. You're not to blame? I began to think sexual molestation was a part of life, something we all had to go through, like our periods (which, by the way, I had to find out all about from a stranger because, again, I was frightened of you). After the man you trusted showed me dirty pictures and told me he wanted to do those things with me, how scared do you think I was of him? How do you think I felt when I begged you not to let him take me for another ride? After many months of him torturing me to just look at pictures, you looked into my crying eyes, smiling, and said, "Oh, stop being a baby. You'll be fine!

How nervous, shy, and embarrassed do you think I was? Were you at all accountable for that? Was I to blame because I didn't fight him hard enough at my young age when he tried to sit me in a chair in his room or on his bed. I couldn't scream loud enough through the hand he held over my mouth! That part could have been my fault? I always shook my head no. I tried to scream. I tried to get away, to run. He was big, an adult. I was a small child who no one was watching over. Even then, I had a coward inside me, telling me to listen to the adult, the man with authority, so as he told me to, look at the pictures! Adults do not lie. *My mom hates liars, so she would not have one she did not trust living in our house! He must be telling the truth, so don't say a word.*

To hear my mother talk, you would have thought her word was law and do not go against it. Maybe that is why her marriage was such a long one. Being married sixty-three years should have had a positive impact on her kids. It did not. What a milestone, though. Kudos to you, Dad and Mom. It would have made it nice if you even liked being in the same room with one another! Or to enjoy each other's company once in a while, at least for retirement. I would have given it to you both, but Dad did his best to stay away as much as he could so you would not have to argue.

Possible resentment toward Dad for keeping her pregnant for the first eight years of their marriage? Could we blame that one on you, Dad? It does take two after all, even though Mom has us believing she was forced. Accountability? Their children were sad to see them work all those years to end up miserable at the end. Not enjoyable to visit parents when they were together. Never helped that Mom complained about her life and everything around herself to everyone. When she made anyone who saw her become somewhat depressed, her fault?

We thought at first it was just a battle of the wills. Dad was not always the most pleasant, but I do not think I would be either. I get my claws out after only three minutes of being in a room with her. My poor dad! Then we heard stories from Mom only that Dad did so many terrible things in the beginning that she had forgiven him for, then we found out it was a lie. We thought she blamed him for everything and from there formed a lot of resentment. Never any forgiveness that we could ever see. She wanted the praise for keeping us all together then blamed Dad for trying to tear us apart with the things he did from his past as a young man. They both deserved praise for the work they did raising all of us. We were all sure Dad was no angel and a harsh man, probably hard to get along with. I am sure Mom deserved better when she was just a young teenager starting out.

We all deserve a good life, especially when we start out fresh. If we were to believe all the horrible stories told about my dad, obviously, we would see her disappointment. I never once heard him tell one bad story about her though. I cannot see her being perfect! There were a few times I recall seeing Dad get carried away with a belt on my little brother, so he was not perfect either, and that meant he had a temper, but we all know; so did she. I only know if you say you're going to forgive someone, that's what you do. Do not use it as a weapon and torture someone with it until their last dying breath!

All of us at times felt really sorry for Dad. He tried being the person Mom wanted in the end. That is how you paid him back, didn't you? He worked hard all those years. He had a motorcycle, a four-wheeler, a truck, but he never had you! He did not have to take his accountability his whole adult life (if it were all true). We would not have wanted that for you either. Find some peace in your heart already. May Dad rest in peace! When my dad was ready to retire, Mom told him, "No, you are not going to retire just yet." Then another year, then another. With your meanness, you never gave in, never gave up. The torture, the name-calling, the fighting. We felt so sorry for him, with good reason.

For the time, you could have been happy. Now it is too late. He is gone and never got to enjoy his retirement. You will never enjoy yours. You are too busy worrying about your kids and grandkids and what they have in a relationship and if it is good. You are so jealous and are going to make it your life's goal to mess that relationship up for them somehow if you possibly can.

She made Dad work many years past the time he wanted to, and he was miserable, never enjoying his last years. That made him have resentment, and it got worse between them. We know that Dad would try many times to make up the past to Mom in so many ways, but Mom would not have it. He would tell us girls how much he tried.

She would rather make his last years, his last days, his last breath, as miserable as it could have possibly been. With no accountability, she would never do anything wrong. I saw with my own two eyes the way she had no compassion for Dad or his illness his last few weeks. Even a couple days before he died, Mom said she was just playing when she got in his face and screamed, "You want to hit me, don't you!" Yet she did no wrong, and again, there was no accountability. She showed no compassion for Dad while he was dying at all.

This is no excuse, by any means, but we discovered Mom to have been taking painkillers for at least twenty years now. We are fairly sure it has been many years beyond that. She had jobs that could have put her in jail had her employers found out at the time. She has a doctor to this day that gives her just about whatever she wants for pain medications, then she also has a few other doctors doing the same thing. She eventually became dependent on pain meds. Even if she had been taking those kinds of drugs when she was abusing her children, which we do not think she was in the earlier days, it is in no way an excuse, and she should be held accountable at least talk to us about it, admit her guilt, what she has done wrong, finally own up to something. Say you're sorry for once and mean it.

We have had family members who have been hooked on pain medications and others who have smoked marijuana. My mother thought that was the biggest sin you could have told her, and here she was doing one of them herself. How dare you! That is called being a hypocrite! Just so you know, Mom, no one is perfect. We all make mistakes. This would have been something we could have helped you with had you asked. You hid it from us. You knew what you were doing, knew that it was wrong, never thinking you would get caught. You are accountable, are you not? You should be ashamed! After the way you have talked to people! The way you have treated your own family members who had a drug addiction. You even disowned some family because of it. How do you sleep at night? I am sure if we would have seen when you and Dad were young, we would have felt sorry for you, Mom, but forgive or do not! He did not have to take his accountability for the remainder of his life, did he really, (if it were all true)? We would never have wanted that for your life either. But how could any of this be true? You tell no lies, never say you're sorry, and never take accountability!

I Did It

If I cry loud, and you're not here,
I'll hug myself instead.

I'll close my eyes, in hopes that there's
No monsters in my bed.

When I scream out, and you just laugh,
I'll know you never cared.

I'm still the little girl you left
In that scary "nightmare."

When I awake from hurt and fear,
What would you've had to gain?

Remember now your "misery."
For you have caused my pain.

You're all alone, as you should be.
Like I was as a child.

The hurt you have, the pain you feel,
Believe me, it is mild.

I wish no harm upon your life.
But love I cannot give.

Please rest assured, I'm happy now.
I found out how to live.

Chapter 44
I Did Not Understand

I did not understand how our mother had so many important things to do that she could not account for where her kids were, at least part of the day. I wondered, if we had been abducted, how long before she would have known it? I am glad none of us were. I am just trying to understand where the heck my mom was at when all these bad things were happening to me, to us. I laid in bed at night, crying my eyes out, scared to go to sleep, never understanding where Mommy is right now. I would give anything to have her come tuck me into bed just this one night, check in on any one of us, me especially, because as she said, I am kind of selfish! She could have made me feel so much love. It never happened.

Well, except that one Christmas day. I did not understand what happened to her that night. If only she could have been focused occasionally on seeing me, she might have known me as a child, maybe even liked me. But you did not want to know me, did you? There was nothing for you to even like! Things might have been so different for many family members, mainly your own children. If only you would have paid attention to all of us more often, known where we were, cared what we were doing, known where your borders were at all times, found out where your overnight guests were spending most of their nights, cared that your children where safe at all times when you were right there!

Why was your attitude always "Oh well"? What did you care about when we were growing up? Even more, who did you care about? Why did I even ask that question? We all know the answer to that question, don't we? It has always been about you, hasn't it? If you could have recognized or wanted to see me, you would have. Instead of the resentful way you looked at me, making me feel so horrible about myself, I could have liked myself. Instead, you tolerated me, wanting me to not understand the way you hovered over my suffering, making me feel afraid of you, not loved. I could have told you way before now my fears and monsters, my secrets, my horrors. Instead, I had to wonder why I was allowed a touch of your love here and there, just to have it ripped away if I did not do exactly as you expected of me, making me not understand you once again.

It saddens me that you think all is well today, that no one should have any type of problem when it comes to anything you have said or done. I cannot speak for anyone else, but you never wanted to understand me. So I do not forgive you for anything, and I doubt I ever will. Would it have been okay with you if your children ripped our love away from you every time we thought you did something wrong? Would you understand? Only then would you know some of the pain you have caused me. I am better than that, though! You received a lot of my adult life too after you stole my childhood without me knowing it. You had the joy of seeing my kids being raised. Then their kids. Included in my husband's life also.

What was it you did for that? Told me everything I was doing wrong with how I raised my children, really not understanding. My kids make me proud. They did not turn out like you thought they would, maybe even like you were hoping they would? What child would think that of their own mother? They are great kids, honest and respectful, decent human beings, who love with all their hearts. I did not understand why I did not get an apology for all the wrong things you thought I did to my kids. Not once did I hear, "Wonderful job." No one would understand why a mother would wish their own child a horrible life, but I think Mom wants everyone to have the same kind of life she has—miserable. It is not fair otherwise.

Something you did give to me was the feeling of abandonment at an incredibly young age. I do not think I would have become this scared, weak, or such a coward with no confidence that I sometimes could feel myself to be today if I let myself had I not felt your abandonment. So thank you for that also!

The pain you caused even then, you could never take back. It will stay back with that child you left behind all those years ago. I became a stronger person as my life started to grow. As soon as I was out of that house and my memories began to vanish, I was fearful to find out all that I did not know, but I am glad my past has come to life. I know I will not be hurt by you ever again. You do not matter to me like you did when I was a child, when I needed you so desperately! Who is the one needing who now, Mother? That I do understand, and I know you do too, finally!

Something else that is hard for me to understand though, how you laughed and joined in thinking it fun to scare me; to chase me with things I was terrified of; to make fun of me when it caused me pain, and yes, it caused me pain. When you would find a snake or mouse and pick it up by the tail, chasing me until I was ready to pass out from running away from you! How could you do that to me, seeing that terrified look on my face? I truly do not know how you slept at night when I could cry if my child was just scared from a dream. It makes me sick to think about all the different smiles I saw on your face as you frightened and terrorized me. How could you do that to a child, your own child?

I would actually look back while you chased me and see you with this evil smile on your face, enjoying entertaining yourself or anyone that would watch you scare me, laughing when anyone would make me scream from being terrified. Help me understand how a mother finds that funny or entertaining? You would encourage other adults and family members to scare me in some other ways also. No matter what, you traumatized me as much as you could, it seemed to me. I know you liked to. You would laugh and say, "Watch this!" You enjoyed it! Was that also a way to toughen me up?

It only made me fear everything more and add to my nightmares. I was very young when you did that the first time. What pleasure did you get from that? Oh yes, that idea to get me terrified of you. Well, it worked! I will never forget the first time we moved to the family home we have now. You found a black snake, you called my name, and you chased me around the house. I remember feeling like my heart was beating out of my body and that I was going to have a heart attack if I did not stop running. But if I did stop, you were going to put that snake on me, and I knew I was going to die if that happened. I did not understand then. I do not understand now.

That is what I told myself then. Because when I had nightmares, I thought I would die if something like that touched my skin. I was supposed to understand why when I grew up, right? I felt that I needed to go to the hospital, or I would die so many times and knew that no one cared if I did die because my own family was doing this to me. I told myself that was how bad I felt and how no one else cared. I thought someone was trying to kill me. Why would everyone be laughing otherwise? I talked myself into believing things like that. I would have a tough time falling asleep or not wanting to go to sleep, afraid something was going to crawl on me, terrified of dreams, nightmares.

If I had told Mom I woke up from a dream that something was going to crawl on me in my dream, Mom would always have this evil laugh that would echo, scaring me more. I will never understand why I could not go to my mother with my fears because she was the one causing them. In my dreams, my adult family members were always trying to kill me. A young child worrying about going to sleep because of dreaming something so horrible—Mom would have loved that had she known!

How many children could say that about their own mother? Would you want me to understand now why I could not trust my own mother? Why she found joy in my pain, smiled from scaring me, enjoying beating on me or watching me get beat on in the circle fights? I did not understand. Yes, I know, all to toughen me up, right? I had feelings, just like you have feelings right now. You made me hate my life. When I was eight! Younger when I started to really realize that was what I was feeling and did not know it. I felt tormented when you smiled, laughed, looked at me in your evil way. Should I understand how you could turn your head when I screamed out in pain? If only you would have helped me just once! For so long, my pain never left me, my story never told.

There were no secrets, no heartbreak, that had ever slipped my lips. I had kept it hidden way too well. You never knew. You never watched. You never cared. That you will never get me to understand. I will always say, I have learned some unbelievably valuable lessons from you. I was determined to do just the opposite of how I was raised. I never would let my kids fistfight. I never let strangers sleep in our home. If there was anything bothering my kids, I knew it, and I was there if they needed me, as I have always hoped I have been. Not you though.

You are still trying to control my life, with the husband you dislike, the grandchildren you think should be raised differently. So many things I could name. I am done with your control and done wanting to understand you. I never beat on my kids, like you would have liked me to do. I let them feel my love easily, without having to work for it. I respect them as much as they respect me. I praised them, encouraged them. I knew deep down it must have been fate that I knew to be the opposite of the way I was raised. My childhood somehow made me a better person, mother, and friend. Thank you for showing me what not to do.

Help me understand why you could not give me one thing to hold on to, to wish upon, to hope for. I was hurt physically and emotionally, but I survived, alone and without your help. I was abused by your hands, molested under your nose, and you were too busy to be my mother. Robbed of my innocence, my childhood, your love. Not understanding then. Not understanding now. Only now I am not that caring person anymore when it comes to you. I am always trying to move forward, as I will remain doing, without any guidance of yours, even without answers. I am okay with that if you are okay with being alone.

Not my doing, but now you have no one, just as I had no one, with nobody to blame but yourself. I am hoping I am better understood now by writing down all my feelings. I am at better peace with understanding what I needed then. I wanted to only be understood. That's all I wanted. That is all I needed. No sympathy or pity and, I truly hope, not your hate. These are some facts about my tragedies, the horrors I have lived, the loneliness I felt, and my pain. But I let myself live, and I am free of most of my nightmares now. I have always tried to be brave when others were around.

My life is good. I have some issues, things I will never understand, but I was so blessed with two of the most wonderful boys, daughters-in-law, and grandchildren. I could not have been more blessed. Finally, something I do deserve!

Chapter 45
Mom's Way

I was not the only child to want to have a conversation with my mother about my past, my childhood, essentially things that took place that deliberately had an effect on my life after I became an adult. I know we have all tried to talk to Mom about when we were young. Happy times, anything that is pleasant, we can talk about those things for hours; she never minds those conversations. But we cannot even bring up the subject of anything bad that we want to discuss. That is never brought into any conversation. It either never happened or we will never discuss it! I remembered a couple of years ago when my younger brother was trying to have an adult conversation with Mom, trying to be serious.

Mom answered and talked like she was a child who did not want to talk. When he asked her a question, her answers were always, "yup" or "nope," something she would do to let you know she wants no part of this conversation. The discussion started out to be mostly if she thought she was happy with her choices in life, about forgiveness, righting any wrongs, being grateful, and ending with learning how to apologize to someone or how to say, "I am sorry." Mom commented little, letting my brother do all the talking. Mom does not like being told anything, especially what she should discuss or whether she needs to say sorry to anyone for anything.

Was she happy? Then she told my brother, "I have nothing to apologize for. No forgiveness is needed."

Then my brother wanted to talk about a few instances he thought she could make amends for. She became so angry. She had nothing to apologize for, and she became incredibly angry again. She had nothing to apologize for and no one to say she was sorry to. Because she had done nothing wrong.

My brother then asked, "How about your daughter? Have you ever apologized to her or said, 'I am sorry' for breaking her leg?" He was talking about when I was three and she broke my leg by accidentally throwing me against the wall. At least we think it was accidental.

Then he asked, "Do you think you should say, 'I am sorry,' to her?"

My mother got truly angry then. She did not say a word, stood up, left, got in her car, peeled out with her car, drove to my house.

She got out, stomped into my house, found me, and hollered into my face, "I'm sorry," very sarcastically.

I had no idea what she was talking about, so I asked, "What are you sorry for?"

She said, "I guess, for breaking your leg. There. I have said I'm sorry."

She turned and peeled out with her car again, but never saying another word to me. I had no idea why she had done such a fake apology, if it was some kind of joke or what just happened. Then my brother called, explaining that he asked Mom to apologize.

I told him to forget it, that she did but she sure did not mean it, and I did not want a fake apology. Still, that is Mom's way always. I was still in shock nonetheless to hear those words come out of my mother's mouth for the very first time and I was sure the very last time. Even though it was fake, it was shocking. If I wanted to, I could have let it hurt me all over again, but I kept my chin up and forgot about it because it is Mom's way.

I think of Mom laughing at people who think they have to show off to get attention, which makes me laugh because she wrote the book on how to show off, especially for attention. She loves having people laugh with her when she is making a joke about someone or making fun of someone. She thinks it is great if it makes her the center of attention in any way at anyone else's expense, as long as it is never hers!

I also hear her complain about people who talk about their illnesses too much or show off their broken bones when she thinks they only broke something to get attention! Those kinds of things coming out of her mouth seem so funny to me. If she can fall down and it causes bruises, she is so happy! Especially if they are easy to see, like on her face or arms. If they are on her legs, she will roll her pant leg up even in public to show the bruises on her legs.

She likes going to get blood work done because the needles cause bruising, and she wears short sleeve shirts so everyone can see. It is just Mom's way. The last time she fell, she hit her face and had a pretty bad black-and-blue eye, with swelling in both eyes. She looked like she had been in a fight. We asked her to please put ice on it before she went to visit her sister, getting on a plane to go to another state to help the swelling go down. Not once would she do it. She loved the attention she got when people asked her, "Oh no, what happened to your face?" She could tell them any type of story she wanted. That is her way.

She does like it all about her, so I made sure she got her share of fame that she deserves in my story, all about her ways and what she has done! Not only was she the biggest part of it, she was the common denominator in every stage of my unhappiness. That was Mom's way.

It was Mom's way to make us strive for a good education also. At least that is what we thought. We were enormously proud that after forty years, Mom decided to go back to school and receive her GED. She always told us how important a good education is, and she wanted to prove it. Then we became confused about Mom's ideas about a good education. My younger sister and I were in high school, not getting straight As but not flunking anything either. Mom wanted to control who our friends were, and she did not like the ones we were spending time with. They were the bad crowd. The thing was, it was not true. There was not a thing wrong with any of our friends. It was another control thing for Mom, another one of her ways!

We were not getting into trouble with our friends, not getting bad grades. She wanted things her way, and our friends were not who she would have picked for us. So one day we were in school and were both called to the office. Mom was there and told them we would not be attending school there any longer. We both thought she was pulling a prank or telling a joke. She told us to show her to our lockers. So we did. While friends and classmates watched, we cleaned out our lockers, and my mother would say every once in a while, "Nothing to see here. Get lost. Nothing to see here!" Some would mock her. Many looked scared for us just because of the look on Mom's face, but we thought she was really enjoying this power she thought she had. If anyone tried talking to us, to ask what was going on, Mom would tell them to mind their own business and move along.

As soon as we were done, we got in the car, and Mom announced we were going job-hunting today! That we will be job-hunting every day until we both have jobs. We looked at one another like this was some kind of trick. She could not be serious! She must have read our minds because she looked into the rearview mirror and said, "Oh, I am dead serious." We both had jobs within two days.

My parents bought an old car for me to get back and forth to work with. Of course, I was also scared of driving by myself, informing me that I would be making payments until every penny was paid back. My job was farther from home than my sisters, and I would be working longer hours. It was an extremely reliable car since it was such an older model, and it always got me where I wanted to go. Mom thought she had gotten her way, that she had won, getting us away from the kids that she called the wrong crowd. We still saw those same kids only after work and weekends, which meant seeing all our friends more than when we went to school with them now that I had a car to drive when I wanted to, on my time off from work.

A few years later, my sister and I both returned to school, receiving our own GEDs, with our educations extending further into the field of caring for the handicapped and disabled, as well as our oldest sister, who went on to even further her education, receiving her BA in psychology. So enormously proud of her.

Mom making the two of us quit school was only for her control. Our education became an important part of all our lives, as well as our siblings. So proud of all of us! Although Mom had many control issues. That wrong crowd did not have any type of bad influence on our professional careers. They were encouraging and helpful for us and would have done nothing to damage our lives. If anything, they have enhanced our lives and are still doing so to this very day, moving on with us as we encourage one another. Parents make mistakes, but with our mom, that was just her way!

I have given up so much of my life while you have taken more than you deserved of it! When I only wanted your time and love. Again, now you want mine. You now try to play the victim. That is definitely your way. You want my help, my sympathy, my pity. Where was mine when I needed yours? Where were you? Now things have changed. I am an adult. I should act like one! Be respectful, kind, protective, sympathetic, and helpful. The hell of it all is that I am not you. I do want to be those things. I raised myself to be all those things, just not for you. Even still to this very day, it's your way or no way. It does not cut it for me anymore! Like when I get to go out of town to go on vacation or go out to dinner, on a short or long weekend, or try to have any kind of fun, if you are not included, you're not happy. I hear from you, "It must be nice!" If you get no sympathy from that, you have been known to clutch your heart, say you have a pain or something is wrong.

I have heard, "Just wait. Don't go yet. Let's see what this is going to do first," bringing the attention back to you by any means necessary. You do this more to me than any of your children. Just Mom's way! You call while I'm away, asking, "When you coming home?" Because then you would have had me under your control. Like all those years when I was a child, and now you want that still. How many times have you called me late at night and said, "Can you come over and follow the ambulance to the ER?" You don't know what is wrong? We spend all night and morning for tests with no findings again of anything wrong with you.

You call me and ask, "Can you call an ambulance. Something is wrong." You can call me to tell me to call an ambulance, but you cannot call yourself? You have called me in the night, saying, "I have fallen down. I am bleeding. Can you come over," when your other daughter is in your house, in the next room. How about calling an ambulance first? An ambulance is called. You get to the hospital.

Entertaining Mommy?

They run tests. There is nothing wrong. In the middle of the night, you need a ride home from the hospital. More of Mom's way? You heard about the boy who cried wolf? If you are looking for sympathy and pity, I am fresh out. How's Mom's way going for you now?

Chapter 46

Getting Me Through

Now the fun part of my life as a child. Yes, there were some fun things in my life that easily came to mind. All the good memories I did not have to search for—I wished there were more of those. They truly got me through. My very earliest meaningful memory and one that I will cherish forever. It is the only one of its kind that I recall and was at Christmastime. It must have been a special one. My mom was in some kind of a mood. I do not remember my age but know that I could speak, walk, and able to remember such a great memory of my mom. We will call it a moment.

I was thinking as I laid in bed that night that I would never receive another gift more meaningful or more beautiful to me ever again as I tucked it carefully under my pillow. Mom had given me an antique brush and matching mirror. I thought it was the most beautiful thing I had ever seen. I am sure my mom picked it up at a lawn sale or pawnshop when I think of it now. I didn't care where it came from. Mom bought it for me. That must have been a lot of money back then. I was glad she had found it. I believe that was the gift that put me on the path to looking at myself in the mirror, wanting to experiment with makeup, jewelry, hair. Since that day, I loved it all. The special thing about that Christmas night was when I put those two items under my pillow for the very first time.

Mom had been standing there in the doorway. I remember because she smiled at me when I looked up at her, an exceedingly rare occasion for me. I think she knew how excited about that gift I truly was, and it probably made her happy because she had picked it out for me. I was not truly sure why, considering the way I thought she felt about me. But an even bigger gift was when she helped me pull my covers up over me, and she placed a kiss on my forehead. That was the first time I could remember my mom showing me love or affection of any kind, the only time it ever felt genuine if she had. I do not recall another time that it happened. That is why that memory is an incredibly special one for me.

The very first happy tears I ever remember having as I went to sleep that night. So I will always remember and cherish the feeling you gave me from that night, Mom. One of the only good things you gave me in my life. I am not sure how many nights I put that under my pillow, but it was many. Also, during those few nights, I had no bad dreams. No nightmares. That mirror was so special, until it had been broken. I am aware of every good thing that ever happened to me during my childhood. As single moments, there were very few. I never understood why you let me have that one moment with you, that single bond. But it was something else that got me through. Even though I did not have another cherished moment with you, it is something that gave me hope and one thing to wish for.

Then there were those special tea parties we would have. All the girls that were old enough to have them and wanted to have them. We got to have little cookies or cut up snacks of some kind, but I do not remember what our drink were in our teacups. Other times would be with friends or our dolls. We even had a couple with Daddy, but he could not fit in our chairs, so he sat on the floor. Mom sat with us a few times; I remember those too. Dad was always a good sport. Mom would also let us have dress-up parties, wearing her dresses, shoes, long gloves, jewelry, and lipstick as long as we did not get it on her clothes and the hats. I liked the hats and wore them once in a while, but did not tell the others I really did not want to because they messed up my hair. How funny I was then.

Speaking of hair, I would get into so much trouble for hogging the bathroom because I would lock the door. I would say I was using it, but I hardly ever was. I was in the mirror, fixing my hair, looking at myself, putting on makeup, then washing it off. I do not think anyone ever knew, and I never told what I was doing! Good memories.

They would get suspicious at times. Bang on the door. "You cannot be going to the bathroom this long! What are you doing in there?" Still makes me smile. There were very fond memories of packed coolers, going to some type of water for the day, sometimes staying there until it got dark. Many times, we would have all three of our meals at the water. Sometimes just for the day, while Dad was at work, we would go for a hot, sunny afternoon and have lunch. Dad always enjoyed getting away on the weekends after working all week. He seemed to enjoy himself while we were at the water. There would be someone there most times Dad knew, or he would make many new friends during the summers.

Mom liked it once we got to the water, but I did feel bad for her. It was always work for her. Not that she did not have us girls to always help her out because we always did. But she planned the meals, always making sure there was enough. Drinks, towels, bathing suits. Packing, unpacking. I did it with my kids, but I did not have eight kids either. She had to make sure we had everything because once we were there, we were not leaving. We played and swam all day, always making friends of our own. I do not think anyone ever noticed. I still never went over my head in the water. I was so afraid of drowning, even when I got older. I swam over my head but to this day have a fear of drowning. I'm still not a particularly good swimmer.

During our outings, there would be the usual arguments between siblings and other kids at the water, at times getting us a time-out on a blanket by our parents or on a picnic table or chair, watching everyone else having fun. So you try not to get into trouble while you are there or learn to not get caught. When our parents could hardly see us in the dark is usually when we knew we would pack up and go home. It was always, "Awe do we have to?" Some nights, if it was hot after swimming, we got to stop off and get an ice cream cone before we headed home. Those were such great times.

I never understood, if everyone enjoyed these times so much, why did we not do things like those more often? I should say, if we did them so much as a family, why would our mom still be so angry? So unhappy? She truly seemed to enjoy herself all those times. Even when dad would make new friends, she usually did also. She seemed happy during all our summer outings. Maybe that was just another of her hats she wore, I am not sure. I will never understand my mom. Some nights we would even get told to get up out of bed late at night. If it got really hot, our parents would tell us to get our bathing suits on, grab a towel, and they would load us all in a vehicle, find the nearest water, and let us cool off for a couple of hours. It did not matter what time of the night it would be, or early morning. As long as we stayed quiet, no arguing, and we behaved, we got to do those things.

Sometimes we would pile in the back seat of a car, eight of us sitting on each other's laps, or all piled into the back end of a pickup truck, no seat belts required, and go get an ice cream cone after dinner for dessert. There would be times we would just travel until we found water to swim in, never knowing where we would end up. Or a relative would tell of a nice swimming hole they had found way up yonder, and we would take off to try and find it. The best part was, while we traveled, we would play games during the trip, using our minds only. No board games, no technology, and it was just the best of times. It was always the happiest the family was together that I can ever remember.

We had some games we knew from our parents' days. Some we had made up ourselves. We played and laughed together; even our parents were included and played along. When we got tired of the games or run out of them, we sang songs. When we found a store along the way, we would sometimes get soda for the cooler, buy stuff to make sandwiches, chips, and something for dessert, or fruit. Sometimes Mom would pack a cooler and bring everything we needed for a picnic. A lot of old country music, that is what our parents listened to. Sometimes we could talk Mom and Dad into singing a song, just the two of them, while we all quietly listened. They sang so well together. We thought they sounded like angels. Those were the happiest of memories, days that got me through.

I have told you about the gravel pit, but I would not have had a place to run or to hide all those years, all those moments. It sure was my escape. There were so many places to be alone when I needed to be and no one could find me. The best place for all of us to play through the years and grow. We all escaped there a time or two; that place sure got me through. We had many toys to take to the pit also. A mini dirt bike they could get it to fly if they wanted it to. It was tiny but mighty and a miracle no one was killed on that thing. I remember being so scared to go over this one narrow hill. If you went to the left just a couple of inches, you would have been rolling with the bike down over that steep hill. Of course, it doesn't look so steep now. I know I closed my eyes every time I reached the top and prayed I got to the other side. I was always afraid of everything, but it was still fun. There was only room for one person driving, but many times, there would be a passenger tagging along, even though we were kids and small.

How we fit I will never know, another thing that could have hurt someone but thankfully never did. The things we got away with at that pit. I don't know how we survived. This was not something that got me through, but such a good thing I had been taught was how to do simple chores—a must for any child to learn. It only got exciting if our dad got involved, and he did a few times I can think of. I hated it back then but would give anything for him to do it one more time. I am thankful to both of my parents to be taught the proper way to do many things. I really enjoyed the cooking part of the chores and was told, "A messy cook is a good cook." Well, I must be one hell of a cook. I never quite got how to keep everything together without making the mess.

When I was young, I hated the cleaning up and doing the dishes, which is where Dad made it exciting, but now I don't mind any of the cleanup. If it happened to be your duty for dishes, for any meal, you had better know the word *spotless*. If my dad looked through our cleaned dishes and found one thing dirty, one piece of silverware with food, you would start to cry. He would open up the cupboard and start pulling out stacks of plates, glasses, pots, and pans, empty the silverware drawer into the sink, and make you wash everything he pulled out, and get it right, or you start all over again.

We always cried throughout these painstaking extra chores, especially watching our siblings played outside and thought Dad was cruel, but now we laugh about his pranks, and that is not the only one. No, he had many! Then came the laundry, which we had a lot of with eight kids. If the laundry was all done and everything was supposed to have been washed, Dad would check our rooms. If he found a piece of dirty laundry in one of our rooms, and I mean in anyone's room, he took every drawer out of every dresser in everyone's bedroom and dumped them together into one room, into a great big pile, mixing everyone's clothes together.

Then we would have to sort through, find our own clothes, refold, find our dresser drawers after Dad had stacked them, not in order, put those back in the dressers, then put away all our clothes again. Not a fun way to spend a morning or afternoon. The one who missed a piece of dirty laundry in their room was not a very popular person for that day. Yes, my dad could be a lot of fun! *Not.* He would do things like that then tell his friends and buddies and laugh and laugh in front of us then say he was thinking of something else that would be fun to do. Then they would discuss other things they could do for torture, and his buddies would get involved and help with ideas.

A thing of our mom's was hanging laundry on the line. Saving money, not using the dryer, we all understood. To this day, we are not sure if this was logic or some form of punishment, but we can laugh about it now. We sort of laughed then because it did not make sense to us. If it rained, we hung laundry in the kitchen on racks, where the woodstove would dry them faster, very logical. Summertime, on the clothesline. In the wintertime, you would think the racks. We were made to hang them on the clothesline outside when it was freezing out. They were stiff before we had the last thing hung. We would wait a couple hours, go get them off the line, stand them up, stiff as a board in a row on the floor until they thawed, then hang them on racks or hangers to dry. Joke, cruelty, or logic? I know, we never got an answer to that one.

This one sure can still make me laugh. Our foster brother introduced a lot of us to smoking cigarettes. We thought he was so cool back then. We all learned to smoke under the barn. Really dumb when we think of all the flammable things that we had in there besides the hay. I remember my youngest brother who would tattle for a quarter. Truth be told, back then, he would have done it for nothing. You little mama's boy! I do think Mom still owes him a lot of quarters by the way!

He was never allowed to know anything about the many things we did. So we were always hiding from him or hiding something from him. We had a really hard time finding hiding spots from that one! After an incredibly long time and not tattling for a while, he convinced us that we could trust him. So one day he came under the barn, and we did not hide smoking from him. He looked extremely interested in trying it. He began bugging us about letting him smoke with us.

"I will tell, Mom, you guys," we started hearing from him.

"Go ahead," we repeated right back to him. "But if you do, we will never tell you another secret."

We knew if we let Mom's baby smoke with us, with him having asthma, we would be in the worst kind of trouble. So us being the responsible siblings (oh, how we laugh now) told him no way! He begged and pleaded every day. We gave him the same answer every day. About the fourth or fifth day, he left really mad. He was gone for a good amount of time, so we were not sure yet. Well, that was the end of that secret. We knew we were all busted and knew not to trust him. We figured we had better pack up and take off before he leads Mommy out here by the hand. But wait, he came back all alone. He had some hay and some toilet paper.

Really surprised, we asked him, "What is that?"

He began to roll the toilet paper around the hay, and it began to look like a cigarette. We all laughed a little but tried not to make him mad. He asked for the lighter as he put it to his mouth.

"No way," we told him.

He asked over and over, "Lighter please!"

We would tell him, "No way!"

Little brother was determined that he was lighting his homemade cigarette.

Finally, someone said, "Oh, let him have it. It's not like he's really smoking a real one."

He was handed the lighter while we were all silent as he lit his fake smoke. It took less than five seconds to light up, and it was gone. But so was most of his eyebrows and eyelashes. We all sat there in as much shock as he was in, all knowing that if one of us laughed, he was going straight to Mom. We knew the story was going to come out anyway because of how he looked. Just...funny. He was the funniest-looking little brother we had ever seen. We could not help it. He had no eyebrows. What! We didn't do it. He did it to himself! You all would have laughed too if you had only seen what he looked like, just seen what we were seeing, especially when he repeatedly kept lifting his eyebrows that were just not there.

Someone started to laugh, which made all of us laugh. Except little brother. He began to cry, running out of there so fast. We did feel sorry for the way he looked, but we just could not stop laughing. We might as well get used to this right now because hell to pay was coming. We knew Mom would be on her way soon enough. Time to pack up, run, and hide, at least for a while. Our whipping could wait. It did not take him long to tattle. All of a sudden, we heard Mom screaming our names before we all got out of there. Yes, we got it good for that one later that day and her thinking we did that to her baby, also for smoking under the barn; we could have caught the damn thing on fire!

Our poor little brother who we made fun of was sitting there crying and looking pathetic, with no eyebrows. Sorry, brother. Later on, we found out that one of my sisters told my brother he could have his own cigarettes, told him exactly what to do. I won't say which one you are, but you know! I also will never forget the time some of my siblings (still not knowing which ones you were) tried playing what they thought was a joke on me. I think they found out it turned out to be not so funny. Still a prank that got me through, I think. They had taken the screen off my bedroom window and opened the window wide then had taken the lampshade off my lamp, turning it on, which helped to fill my room with moths and late-night bugs. Somehow, they talked me into going to my room, then they shoved me in there and held the door so I could not get out while the things I was terrified of were all around me. Talk about a panic attack. I thought I was going to die that night.

I ran to my bed. It was extremely hot. I pulled the covers over me, but some of the bugs got under the covers with me and was getting on me, and I was crying and screaming get them off me at the top of my lungs! While they were outside my door, laughing, thinking it was funny. Between the bugs that got under my covers and the heat, I did not feel so well. I had passed out and do not remember anything after that. They thought I might need to go to the hospital at the time. I was scared of any kind of bug then and now. My siblings felt really bad for me. They never tried to scare me again. I developed a phobia for almost anything that crawled or flew after that. It was not a fun memory, but I can smile about it now. I never went to the hospital. Mom also thought it was funny and thought I was being a sissy.

One fun thing we always did was have family, friends, and the neighbors over for barbecues. Those were always a blast. There would be phone calls made, menus planned. Everyone would pick something from the list, and all that would come would bring something, and what a party it would turn out to be. There never had to be an occasion or holiday. Many times, Mom and the five girls would get out the guitars and microphones and sing for everyone. We did that at a lot of family gatherings. Mom would also play the piano lots of nights after dinner, and we would always stand around and sing for Dad. He would request songs and just enjoy it. We would sing you many more if you were here, Dad. Missing you and singing you a favorite right now.

Chapter 47
Understanding the Hat

She wears many hats. Most women usually do. I have heard that many times before. But I never understood what it meant until about the middle of my adulthood. Some hats I have found are not always good for a woman to have, not even to try on. Where do I start about the many different hats my mother has worn? All the usual a mom would wear, at times being the mom and dad when Dad worked away on jobs. I know she has chopped, split, and stacked wood; carried plenty into the house; shoveled out a car or two when it got stuck; walked a long way if she ran out of gas with her car. A few good hats so far. Shoveled snow off our walkways and driveways, did some plumbing/carpentry work in her time.

I have even seen her fix a few things on an engine. My dad taught her well. She has also made some amazing meals for ten people when we did not have anything to start with. She could always come up with something. A few very great hats so far. She knew how to make a dollar last, always paying the bills that were most important to keep our family above water. I have seen her play some football and kickball with us a few times. If only she had kept those few hats on. What a super life we possibly could have had. I truly loved those hats you wore. Help me understand. Did they get lost in your closet? Did you give them away? Sell them? I know to me it does not even sound like the same mother I had growing up.

She was the most confusing woman I have known in my lifetime. I have loved her, hated her, been puzzled by her, felt sorry for her. Do not worry. I will not forget the two biggies—neglected and abused by her. I am not sure what those hats were called, but I hated those. I am not the one to tell my mother's story. I do not know enough about her, how she was raised, what she went through as a child, mother, or wife. It is really not my story to tell at all. It seems I have never known much about Mom, except the bad things I have witnessed and endured. I only know my mother is an overly complicated person to say the least. Like that beautiful antique brush and mirror, why did you step on that, Mom? Was it just to punish me? You broke my one memorable bond we shared. Why would you do that? When you knew I treasured it? I could not understand that at all. A great way to hurt me in a way you will never feel. But why? I could not have known a true mother could hurt their child like that. It was awfully hard to get to know the real person deep down. I wanted to understand those kinds of hats!

Then another kind. Why do you have to tell us that you kept us all together all these years? I thought that is what mothers are supposed to do. Then if you know something that upsets me about one of my siblings, or I state a fact, you would go and tell them, knowing it is going to cause trouble between us. Why? You do it between all of us just to cause trouble! What hat is that one called, Mother? If you wanted to keep us all together, why now do you want to tear us all apart? Help me understand that one! Were we a burden to you, truthfully? Are you sorry you kept us all together? I am simply confused. You made us believe that we owed you! For being our mother! Because of all you have had to do for us. The sacrifices you have made for us. Never have I heard of another mother wearing that kind of hat, thinking that way, talking the way you do. That we owe you. Your children have been so good to you. You should be so thankful for that after all you have done to us and not done for us.

Those out-of-control beatings—yes, they were beatings—I guess you can say, some have forgiven you for them, maybe even forgotten. What was that hat called? Talk about someone being ungrateful. We treat you well, and it's still not enough? Shame on you! You still have respect; you're treated better than you deserve. The other thing I do not understand is, you have never truly welcomed any of our spouses into our family. I do not understand that one at all.

Entertaining Mommy?

If you're trying to get rid of someone who has been married to one of your children for over thirty years, I do not think they are going anywhere. Give it up already! I am just thankful we got Dad's caring kind of heart and not a selfish, greedy one.

Help me understand this hat, why you feel the need to know about any one of your children's financial issues, their children's daily problems if they have any, your own children's sex lives! Why do you feel the need to know anything sexual that goes on in your own kids' lives? Telling you're only concerned for us? That is just *wrong* on so many levels. How in the world does something like that benefit you in any way? You have even made up stories about your son-in-law's sexual performances before, gossiping about that. Why would that be any of your business in any way? We'll call that a disturbed hat, shall we! How dare you even ask about those things. Why do you have to know anything about our sex lives?

You have asked! Telling us you want us to have a fulfilled life? Should I understand what that is all about? What kinds of hats do people call those kind, Mom? Makes me feel ill. Most mothers want their children happy. If yours seem to be happy, it makes you seem more miserable because you were not included. I am truly not sure about some of the hats you have worn. But some have never fit you well or ever looked good on you! You always seem unhappy if the siblings are all getting along. So you must do something to pit one against the other to get the ball rolling. If your grandchildren come to visit, you will talk bad about their own parents to them. I am trying to figure out a name for that hat! That's your own children you're bad-mouthing. Then you get upset when they have had enough and do not come back. You're lonely again. You know, you could have had this huge, happy family life. Instead, you chose to sabotage it by causing chaos and dysfunction in everyone's individual families. What is that hat called?

I just cannot understand this. Why did you only become a decent mom to me, or any of us, most of the time when we were sick? Why did you become this stranger? Why this one bit of confusion? A hat of convenience, possibly? I have no idea! Help me understand some of these confusing things! You fed and clothed us to the best of your ability. You taught us things a good mother should do. Some of your kids even received and felt love. I was not one of them, but I am past all of that. I could never understand why you wanted to feel my resentment and I got to feel your tension, disgust, and fakeness from you. You treated me differently. I always wanted the truth as to why, never understanding your point of wanting me afraid of you, any of your children afraid of you.

It's not as much what you did but how you made me feel, how you made me feel about myself, how you looked at me. Your whole life, you seemed so unhappy and a whole lot of angry. I could see your anger. Could you not see mine? What hat was this one? How about my pain? You must have noticed that while you beat me. Was it something enjoyable to see on my face? Or just for entertainment? You never cared about my tears, that is obvious. Did you ever hear my screams, or ignored those too?

What about seeing men get into my bed, being dragged into theirs, going off to secluded places just to be molested again and again? Did you just ignore that? Did you have a hat name for what that would have been? Letting them into our house for overnights or letting them move in with us. You couldn't have known what they were all capable of, could you? Not known what they had done in the past, correct? You are not the kind of mother who would wear that kind of hat, are you, Mom? You did not know what they were doing to me, to all of us, you're certain?

Shame on you when you purposely ignored me! This should be some of the hardest things you will ever read. I am not sure that it will even affect you in any capacity. It sure affected me and the hardest thing for me to live through. I have been silent for over fifty years now. It is time for me to have a voice. I needed to speak, to ask. I need answers. If this were all just to say it out loud, getting it off my chest, I am okay with that. I wanted nothing to ever be contained within me again.

The coward I thought was inside me is gone forever! As I stand on my own two feet, strong and brave, let us finish this, shall we? Your anger toward me, the way you wanted me afraid, was that for fun also? Did you laugh about that too? Or was that, too, for your

Entertaining Mommy?

enjoyment? I did want answers, but I will still be okay without any. You laughed when you chased me with something that frightened me. Another kind of hat? Why neglect and humiliate me so much? You never seemed to want me happy. Were you truly trying to beat me into someone you wanted me to be? I think I have them all off my chest now.

I will not ask you anymore whys, but with the understanding, it would be helpful if you could put on the hat you have never had on before, if only to wear it just to answer at least one of my questions truthfully. Wear the honesty hat for a few minutes. Knowing up front, this will not bring us any closer together either way. But it would be nice if you could wear that one hat you've never even tried on. Or do I really want to know? Maybe you already know the answers would hurt me just as much? Something else you always found entertaining! Another appealing game you have loved from the start? You have already worn this hat for far too long. It's time for a change.

You only wore a couple of hats well indeed. But never have you worn them long enough for me to notice. If you could have kept those few nice hats, think about where we might all be today.

To this day, you're still wearing a hat that does not look good on you now nor does it fit you well. Try another one on! Not that it will have an effect on me at all. Keep trying them on. Maybe one will spark someone's interest one day! But it matters none to me.

Chapter 48

Control

Here we go. All about Mom once again. She really does like it this way! If only you understood how she controlled me, how she secretly tries to control all who cross her path. I find it remarkably sneaky how someone can think of ways to control another's mind. Just one more way she made me frightened of her. She not only did things in deceitful, sneaky ways, but she was no idiot. She also had some well thought-out, skillful plans many times in many ways. Mom was a difficult person to deal with, even if she was not trying to manipulate someone else. When she gets anyone to do something for her, it's usually some devious kind of way. We have all seen it and have all been a victim to it.

Guilt motivated. Some type of proposition, or you do not know she has done anything at all in an effort to guilt you into doing something you wanted her to do for herself. Always controlling! First comes the complaining.

"You do things for your mother-in-law all the time, but I cannot get you to do one little thing on my list. I have been asking someone to do this for months. After all I have done for you throughout your lifetime! You will not do this one thing for me! Why do you spend so much time there when I only get to see you for thirty minutes, sometimes less? I do not understand why I had all these kids. What do I get! One of you get a phone call while visiting, and that always seems to take priority. You forget all about me just like that.

"Your phone rings, and it is like I do not exist. I am not even in the room with you anymore. I am your mother. I should not have

Entertaining Mommy?

to ask you to come for a visit. You should do it because you miss and love me. I should not have to ask you to do anything for me! You should automatically do it out of decency! I have been asking you to do that now for two years. No one does anything when it comes my time. When I need an emergency project done, it doesn't happen. But boy, when you first started out, I bent over backwards helping you out. You never had unpaid bills. I would never have let you go hungry!

"I did everything for your children when they were growing up. I bought them everything. Now they cannot even come to see me? How ungrateful can all of you be? You should remodel my bathroom. It needs to be done. I did lend you money when you needed it five years ago!"

These are just a very few of the many things she repeats to guilt someone into getting what she wants in any way she can. There are so many more. Just demonstrating the few ways she makes her best efforts to let everyone know. If she did something for you, even if it was twenty years ago, she never forgets, and you owe her. Do not worry. She will never let you forget! We all think she has a little black book of things written down that she has done for anyone throughout her lifetime, or yours, not only her own children either, whether that debt has been paid back or not.

These are some annoying, irritating things she does to guilt someone for control! We all hear about them. Even if they are not our debts, she complains to each and every one of us, hoping one will tell the other and eventually get back to the person owing the debt, upsetting that person enough to come see her, and boom, she has someone to visit her. Somewhat smart, controlling, but smart. She does not get that trying to control your adult children or grandchildren in this way makes them run for the hills. No one wants to hear her talking about other close family members, her friends, or her constant complaining about this and that: her life, she is lonely, her family is abandoning her or being nothing but negative.

Then there is the talking about her many children, what they are doing wrong, what their spouses have done wrong. You always have the perfect solution for every problem with anyone, don't you,

Mom? Who wants to hear that? I have been guilted into taking her to doctor's appointments before, even if I tell her I have an appointment of my own on that day.

"Well, could you reschedule yours?" she asked me. "I cannot mine, and this one is important." One that she could have driven herself to. I find out when we get there, it was only for some type of checkup! Something she could have rescheduled. When mine could have been important. Even so, she would have loved it if it had been. Just another thing in my life she could control. Any type of kindness that comes from Mom, anything nice she does for anyone, taking them to lunch, buying them a soda when she goes in the store when they did not ask her to, she will write that in her little black book also, and it always becomes an agenda with her. Whatever her kindness was for any of us, there is always a price to be paid later. Eventually, you remind us about that kindness, and it is payback time. "I did that for you, but you will not even do this small thing for me?"

There have been times when we have spent the entire day together, going to yard sales, antique stores, secondhand places. I love doing those things. We go out to lunch. When we finished at the end of shopping, you would say, "We are not going home yet." Always an agenda. You wanted to keep me out as long as you possibly could just to see if you could make my husband angry by bringing me home after dinner. Another way you thought you had control. That is why you always wanted to be the one to drive. After dropping me home, you would go home, call family members, laughing that you hoped it caused problems between my husband and me! What mother likes doing that? For some reason, you would have loved my husband to be angry with you. Funny thing was, it never worked. He is not that way.

You loved confrontation and got upset when never receiving it from my husband. So you would always try something else next time. I wanted to go with you and do all the things you wanted. I enjoyed them also. But you were miserable the whole time we were out. Per usual. Never happy to just be able to be out with one of your children, enjoying something you loved to do. You thought you were controlling something, which made you happy. You are never positive, never cheerful, or truly happy, never just glad to be alive! So I never wanted to spend that much time with you after a while. Because you did nothing but complain, mostly about my dad and your own friends! It was exasperating and depressing!

Also, you gossiped about all your other children, their spouses, your grandchildren. It was always the same every time we were together. It seemed like you were reading off a list. Dad was always the first one to complain about. Then down the list you went! I was so sick of it every time we went anywhere. But being respectful and scared to say anything to you, I always stayed silent. Now you're lonely, not understanding why your children and grandchildren stay away. Your way has never worked. You have pushed away friends and family, mainly from your gossiping, complaining, and your unwillingness to change anything about your unhappiness.

Do you think your children like you being lonely? Do you think your children do not want to see you? You think we don't want to love our own mother? You did this to yourself. Push and push until we all had enough, then cry because you pushed it a bit too far. I do like to laugh when she laughs and gossips about people, lies, or tells tales about others. She reminds me so much of a woman she despises. Just because she was this exact way herself is why Mom and she did not get along all those years! She did not like her mother-in-law whatsoever (for good reason) because she always had her nose in her children's business and never liked the spouses of her children, making it difficult for her children to live their lives.

We all laugh and call her by our grandmother's name behind her back because she is so much like her and sounds just like her. Sadly, she is doing some of the same things she detested our grandmother doing. As you heard, asking her adult children personal business, questions mothers should not be asking. To listen to Mom tell stories of how much other people complain, it is comical to say the least! What I say to this is, Wow! My mom does nothing but complain, as you have already read. I forgot about the complaints about all the sacrifices she has had to make for her children, hating her life, what her children do not do for her. She tells anyone who will listen, her children never do anything for her, and much worse, "Why did I have all these kids anyway? They never do anything for me or visit," telling strangers bad things to get sympathy. We do have family night every Wednesday night. Sometimes we take turns cooking a meal or we order out. That is not good enough. She wants more of us! Some of those same kids visit during that same week. Still not good enough. One of her children and spouse live with her. Seeing them every day was not enough. She complained about them to every one of her other children. Whatever they do while they live there, taking great care of our dad while he was sick was never good enough.

My sister who lives with Mom and Dad had a great relationship with Mom. That did not last long. Mom spoiled that with her negativity and by complaining constantly, also making my sister feel like her servant just because she temporarily lived there. Mom also made her feel like she owed our mom because she was living there. Even though she and her husband were taking very good care of our ill father and cooking their meals.

I know this story is not about my mother. It is about me. But she wanted to control my sister, her life, her husband's life, the way she did me as a child. Even as an adult, she had me as her puppet, pulling my strings as much as she dared. There is a reason my life turned out the way it did when I was a child because of my mom's actions.

While my mom tried to control everybody else's life, my life was being turned upside down with nowhere to run. I was finally waking up! Just because of all you have done to me, all you have said about me, I still do not want you to be alone or ever lonely. I have told you time and time again, only you can change your life.

You thought after Dad passed that you and I were going to be best friends, spend all our time together hanging out. Not happening! Control what life I have left? Are you kidding me? Because you have not liked my husband, you have tried to control how I should feel about him also, making fun of him to me, telling stories to my siblings about him, as if they would not tell me what you're saying. You're an evil, vindictive woman; and if you're alone, it is because your done controlling your family, especially me. I should have told you how I felt from the first day I got my memory back. Your malicious ways are done being in my life. Your toxic bull has gotten you where you are right at this moment,

It is ruthless and unforgiving, what you have done to me. You do not like anything about my life, deep down. You only like me because you could control me. You have never even liked anything about me or my husband. You now think and tell others that he controls me (that is priceless coming from you), keeping me away from you. All the things you have tried to do and say about him. I do not have to tell you what a good person my husband is. I do not have to defend him to you or anyone. It is not worth my time or my breath. I know what and who he is. You could have seen that for yourself. Another loss you caused all on your own.

Funny that I believe you're the only family member that has a problem with him. I feel nothing but pity for you. I'm not sure that you even deserve that. I wish you would learn to keep my husband out of your controlling game. He does not want to play! My husband has not or ever tried to control me. All people are not like you. No one happy, genuinely happy, would want to control another person or their lives. The way they think, what they do, how they should feel, who they should like. That is all you. Control is exactly what you do. It's your game. No one wants to play. So if you are looking for someone to blame, instead of my husband, please look in the mirror!

What you would call your perfect life now would be to have only your children to come visit you, no spouses allowed. What power you would feel then! What control you'd have. We will not even have to talk about our spouses. For you to have us all to yourself for as long as you possibly can. That is a controlling game you would love to play. If keeping us away from our spouses upsets them, that would be an added bonus for you! Anything you can do to upset the enemy without showing them. Only that is not what you would call them to their faces. Oh no. You have to keep up the appearance that if anything goes bad between you and any of our spouses, it could never possibly have been your fault in any way.

Next, you would want us to be doing your honey-do list that seems to grow every time we see you. The maintenance jobs. The separate cleaning list you have. Cooking you a few meals ahead of time that should last until the next person is to come over and cook some more. Organizing all your rooms full of crafts (again). Organizing the throne where you sit in the dining room (again). Organizing all your sewing projects (again), and those are all because you just will not take care of things yourself. You are able to do most things yourself. Maybe not the maintenance but most everything else. You just choose not to because you have all these kids who owe you for having us and raising us. Oh yes, let's not forget. We should also be the ones who take care of your cat litter box, food and water dish, for a cat you truly do nothing with and only requested him because you were jealous of our dad's dog, whom you despised that poor dog, as we have all witnessed.

The cleaning of your fridge from spoiled food because you refuse to throw anything away. You might eat that later. But it never comes to later. All a way to control your children when you are perfectly capable of doing all these things yourself. If now that we were done with your chores, we could all gather around you so you could tell us how disappointed you are with each one of us, what we are doing wrong in our lives, ways we could help improve our lives, get your opinions in (again) our choices for a spouse or partner, ways we could control our own spouses—that you would have some real good ideas—talk bad about each and every one of them for a while, or telling you we are leaving our partners/spouses. That would truly make your life so much happier.

How am I planning your perfect day so far? We all know how much livelier you would be. At least for the amount of time we spent there. You would still do your complaining about our children, gossiping about someone who was not there with us, or talking horrible about our dad and the things he used to do wrong or while he was still with us. You already said horrible things about him with him sitting right there. You always wanted the challenge of him trying to defend himself. You were in your prime when you could have a good argument with Dad, always pushing his buttons until he would blow a fuse. Then you would look at us, smiling, and say, "See how he is? What did I do?" You always smiled, knowing it made him more

Entertaining Mommy?

upset, even worse, thinking you always won. What control! The only thing you did to Dad was make us feel sorrier for him having to put up with you the rest of his days.

Before we left, you would want us to put you on a pedestal, tell you how much we love and adore our mother, that we can't wait to see you again, tell all the good you have done for us, the perfect mother you have been, how much we worship the ground you walk on. Wait… WAIT! We really have to start all over again. We forgot to turn on your tape recorder to record us all talking so you can hear it while we are all away from you. Then it would be back to you being bitter and miserable. Until one of us came back so you could throw one of us under the bus about the horrible job we have done while we were all there doing your chore list. That would be the kind of control you have always wanted over your family, your perfect life, your perfect last years. That would be your idea of a perfect day. It could be spoiled if one of us did not come back for that visit the next day or one of us could not make it for that day of children's visit only. We would not want to spoil the whole thing for you.

You think I am joking, all you readers out there, but I am not! That is how our mom would like to control each and every one of us, and worse! It would become her idea of a perfect life. When one of us gets to purchase another new car or to buy a house, it has never been "I am so proud of you." No! We hear, "Why did you have to buy something so expensive? You think you're better than the rest of us?" A family vacation or going out to dinner that does not include her, for her to say something nice for a change, oh no, she cannot do that. It must be your controlling ways. "Well, it must be nice," or "You didn't ask me! Bring me back something!" When everything is not about you!

If you have nothing nice to say, keep it closed. Also, if we could just get through the door, to say hi to anyone else that may be sitting or standing prior to the end of the room where you are always sitting on your pedestal before you start hollering, "Where's my hug!" It is not in an enjoyable way you ask or an enjoyable way to want to greet someone. You are not happy to give us a hug, kiss on the cheek, or a fake smile. It is just another way of control, demanding us to get over to you first while you sit there on your throne! For that brief moment, it makes you feel power, to have us walk to you because you have demanded us to then to have us in a hug, or should I say, in your clutches.

I never understood what that meant to you, the demanding of the hug. I have a better understanding of it now. I do hug because my siblings do. It never feels fake when they hug me now or when they give me a smile. Although I still do not like the feeling of hugging because of what happened in my childhood, not because I do not love my siblings. I do. Does it sound like our mom does? That she knows how to love without control? Does it sound like our mom has been proud of her children, happy to see them carry out goals? Just glad to be a mother? Things that she did not ask us to do for her! You think she has ever told any of her children she is satisfied with how they have turned out? Glad they have a rewarding, full, happy life? That any part of our lives appears to make her proud? Of course not. That would mean she is giving up some kind of sick power, giving into someone else's control. She will not allow that!

Something else we found odd that our mother did. I guess you could call it for control or a hat issue. I'm not sure what to call some of the strange things she did as we grew up. For some reason, Mom liked to keep a sewing needle in her hand all the time. If we had friends over, she would go around the table and start jabbing her children with this needle. Not enough to draw blood every time. Just enough to irritate our skin. How she loved making us cry out without warning. She poked us anywhere too. If our friends were around a lot (used to being there), they, too, would be poked by the needle. She tried making it to be some sort of sick game, but it hurt, and she would get this evil, satisfied look on her face every time she got a huge reaction from one of us, licking her lips with a smile. It was sick, hurtful, mean, and embarrassing for her to be doing things like that in front of our friends, especially if they were unfamiliar with mother! Another control issue!

Also, my parents used to love playing cards. We used to play only regular four-person card games. Then we somehow began to play poker. We played for nickels and dimes, quarters once in a

Entertaining Mommy?

while. Most of the siblings began to play, and we would sometimes have two or three tables playing at the same time. It was so much fun!

We all took turns hosting it at our houses so one person would not have to do all the work every week. We might lose five or ten dollars, nothing big. It was mostly playing for fun and just getting together. We would all bring something to eat. Sometimes the host would cook dinner; others would bring snacks for the game afterward. Just something fun to do together as a nice family get-together once a week.

Then trouble started brewing whenever Dad would happen to be dealing and Mom lost a hand. She would get upset with Dad, like it was his fault, like he had control of the cards and how they were dealt out to her. It started getting worse. Some people did not like hearing it every weekend, so they quit and never played again and even stopped coming to watch. It got so bad verbally. Mom spoiled it for them. She wanted to control how Dad dealt the cards to her, we assume. Impossible to do, but she stayed angry at him most of the night from then on. Then other relatives wanted to start playing. Even friends would join. The ones that knew Mom well stayed the course for a long while.

Others just could not stand the bickering or the name-calling, then she started the swearing, throwing cards, knocking other people's stacks of money over if they were winning. Dad began arguing back, which caused more turmoil for everyone, but we could not blame him. More and more people dropped out. I eventually received phone calls from each set of couples, saying they were sorry, but they just could not take her anymore. Mom was too serious and angry. It was no fun to play with her. Even if she won, she was a poor winner, showing everyone around the table, "Look. I won. I finally won!" Then she would always say (no matter how much she would win), "Well, it will never make up for what I lost last week." She could not enjoy it!

The reason we were there was to get together and laugh, have fun. Needless to say, no one wanted to play anymore, so we have not done that in a several years. Play without her, you think to yourselves? She would never allow that! You can bet, somehow, she would make all our lives a living hell when she found out, and she would find out someway, somehow. She has eyes in the back of her head, remember? It seems to me, deep down, everyone seems just a little intimidated by her. Our family barbecues, dinners, birthday parties, any gatherings fizzled out because she spoiled the mood and any fun we may have had for everyone she talked to.

She is a very depressing person to talk to—never happy, never positive—always complaining, talking about anyone there she could. I cannot put all the blame on my mother for all my childhood problems, but she is the seed that grew to get it started, and it sure started in a bad way. Putting into words all that has happened to me, all my feelings, all that I have never dared to tell, has been a tremendous burden lifted not only from my shoulders but from my heart. I feel at peace. I have joy. I feel loved. My life moves on.

My voice has been heard!

Chapter 49

I Found My Voice, the Coward Lives No More

The only way for me to get any answers and for me to begin to think about having a voice was to have a plan. I knew it had to be for me to fight hard, whatever it was. It would be the only way for me to progress forward. Get my answers and move on. What a breakthrough I have finally made. The coward I was not sure existed for so long, beginning for me as a young child, was just something unknown to me yet something I was so fearful of. I'd known it may be living inside me, growing as rapidly as it possibly could while not giving itself away too quickly and without my preventing it to fail. That is what it was counting on and living off, convincing me just how real it was without showing it existed.

Whatever it had to be for me to find, to have been hiding in the shadows like the frightened weakling I would find out it could become, building itself on my fear, lack of control, and the pain it has fed on for all of my years! I do not know what age I had been when I thought I felt that coward building its predatorial life inside me. I know that I had ignored it. I thought in the beginning, *I am too weak with no courage to help myself or begin to do this on my own.* I now know, that was not the truth but that I would definitely need someone's help to fight whatever this is. If I had only waited, listening to my own voice, to find out that the evil coward was something or someone who had not truly been there this whole time, counting on never expecting to be discovered.

I would find this all on my own, only thinking I needed someone else's help due to the pain and horror it has caused. I should have been brave then. But I knew it had to have started building its walls back then before I had gotten my very first bad spanking, when I had heard its vicious cries and became frightened of something that I felt yet had no idea of what its worth would become to my life. Something so different yet so strange to me, following me whenever I closed my eyes. Then being so young, not knowing they were called nightmares, with evil. For me to keep rediscovering them throughout each battle I fought in my world, I wondered, could I have possibly stopped what happened to me in the next series of events in my life just by being brave and asking for help?

Being so scared, so unsure, it was not easy. What a dangerous place to be. I only knew it was the way for me to beat those hidden emotional battles I had been bullied into feeling. I always knew one day I would have to fight that cowardly threat that had lived inside me for this long once I had found out. I also knew, this would be my last chance to find my voice. I was not aware that cowardice had not really been there the entire time, but I knew confrontation head-on was the only way to achieve the end of my suffering, to become that brave fighter I had always dreamed about becoming I knew could come. Throughout my very frustrating developments, I have tolerated more pains of the heart.

I cried too many tears for that lost innocent. I have had my hidden nightmares and memories come to life. Then to relive my painful childhood all over again, how scared and alone that little girl must have been. All those painful thoughts unveiling one after the other. What could I have possibly done to make my mother want to look at me that way? Torture me all this time, in this manner? Hit me like that over and over? As a little girl, I did not know what to believe. But I came to the conclusion that it must have been something bad enough for her to just forget I existed. That is, until she needed someone to take her rage out on, for her to have me to just belt around some anger with. Only then would I feel useful to my mother.

That is why I can only think she did not love me as a child. Do you think she could hate her own daughter? I always wondered. But why? I was not sure, hoping I would somehow one day find out. It could not have been for just to be in control, could it?

My suffering and nightmares, there could be no way a mother would know about that and do it anyway for money and bribes, could they? Please tell me I am wrong! To know that your child was off with a man somewhere, being molested, and yet possibly getting something out of it? No parent could really do that! Having your daughter confess sins of a man and what they have done to them then calling your own child a liar! Not checking into what you called a story like that. Letting your other daughters go with that same man? What is it you could possibly have gotten out of it all had you known what all those monsters were doing to me? To any of your daughters? Not for a free babysitter! That just could not be true. Mothers really would never do that, would they, Mom? Money, truly?

What could really be wrong with my mom if that were to be the true reason? That is a question I guess I would really like to have answered! Had you seen my pain all those times, you would have helped me! Seen my tears, felt my weakness from touching me, you would not have let them do it for any price, would you? Was my mother the monster? Were you really that evil? What would make you hate me? Your own child! How could you beat a three-year-old? Or your own child when I was any age? Any of your children! What did I do to you? Why could you not give me your love? I fought a battle, one that I had come so close to giving up on so many times. That coward would always be there to frighten me, make me always think before I waged a battle I knew I could never win. But why me? I kept fighting, and I never gave up! Why would the coward never give up? Never even try! Never get any weaker? A will that was so strong! But it found one that was stronger.

I was not finding help, not telling someone like I should have. I almost gave up, giving in to myself, to my own weaknesses so many times, but that is what that coward wanted, just waiting for that! I thought I was staying as strong as I possibly could. Starting at such an early age, I thought I could handle it alone. Because I was fighting something that meant nothing to me and that I could possibly destroy it without any problems. Just another monster I despised. I could do this. I made myself believe!

At any age, you can fight any monster, any coward. Those were my only weaknesses, and the coward knew it. But I have found my voice. It took me too long, but here I am. I did it! I fought my demons, my monsters, and I did it all alone. No one must be alone. No one must fight alone. It was too hard to do. I began thinking I had lost. I fought what I thought was the coward living inside me, making me afraid, frightened and scared of all and everything. But I was so wrong! It was its own devious monster, a brutal, evil person trying to control my mind, my spirit, my voice, only playing emotional tricks on me for such an awfully long time, whenever it felt necessary to do the most horrible damage.

Someone who could have helped the coward inside me, and not be the coward inside me…my very own "mother!" She had been the coward building its predatorial walls inside me. She was the one making me fear everything, everyone, making me feel weak, purposely hurting me time and again, wanting me to fail, wishing and hoping I would give up, give in. Little by little, she was teaching me how to abandon myself and everything that mattered, how to give up on myself, telling me how unworthy I am, that I would never be anyone. No one would ever be able to love such an ugly child. I believed her like I believed all the other monsters in my life. Then I could be her puppet forever. Afraid and terrified of my own mother. She looked forward to that, making it her little game for a very long time. That was what she was working toward. That was her eager goal. She almost had fulfilled it.

She stayed inside my head, my mind; she never left me. She held on to my fear and fed on it, making me terrified of all that was alive around me. She was the voices in my head, making it dangerous for me to live a complete or a healthy life! She had me in her clutches. My own mother was that coward, not me, making me too afraid, knowing what would make me frightened and using it against me! She knew the whole time how to keep me subdued for your own calculating, sly intent. What kind of mother does that? I was never a coward! Just led to believe I was.

I never gave up. I took pain and heartache, but I still fought my way through. I took you on, I fought you, and I beat you! That coward lives no more. You did not win, Mother. I am not a coward. I was never the coward you had led me to believe in. I did everything you tried to stop me from doing that was good and so much more. I believed then that I had helped my sisters. Most of all, I have now helped myself. I am now loved, something you said would never happen for me and hoped I'd never find. I have found strength and more determination than I will ever need again in my lifetime.

You may have had all the control and power in the beginning, but I have it now, when I really no longer need it. My weapon is my love, my dignity, my respect. None of it is for you though. That is the price you will have to pay for all that you have done. You may not think it much of a price to pay. But when your children have all decided that should be your cost, then you have little left but loneliness. That feeling of being unloved and the loss of feeling unwanted or needed—not very good feelings but ones just as you made me feel all those years ago. So many hurtful, painful times that stung me every damn time! I am okay though. I am fine now with all my decisions. Are you? I have made it throughout my emotional story, my out-of-control battles I have had to stop, of course.

The pain of my emerging memories still try to defeat me. I have not and will not ever let them again! I have finally, without a doubt, made it through it all. Though not without tremendous pain in my heart, deep down in places I did not know had existed. Opening up to a little girl who was once lost but found the little bit of peace and happiness her siblings had shown her throughout her childhood and now as an adult still giving her peace. Thank you all so much for that. I know I wouldn't have made it without all of you. It's because of you that I did make it! It was only where my agony, my misery laid, holding on, trying to inflict the worst kind of torment that is hard for my reality to keep at bay. This may have been a challenging thing for me to live through, but the real pain and suffering is in everyone now knowing that I did.

To tell my story, it hurts. Oh, how it deeply hurts. But now my heart is finally set free, and I can live! I have never had the opportunity to confront my mother. Here I am now, painfully saddened. I still needed my mom in my life, but I know, it is not possible. She is not a good person and still too scary. But I'm not afraid of you anymore. Not frightened of your eyes, your voice, any of your weapons, or of your hands. I still feel sorry for you though. Only because you missed out.

You have a wonderful daughter who needed you, then and even now. You will lose all these years. What about your other daughters? You have missed out on their lives just as much. It is really sad for you, especially that you have had to be right, not owe anyone apologies, never saying you're sorry. You have it all, Mom, sitting right in front of you, staring you right in the face. If you're looking in the mirror, that is. Blame no one but yourself. I used to beg for your kindness and love. Now you want mine. Sorry, I have none to give.

I used to love the mother you should have been, the one I wanted and needed you to be, the one who wore all those nice hats in the beginning. You could wear those now. I would not know you, and I would not care. Keep on the one you have. It matters none to me. What about your other four daughters? What you have done to them, how you have made them feel? The hurt and anguish you have put them through, would you ever be sorry about that? Say you're even a little bit sorry for the pain you have caused them? I didn't think so. As you have always said, you owe no apologies to anyone and have nothing to be sorry for. Well, shame on you! It doesn't matter because I have made it. I have never before felt better. I feel empowered knowing I can tell someone else to take that fighting step.

Help yourself. Do not let anyone make you feel small, worthless, or unloved. Find your voice and let your own coward—whoever or whatever it may be—to be removed from within you, your mind, your spirit, your being. Let it be completely removed from your life. What a freedom it is to fight the battle and win the war. I had made all the wrong choices in the beginning, ones I will always regret. I did the right thing in the end; I know that now! No more running from my fears.

The tearing down of a lost confidence could start to ruin a person's soul. Something or someone making you have low self-esteem could make you not believe in yourself. Do not let that happen. You let them win that way when you do have a say in your own life. You can lift that head up and fight. Anyone can do it. Do not be afraid at any age. We all can do this. Fight anyone or anything you are battling. Mine became a winning battle, just like yours will be. I am free—free of the demons, the monsters, the coward inside me. If you think this innocent child did not deserve those dreadful memories, horrible nightmares, that painful physical and emotional abuse, then think deeply within yourselves! Is there a reason that you deserve yours? Of course, there is not! No one deserves any kind of ABUSE! If you or someone you know is being abused, please tell someone!

If you are being neglected or abused, tell someone!

Fight your coward. Let someone help you. Stand proud! Be a fighter!

As I woke, I had to think about where it is I am. I looked around, a bit dazed, as I spotted my therapist. I realized what this was, what it is we just accomplished. She had the biggest smile on her face that I had ever seen before.

"How are you feeling?" she asked.

"Like I have been hit by a truck," I replied.

I knew why she had that smile. I felt it too all of a sudden. At that very moment, I could feel the impact of this session. Somehow, I knew I would not have to explain why I felt this way. I knew that she had known. I suddenly felt at peace.

I felt a calm rush over me and returned her smile. It was the strangest thing. All of a sudden, I knew I would not be frightened anymore. Even though I also knew everything that had been hidden has surfaced. I was not afraid of it anymore. What a tremendous feeling this is for me, like nothing I have ever felt before.

"You did it," she finally said to me. "It was some very hard work and a lot of these long sessions, with many uncertainties, but you never gave in to any of the fears you have had all these years, all those many times of starting all over. I am so proud of you."

I knew exactly how she felt. I was pretty proud myself.

"We did it," I corrected her. I smiled at her again. "If it had not been for all your encouragement and knowing when to push me, I could not have done this. Thank you so very much from the bottom of my heart. I appreciate you." The happy tears began to flow.

With that same smile she had before, she said, "You are very welcome. I think this part of our sessions are over. Do you agree?"

"Yes," I told her with confidence. I did not need to relive the past for one more day! "I am so happy how things have turned out."

She said, "If you want to continue with something else or if you ever need to revisit something, anything, I am here for you."

"Thank you. I think I would like that," I replied.

"Then stop at the desk and make an appointment for two weeks. I will see you then, but as always, if you need to see me sooner, I am just a phone call away!"

As we both stood, she looked surprised to see my arms opened wide for the first time since I'd met her. I felt so comfortable with her. I gave her a big hug, which she returned. She knew what all this has meant to me and what it meant that I was willing to hug her.

"I think I will keep you," I said as we parted, knowing this was not the end.

Find Your Voice

The only voice you need to hear is your own.
Do not let anyone else's voice in.
You are the most important person so…
listen to your heart.
If ever there was a voice to hear, it is yours.
If I had listened to mine in the beginning,
found someone to hear my voice,
my suffering may have stopped.
Instead, I let it live on, longer and longer,
listening to the voices in my head,
and not in my heart.
"They" became the champion
for far too long!
Feel that heart of yours,
begging you to fight.
Just believe in yourself.
You will always win.
There will always be someone, somewhere,
who will listen and be there for you…now!
There will be no more suffering alone,
if only you find your voice.
Find someone you trust,
someone who trusts you,
believes in you,
as you should do.
There is always
someone who will listen.
You cannot do this alone!
No matter your age.
You are the one deciding its time…
Just listen
to "your own" voice!

Nationwide Hotlines for Abuse

There are nationwide hotlines for any kind of abuse:

The national physical abuse hotline: 1-800-799-7233, twenty-four hours, seven days a week.

The national sexual abuse hotline: 1-800-656-4473, twenty-four hours, seven days a week.

The national domestic abuse hotline, or verbal abuse hotline: 1-800-799-7233, twenty-four hours, seven days a week.

The national child abuse hotline, child help abuse hotline: 1-800-422-4453, twenty-four hours, seven days a week.

They are here to help you!

Please make that call if you need help!

About the Author

I have known her a long part of her life. A girl with a lot of love to give, while receiving nothing she deserves. The struggles she fights just to survive will astound you. Growing up with many siblings is the only thing that helps her have hope, and the love she needs to get through it all. To get out of that house, the only way she knows how then to marry the first man who shows her affection is what she feels she has to do to stay away. It is another one of her many ways of chasing after love. She survives but will the pain along the way make her or break her? She has a normal marriage, children, love. What more could she ask for? Then come the flashes, nightmares, the unexpected. What could be happening to her world? Why are her siblings telling these strange stories? Abuse, neglect, who could they be talking about? The visions, who is that small girl crying?

CPSIA information can be obtained
at www.ICGtesting.com
Printed in the USA
BVHW052242160423
662367BV00001B/121